Natural Remodeling
for the
Not-So-Green House

NATURAL REMODELING
for the
NOT-SO-GREEN HOUSE

*Bringing
Your Home
into
Harmony
with Nature*

Carol Venolia
& Kelly Lerner

LARK BOOKS
A Division of Sterling Publishing Co., Inc.
New York

Library of Congress Cataloging-in-Publication Data

Venolia, Carol, 1951-
    Natural remodeling for the not-so-green house : bringing your home into
harmony with nature / Carol Venolia & Kelly Lerner.
        p.   cm.
    Includes bibliographical references and index.
    ISBN 1-57990-654-0 (pbk.)
    1. Dwellings—Remodeling.   2. Ecological houses.   3. Organic living.
    I. Lerner, Kelly.   II. Title.
    TH4816.V46 2005
    643'.7—dc22
                                        2005029075
10 9 8 7 6 5 4 3

Published by Lark Books, A Division of Sterling Publishing Co., Inc., 387 Park Avenue
South, New York, N.Y. 10016

Distributed in Canada by Sterling Publishing, c/o Canadian Manda Group, 165
Dufferin Street, Toronto, Ontario, Canada M6K 3H6

Distributed in the United Kingdom by GMC Distribution Services, Castle Place, 166
High Street, Lewes, East Sussex, England BN7 1XU

Distributed in Australia by Capricorn Link (Australia) Pty Ltd., P.O. Box 704,
Windsor, NSW 2756 Australia

If you have questions or comments about this book, please contact:

Lark Books
67 Broadway
Asheville, NC 28801
(828) 253-0467

Manufactured in China

ISBN 13: 978-1-57990-654-2
ISBN 10: 1-57990-654-0

For information about custom editions, special sales, premium and corporate
purchases, please contact Sterling Special Sales Department at 800-805-5489 or
specialsales@sterlingpub.com.

EDITOR: James Knight

ART DIRECTOR: Kathleen Holmes

COVER DESIGNER: Barbara Zaretsky

ASSISTANT EDITOR: Rebecca Guthrie

ASSOCIATE ART DIRECTOR: Shannon Yokeley

ART PRODUCTION ASSISTANTS: Jeff Hamilton
                                          Jackie Kerr

EDITORIAL ASSISTANCE: Delores Gosnell
                                   Dawn Dillingham

EDITORIAL INTERN: Sue Stigleman

ART INTERN: Ardyce E. Alspach

ILLUSTRATORS: Olivier Rollin
                      Orrin Lundgren

Contents

Introduction

The Joys Of Natural Remodeling

WELCOME TO AN EXPERIENCE that will transform your world. Starting right where you are, you can modify your home so that you are living in harmony with nature.

By "transform your world," we don't just mean redecorating your house with eco-friendly materials; we don't even mean just rehabbing your house to be more energy-efficient. We mean that you can be healthier and more joyful while having increasingly beneficial interactions with the ecosphere. In other words, this book is about much more than remodeling; it's about how you relate with all of life—including your own.

The alterations you make might be as simple as moving furniture, repainting walls, adding a trellis, or redirecting your food and water waste. Or they may involve rethinking the way your house works, rearranging rooms, or adding space. The scope of the project isn't as important as the breadth of your vision. When you become more aware of the sun's path, the wind's direction, and other resources that are all around you, your responses will feel—well, natural. Seemingly minor actions undertaken in harmony with the biosphere can be more powerful and beneficial than dramatic but shortsighted gestures.

But how do you decide what changes are best suited for your home and your lifestyle? This book will provide you with the tools you need. We will show you how to interpret the broad concepts of sustainable living in specific ways that can be adapted to your particular needs and lifestyle. We will begin by showing you how to take stock of where you are right now, and then help you imagine where you want to be. Then we will provide you with time-tested suggestions—from very simple to more complex—to help you create a natural home that is uniquely your own.

And who are "we"? We are both architects, each with a private practice dedicated to making homes that are good for people and the planet. Now we will bring you the combined wealth of our own experience and the expertise of our colleagues, in an adventure designed to help you transform your world.

The goal of natural remodeling is to modify your dwelling so that it becomes a positive mediator—not a barrier—between you and the rest of the living world. A home that is warmed and illuminated by the changing light of the sun, cooled by breezes and the shade of greenery, and blessed by birdsong in the garden is not merely energy-efficient, it is also healthful. By reuniting us with the web of life that is our birthright, such a home naturally nourishes body and soul.

Isn't a New Eco-Home Better?

You may be thinking, "But isn't it better to start over and get it right—to build a new eco-home?" As the green building movement has expanded in recent decades, a perception has grown that unless you're living in a solar home of earth or straw on country property, you're just not doing the truly green thing. Many of the books and articles on eco-building focus on the new, isolated home.

However, staying right where you are and massaging your current home for greater harmony with the living world is one of the most powerful things you can do. There are also many practical reasons for doing this:

You are working with an existing building. It usually takes fewer resources to make your current home more eco-friendly than to start from scratch somewhere else, even using green materials. And if you don't improve the home you're in, who will? Capitalize on the energy and materials that have already been invested in your home.

You aren't destroying more of the increasingly scarce undeveloped land. That bucolic image of the eco-homestead in the country comes with a not-so-lovely price-tag: topsoil torn up and compacted, drainage patterns disturbed, plant and animal communities uprooted, vast material and energy resources consumed in construction, new roads, wells, and septic systems—and, all too often, greenhouse gases produced by driving long distances to jobs, schools, and stores.

You can save money. Chances are you'll spend less on remodeling than you would on a new custom home—and many of the changes you make will lower your utility bills. You also have the option of making changes step by step, paying as you go, and avoiding the cost of interest on a loan.

The infrastructure is already in place. With an existing home, the roads, driveway, water, and power are already there. The civic investment in generating and distributing power and treating water and waste has already been made; you don't need to tear up the landscape or your budget to create them.

You're in an existing neighborhood. You are probably already knit into a community and its history. In addition, you may have schools, recreation, stores, and services nearby. This has social and economic value, as well as having a lower energy cost than driving long distances.

You can revitalize your neighborhood. Investing in your home improves your neighborhood and may inspire your neighbors to do the same. Whether by conscious intention or a more subtle ripple effect, the eco-improvements you make to your home and yard can inform others and encourage them to follow suit. You can even join with others to turn your neighborhood into an eco-village.

In short, ecological remodeling is not the poor cousin of the shiny new eco-home. It stands on its own as a wise, resource-conserving, community-building, accessible, enjoyable way to improve life.

The Heart of the Matter

When most of our time is spent inside buildings and cars, it's easy to forget how living systems function. Natural remodeling is also about remembering what our bodies know deep inside about the interconnectedness of all life. In this book, then, whether we are looking at how to select flooring, whether to upgrade a heating system, where to add windows, or how to plan a garden, our touchstones are: What will be best for all of life? What will bring you home to Mother Nature? The vitality of the biosphere—including you—is our standard for measuring success.

How To Use This Book

This book will guide you through a natural process for remodeling your home. The colorful diagram below shows you how the book is organized. We'll begin with the most basic information and interrelationships, then help you deepen your understanding so that you can make decisions and changes in an effective sequence.

In many chapters, you'll find sections entitled *Low-Hanging Fruit*. These sections focus on ideas and things you can do right away. They will engage you in the process of change and allow you to experience immediate and pleasant results. They are also the steps that aren't likely to create problems if they're taken in isolation.

In contrast, the *More Advanced Steps* sections are intended to be read but not acted on until you've worked your way farther into the process. We list them within the chapters to show how you can eventually apply the material to your overall scheme. However, a guiding principle of natural remodeling is integration—systems thinking. We advise you not to undertake the More Advanced Steps in isolation; keep them in mind for possible use later, as your integrated scheme evolves.

Remember, the essence of natural remodeling is responding to the unique qualities of where you are and who you are, so we'll rarely tell you exactly what to do. In terms of the time-honored metaphor, we won't give you a fish; we'll teach you how to fish—or how to buy good fish if fishing isn't your thing. The result will be a lifetime of satisfaction and deeper ecological wisdom.

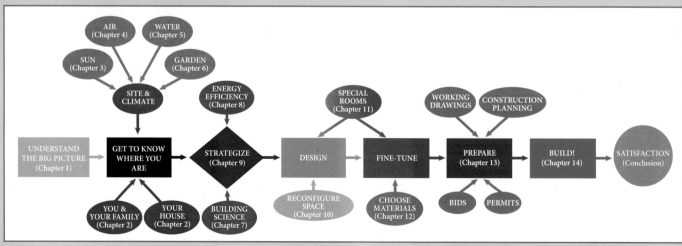

CHAPTER 1

At Home with Nature, Yourself, and Your Climate

Study nature, love nature, stay close to nature.
It will never fail you.

— Frank Lloyd Wright

CREATING A NATURAL HOME is partly about the house itself, but it's mostly about how your house supports your relationship with the rest of the natural world. In fact, the relationship between you and the natural world outside your home is the foundation for all the remodeling decisions you will make. In the next chapter, we will give you the tools to determine your specific needs and desires, as well as identify the attributes of your site. But first, we need to determine how you relate to the world around you.

9

Your Senses, Your World

Your senses link you with your surroundings. But modern living tends to both over-stimulate and under-nourish your senses to the point where you no longer remember how delightful sensory richness can be.

Research suggests that your body is not made for the monotony of most indoor environments. The result can be sensory numbness, boredom, and anxiety. Buildings are fine tools for avoiding the extremes and inconveniences of weather, but by walling ourselves off completely from natural surroundings and processes, we diminish our own vitality.

The solution to this problem is both delightful for you and good for planet earth. Living with natural light, the warmth of the sun, and the coolness of shade trees and breezes is good for your senses—and it reduces fossil fuel consumption and air pollution. Planting trees and gardens nourishes you at the same time that it improves wildlife habitat. But, most importantly, when you really experience your interdependence with all of life and the earth, you are less likely to make harmful decisions.

A vine-covered trellis helps blur the separation of house and garden, bringing the inside out and the outside in.

Natural Rhythm

How you perceive the world through your senses is just the beginning. Another exciting piece of the picture is realizing how much your body needs to be in sync with natural cycles.

When we live indoors under electric lighting, it's easy to forget that our bodies have been intimately linked with the rhythms of nature since life began. But it makes sense: As life on earth evolved, the influence of the sun and moon were constant; in order for organisms to thrive, they had to adapt to the cycles of day and night, a waxing and waning moon, and the seasons.

But most contemporary Americans are out of sync. Awakened by an alarm clock, we tend to get too little sleep, jump-start ourselves with caffeine and sugar, work indoors under steady levels of electric light all day and into the evening, and then—surprise!—we have trouble sleeping.

Not only are we out of harmony with the sun and moon, but our complex biological functions get out of phase with each other. When this *desynchronization* occurs, health declines. We may become tired, depressed, or anxious; coordination and mental ability may suffer; our sleep may be disturbed; digestion and metabolism can be thrown off; sex drive and fertility are lowered; and we generally become more vulnerable to disease.

A simple greenhouse addition provides solar heating and a wonderful place for humans and plants to soak up the rays, even on a cold day.

The solution to desynchronization can be deceptively simple: return to the cycles of the sun and moon; don't allow electric lighting to obliterate your internal rhythms. This has a lot to do with your home: daylighting, passive solar heating, outdoor living spaces, and greater contact with the living world are naturally healing. Gradually awakening with sunlight, getting adequate daylight indoors and out, and turning down lighting levels toward bedtime can make a radical difference in how you feel.

CAROL'S EXPERIENCE *For years, I have wanted to move toward harmony with natural cycles. It's taken a while to change some habits, but my efforts are paying off. I used to stay up late, sleep late, and feel lousy, but I gradually shifted so that now I'm awakened by the morning sun. I only use an alarm clock on the rare occasions when I need to get up extra early. I feel much better these days. I get outdoors every day. I moved my desk near the windows, and I work by daylight most of the time. I'm learning to slow down in the evenings and keep lighting levels low; it feels good to end the day relaxed.*

What could be more delightful than sitting outside on a mild afternoon? A trellis with vines offers the perfect seasonal shading solution, allowing full sun in the winter and shade in the summer.

Thermal Comfort and Delight

Thermal comfort is one of the primary reasons for creating shelter. But many people are accustomed to letting their home's thermostat take over, and they don't know what makes them feel comfortable. If you want to improve your well-being and reduce your dependence on nonrenewable fuel sources, it's a good idea to understand what makes you feel warm in winter and cool in summer.

It all comes down to how your body handles heat. Your body uses food as fuel to constantly produce heat so that you can function effectively and stay alive. A portion of this heat is

HOW THE HUMAN BODY LOSES HEAT

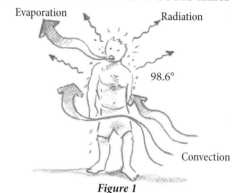

Figure 1

SEEING NATURE
by Debra Lynn Dadd

For most of my life, I hardly thought about Nature. To me, Nature was off somewhere else, in a park or at summer camp. My world and the world of Nature were separate places.

When I first met my husband, Larry, I was surprised that he saw the world with different eyes. One day we were walking in the financial district of San Francisco, where buildings tower so high that you can hardly see the sky. Suddenly he said, "Look at that bird nest!"

Bird nest? I saw only concrete, signs, front doors, people, cars, and diamond rings in a jeweler's window. He walked down the same street and saw birds, flowers in window boxes, trees in planters, and cats running by. He felt the sun on his hair and the wind on his face. He changed forever the way I look at the world.

Nature is everywhere, in everything. I now see the tree my desk is made of, the earth's clay in the bowl I eat from, and the cow that gave its milk for my yogurt. It's all around me, and I dwell within it.

At the same time, Nature dwells within me. My own body follows the same patterns of life as all other living organisms. It must take in nourishment and expel wastes; there must be energy and communication and shared purpose. These functions occur whether we look at

Nature is never far away. It's in the wood grain of a shelf, the clay of a plate, and the stone of a mortar and pestle.

a cell, a heart, a body, a tree, a forest, or a city.

Nature operates on cycles that connect us with each other, all other species, the land, and the cosmos. Though water in our homes comes from a tap, we drink rain and snow. When we purchase food from a supermarket, we are eating sunlight transformed by flora and fauna. We fill our lungs with air that is circulating around the planet, passing through forests and thunderstorms, flying on currents of wind in great cycles from poles to equator.

Your home and yard are already participating in natural ecosystems, in which sun, air, water, earth, plants, and animals constantly interact.

Coming to know ourselves as Nature is not a matter of becoming something unfamiliar; it means observing anew *what we already are*: living beings with the ability to be aware of and act in harmony with the flows and processes that successfully sustain all life.

Debra Lynn Dadd is the author of Home Safe Home: Creating a Healthy Home Environment by Reducing Exposure to Toxic Household Products *(Tarcher/Penguin, 2005) and publisher of dld123.com.*

A plastic-wood composite deck remains a comfortable temperature, even in full sun.

required to maintain your body temperature, but the rest must leave your body so that you don't overheat.

As conditions around you change, your body automatically adapts, retaining or rejecting heat. When you are hot, your body perspires to lose heat by evaporation, and it increases blood circulation so that you can lose heat from your skin's surface, (see figure 1, page 12). When you are cold, the opposite happens: your body decreases perspiration and peripheral blood circulation to slow heat loss.

Most people think of thermal comfort as a function of air temperature, but humidity, air motion, sunshine, and the temperatures of surrounding surfaces may actually be more important. Humans generally prefer air temperatures between 68°F and 78°F, relative humidity of 30 to 70 percent, gentle air

movement, and comfortable surrounding surface temperatures. When your climate doesn't provide ideal conditions, you can alter your environment to bridge the gap.

You can be comfortable in an even wider range of conditions as long as the environment provides the right modifiers and your body can adapt to lose heat at a comfortable rate. For example, breakfast outdoors on a 65-degree morning can be quite comfortable if the air is still (i.e., you aren't losing body heat), you're sitting on a wooden deck (neutral surface temperature), and the sun is shining on you (providing warmth) (see figure 2).

Under different circumstances, an 85-degree evening can also be comfortable; with low humidity, a breeze, and dark clear skies, a cool stone patio would be great for dinner because your body can lose heat to the breeze, perspire into the dry air, and be cooled by the patio and the night sky (see figure 3). In both of these cases, the air temperature is outside the classic comfort zone, but the combination of natural and created conditions can bring comfort and delight. And, of course, you can extend your comfort zone even more by pulling on a sweater or engaging in physical activity when it gets cold or changing into shorts when it's hot.

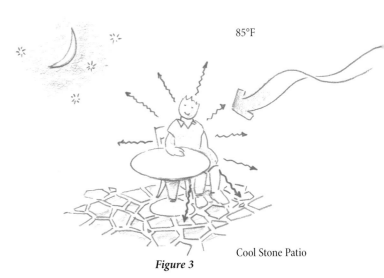

65°F

Neutral Wood Deck

Figure 2

85°F

Cool Stone Patio

Figure 3

With light from a dormer and ample windows on two sides, this room is naturally light, warm, and in touch with the outdoors.

As you can see, just staying comfortable involves a rich dance between our bodies and the climatic conditions around us. Most of us don't want to live outdoors at the mercy of climate extremes. But we don't want to be cut off from our lifeblood either. A dwelling that lets you experience the multi-sensory, biologically stimulating richness of contact with the elements, while protecting you from excessive cold, heat, wind, and rain, is a place where you can thrive.

In fact, designing in response to climate is the great meeting ground where human well-being and energy efficiency come together. Design with climate is the hallmark of a natural home.

THE BEAUTY OF FOLLOWING A NATURAL PROCESS

We often get calls from people who want help in greening up their home when their project is already designed, or even in construction. In other words, the homeowners are asking us to put a green veneer on a not-so-green house. They're not being deliberately difficult; this is what the current marketplace has taught them to do. But at that point, dozens of decisions have already been made that eliminate green possibilities. Many opportunities to save money—while conserving natural resources and increasing comfort and delight—have already been lost.

When people don't begin by working with the ecosystems in and around their homes, they're left with limited, costly options. This can be frustrating, and it perpetuates the myth that ecological building is expensive. But the high costs and frustration are unnecessary. This book is designed to help you think about your house and its surroundings as a whole system from the start, accepting the gifts that nature offers as the first step in creating an affordable home that's good for you and the earth.

Our ancestors built their homes in harmony with site and climate out of necessity. They wanted to be warm in winter, cool in summer, and dry when it rained, so they crafted their homes to take advantage of the sun, wind, and earth. They had no utility grid, light fixtures, central heating, or air-conditioning to fall back on. They also didn't have processed building materials or long-distance transportation, so they built with the materials at hand: earth, stone, wood, and natural plant and animal fibers.

We can learn a lot about climate-responsive design from traditional buildings around the world.

Mexican Courtyard houses create a protected oasis with shade, plants, and flowing water. Their massive adobe construction modulates temperature extremes. (Hot Dry and Mixed Dry climates)

Mesa Verde Cliff Dwellings, carved into the side of a canyon, are warmed by the sun. The south-facing cliff blocks cold winter winds, and the rock walls and floors store the sun's heat for cool evenings. (Hot Dry climate)

Charleston Two-Story, Side Porch Houses are one room wide to catch cooling sea breezes. The two-story porch creates shade and extends the living space into the gardens. (Hot Humid climate)

New England Saltboxes open to the sunny south with a high front wall while minimizing exposure to cold north winds. (Cold Humid climate)

Elevated Pole Houses in the tropics stand above the damp ground and allow cooling breezes to circulate freely. A thick roof provides shade and insulation from the solar heat. (Hot Humid climate)

The Role of Climate

The climate of your region is determined by a combination of the earth's orientation to the sun, your location on the earth, and your proximity to bodies of water, hills, canyons, or plains. The climate around your house is the sum of the sun, wind, and water that flow around and through it. These resources are nature's gifts. The more your home's design works with these natural flows of energy and materials, the more efficiently and pleasurably it will operate.

You could remodel your home without paying attention to the gifts of your climate, but the results would be less than satisfying. For instance, ignoring the heat and light from the sun, the cooling and refreshment available from breezes, and the ways in which moisture moves through your home can lead to higher utility bills, mold damage, and indoor air quality problems—not to mention the loss of sensory delight.

In order to select appropriate building materials and heating and cooling systems, you need to know how hot, cold, humid, or dry your climate is. The better you understand your home's surroundings, the easier it will be to make decisions about design, comfort systems, and materials; as you pay attention to the environment, things begin to fall into place.

What is Your Climate Zone?

Your local temperature and moisture conditions can be summed up in terms of a *climate* zone. Climate zones are general designations, such as *hot dry* or *very cold*, that describe the primary nature of the regional climate; they summarize the

CLIMATE ZONES OF NORTH AMERICA

VERY COLD
Very Cold Winter
Mild Summer

COLD DRY
Cold Winter
Warm Dry Summer

MARINE
MEDITERRANEAN
Mild Wet Winter
Mild Dry Summer

MIXED DRY
Cold Dry Winter
Hot Dry Summer

HOT DRY
Mild Dry Winter
Hot Dry Summer

COLD HUMID
Cold Winter
Warm Humid
Summer

MIXED HUMID
Cold Winter
Hot Humid Summer

HOT HUMID
Mild Winter
Very Hot Humid Summer

Figure 4

magnitude of available sunshine and rain. Understanding your climate zone will guide your choices of general design strategies and building details in the coming chapters.

Based on your observations and experiences, you can probably pick out your climate zone from the descriptions below. For example, most of Arizona is clearly dry, while much of North Dakota is very cold. The accompanying map will help you identify your region (see figure 4, page 16).

An elevated screened porch on a Virginia house extends the living and dining area into the forest. In this hot, humid climate, shade and breezes are crucial to natural summer comfort.

- **Very Cold**: very cold winter, mild summer; high heating needs, low cooling needs; precipitation varies

- **Cold Dry**: cold winter, warm dry summer; high heating needs, medium cooling needs; less than 20 inches annual precipitation

- **Cold Humid**: cold winter, warm humid summer; high heating needs, medium cooling needs; more than 20 inches annual precipitation

- **Mixed Humid**: cold winter, hot humid summer; medium heating needs, medium cooling needs; more than 20 inches annual precipitation

- **Hot Humid**: mild winter, very hot humid summer; medium to no heating needs, medium to high cooling needs; more than 20 inches annual precipitation

- **Marine Mediterranean**: mild wet winter, mild to warm dry summer; medium heating needs, no cooling needs; precipitation varies, but the month with the heaviest precipitation (in the cold season) has at least three times as much precipitation as the month with the least precipitation (in the hot season)

- **Mixed Dry**: cold dry winter, hot dry summer; medium heating needs, medium cooling needs; less than 20 inches annual precipitation

- **Hot Dry**: mild dry winter, hot dry summer; medium to no heating needs, medium to high cooling needs; less than 20 inches annual precipitation

Knowing your climate zone is one of the most basic tools for making decisions about your remodeling project. The conditions of each zone suggest effective approaches to heating and cooling, and rule out approaches that just won't work in that zone. For instance, in both *hot dry* and *hot humid* climates, staying cool is the most important design challenge, but these two zones require different cooling strategies. In a *hot dry* desert climate, adding moisture to the air (via evaporative cooling) provides effective cooling. Adding that same moisture to the already humid air in a hot humid climate would make the heat even more oppressive. When it's hot and humid, only shade and air movement will cool you down; picture sipping a mint julep while seated in a wicker chair on a high porch with a ceiling fan turning overhead.

Your Natural Home

And what about your house itself? How can it begin to do justice to the deep love relationship you have with the natural world? The more you understand the dynamic realms within and outside your house, the more beautifully you'll be able to allow it to dance gracefully between these worlds. Let's look a little more closely at this zone between you and the world.

Your home may appear to be standing still, but it's constantly interacting with the world within and around it (see figure 5). In fact, homes function as a unique kind of organism. They take in water, air, energy, and goods from outside, process them for our use, and expel our waste products. Sunlight, air, moisture, people, animals, fuel, electricity, food, and possessions flow in and out through doors, windows, cracks, pipes, wires, and even the walls, roof, and floor. Waste products flow out into the air, soil, bodies of water, and landfills. The house itself shrinks, expands, cracks, and leans with changes in temperature, humidity, wind, and solar radiation. In fact, decay and aging begin as soon as a house is created.

Even in terms of comfort, your home should not try to be a barrier between you and the outside world, but a system in constant interaction with other systems. It's a zone in which

This home was remodeled to bring its owners into greater contact with the natural beauty around them.

wind is slowed, sunlight is filtered, moisture is deflected, and heat is discouraged in its efforts to either leave or enter, depending on the season. The success of a home is determined by how well it does all these things, how beautifully, and for how long.

As you proceed through this book, we'll help you understand your own nature, your home's surroundings, and whether your current home is doing its job in relating the two. We'll help you determine strategies for making your home function better in keeping with your desires, your financial means, and your respect for the earth's resources and living systems.

HOME IN RELATION TO NATURAL FORCES

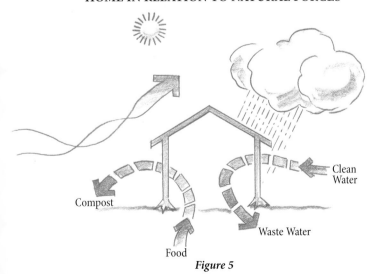

Compost

Clean Water

Waste Water

Food

Figure 5

How Does Nature Create A Home?

by Dayna Baumeister, PhD

You are not the first creature to inhabit the space your home occupies. Whether you live in the city or country, your plot of land was once home to many creatures—plants, animals, fungi, and bacteria. Is there anything you might learn from them? How did they live there? How did they survive and reproduce and create a home? Perhaps they might tell you something about the climate variations or the soil on your site, or how to create conditions conducive to life—yours included. This process

Nature-inspired homes are all around us.

of learning from the strategies of plants and animals is an emerging science called *biomimicry*. It is based on the premise that life has been around for 3.8 billion years and, in that time, has probably figured out a thing or two about what it takes to live on this planet sustainably.

Observe what the plants and animals of your area are doing. Why are there no trees higher than 20 feet in your neighborhood—soil instability? Wind? Notice how the old grasses are lying; that will tell you the predominant wind direction. What sheltered habitats do the migratory birds prefer? What does that tell you?

Biomimicry also suggests that we learn from the general principles of nature. For example:

• Consider waste as a resource.

By recycling materials, the nutrients stay in the system, allowing the whole system to thrive. When remodeling, extend your thinking beyond recycling your job site waste. Could the old iron gate be used in the garden as a trellis or painted and hung in the bathroom to hold towels?

• Diversify and cooperate to fully use the habitat.

Complex ecosystems are filled with creatures occupying most available niches, resulting in a stable and productive system. In your remodeling project, consider how shared walls or adjacent spaces can be used beneficially for both rooms. How can spaces cooperate (rather than compete) for limited resources, such as money, light, electricity, and water?

Local materials fit in with the natural landscape. The peeled poles of this remodeled entryway match the surrounding pines.

• Optimize rather than maximize.

People tend to pick one attribute or strategy and try to maximize it. But consider an elk; the larger his antlers, the more likely he will mate—but the less likely he'll be able to outrun a mountain lion. The optimal antler size will bring him both reproductive success and a chance of surviving to enjoy it. In what ways can you optimize your design?

• Use materials sparingly.

In nature, form follows function because shape is cheaper than material. How can you meet your functional needs without using too much material? Can the bathroom be near the kitchen, keeping plumbing runs short? Can your guest room double as an office, library, and reading nook?

A local salvage yard can be a treasure trove of building materials for remodeling, especially if you are trying to match original materials or fixtures.

• Shop locally.

A mature ecosystem can't pick up and move to gather its nutrients elsewhere. It stays in place and therefore must shop locally. What percentage of your remodeling materials come from your local economy? If you acquire local materials, shipping costs are eliminated, returns and exchanges are easy, nutrient flows stay in the system, and a story is created that grows with the house. Shopping locally also means fitting to local habitats. Perhaps there is a reason why terra cotta isn't made in Northern Maine.

In tapping the power of limits, nature has revealed the best of the sustainable strategies. Respecting natural limits doesn't mean you have to live in a geodesic dome or a paper sack. Consider these limits as boundaries to unbridled creativity, allowing fabulous possibilities.

Dayna Baumeister is the cofounder of the Biomimicry Guild. With degrees in biology, a devotion to applied natural history, and a passion for sharing the wonders of nature with others, Dayna works as an educator, researcher, and design consultant. For more sustainable strategies, take a look at Biomimicry: Innovation Inspired by Nature, *by Janine Benyus.*

In a whimsical expression of recycling, a used Mazda hatchback window provides an entry roof.

With an increased awareness of the natural world, you can transform your home into a welcoming haven of peace and vitality.

Can We Heal Our World?

Finally, let's put this home-remodeling stuff in perspective. Your home is neither a major cause of nor a cure for our global ecological crises. But you can look at the impact of your individual actions in two important contexts. First there's the obvious one: the more people, families, and communities who take individual action, the greater the impact. But there's a subtle issue that may be even more powerful: What is really needed is a snowballing change in perceptions and priorities.

With every person who grasps that we are all interconnected, and dependent on a healthy biosphere, and then changes his or her behavior to reflect this belief, the groundswell gains momentum. There is a tipping point when the impact of all the individual actions and attitudes becomes greater than the sum of the parts. Whole systems can change in the blink of an eye. The industrial revolution took place in a few years; a similar reorganization of society and energy systems can happen just as quickly.

How does this relate to your home? Ideally, you will embrace this opportunity at its most delightful and powerful level. You will begin by becoming more aware of the natural world within and around you, wherever you live. You will make shifts in your surroundings that increase vitality, both in you and the environment. As you remodel your home, everyone involved will be affected; you can cooperatively educate every designer, builder, subcontractor, and supplier you bring into your sphere. You will continue to make shifts that your family, friends, and neighbors will enjoy. When your home is a haven of peace and vitality in an alienating world, every visitor will be affected.

As your awareness and commitment grow, the ripples will carry even farther. Your understanding of life's cycles will deepen. Then when an issue about, say, water policy or development or forest practices comes up for a vote, you'll want yourself and others to be well informed about it because you understand how crucial such systems are. Or maybe you'll be moved to take a proactive stance, joining with others to form a watershed council, promote pedestrian-friendly neighborhoods, or protect a local forest ecosystem. In other words, every step you take to deepen your awareness is a part of the larger journey. There's no need to view natural remodeling as a huge undertaking; the moment you tune into the living world around you, you have taken the biggest step. The rest is details.

Myhrman/Knox Family Compound

Tucson, Arizona

Imagine that you're walking down a residential street in Tucson, Arizona. It's a middle-class neighborhood, built in the 1930s. You pass one small cinderblock house after another, all looking similar under their different colors of paint. They're surrounded by a variety of landscaping: border lawns, cactus gardens, etc. Suddenly, you notice a change. You feel as though you've stepped into a different world.

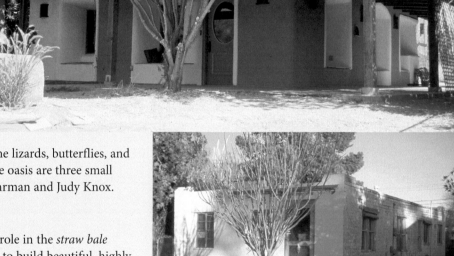

A thick, sinuous plastered garden wall welcomes you into an urban oasis of winding paths, flowers, fruit trees, sculptures, and water features. An earthen bench invites you to sit in the shade of a palo verde tree and watch the lizards, butterflies, and birds that are drawn to this paradise. Nestled in the oasis are three small houses. This is the family compound of Matts Myhrman and Judy Knox.

Being at Home

Matts and Judy are widely known for their pivotal role in the *straw bale revival*—using densely packed bales of waste straw to build beautiful, highly insulated, thick-walled homes. For years, the couple traveled around the country, teaching groups of people how to build community while raising bale walls. At the end of each trip, they returned to their home in Tucson.

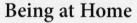

Before Matts and Judy began to work on this house, it was a poorly maintained, uninsulated concrete-block structure.

Benches built into the straw bale garden walls provide a peaceful spot to sit and enjoy the surroundings.

The plastered straw bale gateway beckons visitors into a desert oasis.

The porch roofs not only shade the house, they also create delightful outdoor rooms.

"Matts and I always assumed that some day we'd move out to the country and build our own straw bale house—or at least find an empty lot in town and build from scratch," says Judy. "But we became a little disenchanted with that several years ago. We really had a transformation in the way we thought, realizing the cost of leaving the cities and their existing infrastructure and sprawling out into the countryside. So we decided to slowly turn our own home place into a demonstration of beautiful city living—an oasis. I think it's a much more exciting life, and it also makes Mother Nature a lot happier."

Matts and Judy decided to start with the house next door. It was a 900-square-foot ugly duckling, built in 1938 of uninsulated concrete block. "When we started, it was truly in deplorable condition," says Judy. "In summer it heated up like a furnace, and in the winter it was freezing inside. And it wasn't just an energy hog; it looked horrible. The exterior had not been maintained. It needed major work. Our consciences would not allow us to own a home that was so unattractive—to people and to the environment."

For years, Matts and Judy had been trying to convince people to wrap existing houses with straw bales. "We always thought of it as possibly *the* most sustainable use of straw bale construction," offers Judy. "You're using an existing structure, rather than abandoning or destroying it, and you're making it more beautiful and energy-efficient. So when we decided to remodel our ugly duckling, we never considered any other option."

First Steps

Matts and Judy decided to take their time with this project, paying cash as they went to avoid the pressure and the interest charges of a construction loan. Beginning in 1997, they did most of the work on the rental house over a three-year period. They made only minor changes to the interior, allowing the home to be occupied throughout the remodeling process.

Tucson's climate is dry, with mild winters that require some heating and hot summers that provide the greatest comfort challenge. So the initial steps were to insulate the roof, shade the walls, and upgrade the single-pane steel casement windows to energy-efficient models—crucial features for keeping out the sun's heat.

The first step was to improve roof insulation.

Their first goal was to insulate the roof to R-40. The house had a flat roof with a ceiling cavity about 9 inches deep. It wasn't too hard to blow cellulose insulation into that cavity, but that only gave them R-27. "To get the rest of it, we did something that we felt was a compromise," says Matts, "but we decided in favor of doing it after we weighed the options." That solution was to put 2 inches of rigid isocyanurate foam over the existing roof, then top that with a hot-mopped treatment and a white elastomeric coating. The rigid foam brought the total R-value to about 42, and the white coating reflects the sun's hot rays.

Next, they replaced the windows with argon-gas-filled double-pane New Millenium Andersen windows, with a frame composed of recycled vinyl and sawdust. "I didn't like the idea of using PVC," admits Matts, "but I liked the fact that a lot of it was recycled, and the sawdust was reclaimed from their wood window manufacturing. So it was a compromise—partly in the interest of low maintenance and longevity."

Outdoor Rooms for Shade

With insulation in the roof and high-performance windows, the little house already felt more comfortable. In the second year of the project, it was time to add the crucial cooling element of shade. Armed with a load of salvaged timbers, Matts and Judy added porches on the south and east sides of

Adding a door to the long east side allowed entry near the middle of the house, making a more welcoming, functional floor plan.

the house. The porch floors are concrete, and a post-and-beam structure holds up the standing-seam metal porch roofs; the metal was chosen for its durability; a "ceiling" of reed fencing adds a warmer feeling. In some areas, the porch is roofed with reed fencing only, to let in filtered light.

For the most part, Matts and Judy left the interior of the house as it was; they spiffed up the walls with fresh paint, and they tore out the old carpeting and painted the concrete floors an earthy red. But they did make one change in the floor plan. The original front door was at one end of the long, narrow house. Judy decided that it would feel better to enter in the middle of the east side, between

the living and dining rooms, allowing the new east porch to function as an extension of those living areas. "Just moving the front door to the east side makes the house seem wider," says Judy. "It feels less like a shotgun house, and that east porch is beautiful, private, and cool in the summer."

The porch ceilings are of reed fencing, hiding the metal roof and blending well with the other warm, natural materials.

A patio roof made of reed mats turns the hot western side of the house into a comfortable shade garden.

Matts and friends lift straw bales into place.

Wrap It Up

Finally, it was time to wrap the concrete-block walls in straw bales. First the bales needed something to sit on. Where there were porches, Matts and Judy made a *toe-up* of flat, pressure-treated 2x4s, set out from the wall the width of the bales. Elsewhere, they placed railroad ties on the ground to elevate the bales from the earth. In both cases, they filled the space between the toe-up and the concrete block wall with pea gravel.

As the bales were laid up, they were held tight to the block walls with wire, via holes drilled into the hollow cores of the blocks. When completed, the bale walls were topped with a little metal roof, carefully flashed into the house's parapet wall to keep rainwater from finding its way between the bales and the block wall.

The window openings presented special challenges. Having chosen to mount the new windows in the existing block walls, the depth of the bales made inviting nooks out of the window openings. Matts and Judy decided to go all out to make those into delightful window seats, with a horizontal surface of sandstone handcrafted by Matts. Where windows were unprotected by a porch roof, a galvanized metal pan under the sandstone keeps rain from getting into the bale walls.

Wrapping the house with straw bales.

A metal roof covers the tops of some new straw bale walls.

With the bales in place, the artistry could begin: plastering and detailing the walls. "We decided that we weren't going to use any cement or wire mesh on the exterior walls," says Judy. "That was another reason for the porch roofs: to protect some areas so that we could use earth plaster. On the exposed portions, we used earth with a finish coat of lime plaster." To oversee this job, they brought Axel Linde over from Germany. Axel had taught straw building with Matts and Judy for years, then apprenticed with a master mud plasterer in Germany for three years.

In addition to the earth and lime plasters on the walls, Axel raised the surface around the door and window openings using cob, reed fencing, and burlap. He then finished these surrounds with finely polished white lime plaster. "The plastering was done five years ago, and it's as beautiful today as it was then," observes Judy. "It just transformed the place; people fall in love with it."

Where the straw bale walls aren't protected by porch roofs, the earth plaster received a finish coat of lime plaster.

24

Additional Features

When Matts and Judy shaded the south side of the house, they gave up any direct solar heat through those windows. But they made up for it by adding a solar air collector on the roof, with a small fan that distributes the heat through the duct system. Now that the house is well insulated, the solar-heated air is often all that's needed in winter. The porch roofs also cut down on the natural light in the house, which they counteracted by installing four new tubular skylights; these bring in plenty of light with little heat gain or loss.

Accomplished earth plasterer Axel Linde led the wall-finishing crew.

To improve natural ventilation, Matts and Judy used screened operable windows and doors with security screens. Their daughter-in-law, who now lives in the house with her two children, can feel safe leaving the doors open at night to cool the house with the desert night air. When daytime temperatures are too high to be handled by natural cooling, an evaporative cooler keeps indoor temperatures comfortable. Often, however, the family just lives on the porches. "They really love it there," beams Judy. "The porches are wonderfully livable on all but the hottest and coldest days of the year."

The utility bills for the bale-wrapped house are now about half what they once were. The remodeling project is still evolving. Matts and Judy's plans include solar hot water and rainwater harvesting.

Straw bale walls can easily be carved to create niches.

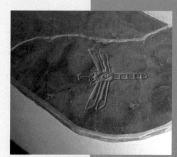

Matts crafted sandstone seats to decorate the many benches and niches in the outside walls of the house.

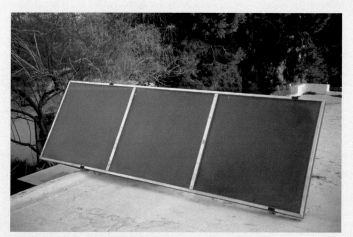

A solar air heater on the roof heats the home in winter.

Warm air is ducted from the solar panels into the house.

An openwork fence defines space and gives privacy, while letting welcome breezes pass through.

The Family Compound

Meanwhile, the extended family turned their attention to the three houses as a unit and the gardens that surround them. Over the next few years, they transformed their two city lots into a lush family compound, fondly known as the home place. The undulating straw bale garden wall at the front and back of the properties provides privacy and noise control while remaining welcoming to guests. Along the east property line, Matts planted a grove of bamboo to provide shade and block the view of the neighbor's house and swamp cooler. Throughout the property, gardens and winding paths strike a balance between connecting the three houses and providing privacy for each.

A few years ago, Judy unexpectedly found herself "landing in a wheelchair." Consequently, all the paths and garden beds are wheelchair accessible. "I encourage everyone to take accessibility into account in their designs, indoors and out," urges Judy. "Anyone could end up in a wheelchair, and nobody wants to have their home and garden inaccessible. It's far easier to achieve if you keep it in mind during every phase of design and construction."

While planting flowers and fruit trees, and creating raised beds, desert gardens, food gardens, and habitat gardens, Matts and Judy did so with respect for the precious resource of water. They invested in a sophisticated

After Judy unexpectedly ended up in a wheelchair, she began encouraging others to design gardens and homes for accessibility.

Handcrafted touches add beauty, delight, and a sense of the artistry of others to a home.

The gateways and garden walls are made of local natural materials.

26

drip-irrigation system and they use deep mulch around the plants, creating lush gardens while reducing their water bill by nearly a third. Behind the scenes, an underground system uses gravity to distribute scarce rainwater to the plants. "Being in the desert, it's easy to feel landlocked," says Judy. "So we employed local artisans to create some beautiful sculpted water features. We get to enjoy the sounds of water while attracting thirsty birds, lizards, and butterflies."

In keeping with the larger landscape, many of the shade structures, trellises, and garden walls in the family compound are made of natural desert materials, such as saguaro ribs, ocotillo cactus, and a desert bamboo called carrizo. "The landscaping has changed the place dramatically," says Judy. "There's something growing outside every door. Our home place has become an oasis in the middle of the city." "As I walk around here, this place is a source of joy for me," adds Matts. "The natural materials, the craftsmanship, the gardens—they give us rich gifts every day."

In the desert, it's crucial to use water with respect while enjoying its life-giving beauty.

Rippling Outward

The impact of all this loving work goes well beyond the people who live in this home place. Hundreds of people tour the family compound every year, for garden tours, solar home tours, and workshops. "People can hardly believe what can be done in two modest urban lots," says Judy. "We love hearing people say, 'You know, we really could do this; little by little, we could make our city place into a beautiful oasis like this."

Beauty is an important aspect of this demonstration center. "We've come to understand beauty as an

Behind a beautiful handcrafted gate is a pleasant, partly sunny spot to sit and enjoy a meal with friends.

Matts And Judy's Top Five Tips for Hot Dry Climates

1. Shade your walls in summer; if you can do so in a way that lets in winter sun, all the better. Look for ways to get shade naturally: trellises, deciduous trees, and vines.

2. Insulate well; use straw bales wherever appropriate.

3. Use materials that can stand up to the sun; it's not green to have good materials go bad quickly.

4. Consider the landscape as part of your renovation. Use rainwater and minimize water use; honor the fact that you're in the desert, and don't try to create a New England garden.

5. Use natural ventilation; keep air moving through the interior with windows, doors, and security screens if necessary, especially at night in spring and in fall, when the air temperatures drop.

essential component of sustainability," says Judy, "because it inspires replication."

Matts and Judy have developed a bottom-line criterion for all their decisions: "If this were replicated 300,000 times in this city, would that be a contribution or would it diminish our area?" Looking back on this project, Judy offers, "The choice we made to stay here, the things we've done to make this functional, beautiful, and environmentally friendly—we would be proud to see it replicated 300,000 times in Tucson."

Asked for her advice to people who want to live more sustainably, Judy says emphatically, "Don't move an inch. You don't have to go anywhere to create beauty. All you have to do is look at what you've got and start thoughtfully stepping through. You can't do it all at once; make a 10-year plan, a five-year plan. But stay where you are, use your existing infrastructure, use natural materials, locally available materials, scrounged materials. Keep beauty very high in your focus. If you keep stepping through the process, you'll transform your living space—and maybe the world."

Tucson artist Sharon Brady created metal sconces that celebrate urban Sonoran desert fauna.

Everyone loves hanging out on the porches year-round.

28

You, Your House, and Your Site

When you build a thing, you cannot merely build that thing in isolation, but must also repair the world around it, and within it, so that the larger world at that one place becomes more coherent, and more whole; and the thing which you make takes its place in the web of nature, as you make it.

—Christopher Alexander

Your home and garden, like a plant turning toward the sun, can thrive by adapting to their own unique circumstances.

JUST AS A SEED NEEDS FERTILE SOIL, sunshine, and water to grow, your remodeling process needs a starting point that's rich in information so that it can take root and thrive. Natural remodeling begins with paying attention to who and where you are. In this chapter, you'll start with learning more about yourself and the others who share your home, then move outward to study your house and its surroundings. People have a tendency to jump straight into design or material selection without first getting to know the ecosystems they're part of (including the house and people). Skipping these initial steps is likely to result in a disjointed product that doesn't meet your needs—possibly accompanied by high energy consumption, high construction cost, structural problems, or even poor health.

Remember that the primary goal of natural remodeling is to restore your vital connection with the rest of the living world. That can only be done by first understanding how you and your family live, what the world outside your home is like, and how your house mediates between those two realms.

Exploring yourself, your house, and your site gives your remodeling process a firm foundation. Knowing what you have to work with will make the many decisions to come easier and more coherent. As you work your way through this chapter, a clearer picture of your available needs, resources, and goals will emerge, which in turn will inform your choice of design strategies.

Studying your current circumstances can also lead to uniquely beautiful, effective design solutions. Because each home and landscape has different features, and everyone has distinctive tastes and needs, each natural home will have its own personality. To return to the plant analogy, no two plants grow in exactly the same way—especially if they grow in different locations. Each plant responds to its unique conditions, resulting in different shapes, sizes, and even colors. What could be more delightful?

Starting Your Project Notebook

As you gather information about yourself, your house, and your locale, you'll want to record it in a useful manner. Designate a three-ring binder for this project. In the binder, jot down your observations, collect pictures, store charts and graphs, and make notes and sketches on plans. We'll discuss how to create and use these tools as we go along. Your Project Notebook will guide you as you fine-tune your design to fit your unique site, house, and preferences.

Use your Project Notebook as a place to collect visual images from magazines and books. Choose photos that resonate with you at a gut level. Sometimes a photo might only contain one material or element that grabs your attention—cabinet pulls or the relationship between the kitchen and dining room. Save it and add sticky notes with your thoughts. These images can spark your imagination as you begin to design.

Later in the design process, your Project Notebook will help you organize product brochures and other information as you begin to make decisions about materials and systems. With everything in one place, you'll be able to access information when you need it.

The better you understand yourself and your family's needs, the more likely you are to be satisfied with the results, and the less likely you are to overbuild. Sometimes people remodel their homes based more on an idea of perfection than on an understanding of what's already there. They may tear down and rebuild so much of their house that they begin to wonder if they should have just built a new one. If their intention is to remodel for greater eco-friendliness, the

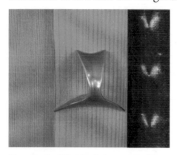

Your Project Notebook is a great place to keep pictures of things you want to include in your remodeling project— like this whale-tail cabinet door pull that goes with a water theme.

excessive use of resources becomes especially questionable. But if you begin with an open mind and work from an awareness of your actual needs and available resources, you may find that you can significantly improve your lives and your level of environmental responsibility without dramatic changes. It's all in the approach.

Taking Stock: You and Your Family

Your personal explorations will help you understand where your current home does and does not meet your functional, physical, and emotional needs. The better you know yourself in relation to your environment, the more accurately you'll be able to massage your home into harmony with everything in and around it. That kind of accuracy pays off in making the best use of resources—from forests and fuels to your personal energy and finances.

To help you with this process, you will find a questionnaire in Appendix A, page 261. Make a copy for everyone in your household and have each person fill one out. This may take a few days. That's fine. The point is to encourage everyone to explore what each wants from your home. When everyone is finished answering the questionnaire, find some way to discuss everyone's answers. Swap them, have a family meeting, do anything that gets everyone communicating about this feedback.

When contemplating how you want to change your home and yard, don't forget to spend time outdoors considering how to best use nature's gifts.

In my architectural practice, I give my clients an extensive questionnaire early in the process—much like the one you'll find in Appendix A, page 261. Most clients are delighted, but a few are downright resistant. I explain to them that the more I understand about their tastes, their wants and needs, their lifestyle, their family, and their personal environmental history, the more readily their design will emerge, and the more satisfying it will be— and the less time we'll have to spend backtracking.

But the best testimonials have come from clients themselves. In fact, the clients who fight the questionnaire hardest often become its biggest fans. "Tell your future clients that your questionnaire was one of the best surprises in the process," urged one formerly feisty client.

Whether you design your own remodeling project or hire a professional, the questionnaire is an invaluable starting point. I think its power comes from the fact that most of us aren't used to paying attention to the habitual parts of our lives. We often take our living circumstances for granted, adjusting around inconveniences and not noticing when our vitality is diminished. Sometimes we forget there's more to life than finishing our to-do lists, making enough money to pay the mortgage, and keeping up appearances—or just plain keeping up! All too often, our self-awareness gradually diminishes. And why should we want to know our true, deep desires if we don't think we can satisfy them?

I've come to believe that most people don't realize what they're missing— how much richer their lives could be if they paid attention to their basic wants and satisfied them in straightforward, natural ways. Taking time to work with the questionnaire is a gift to yourself that will last a lifetime. If the questionnaire seems long, just try setting aside a few minutes a day to work on it.

Everyone's awareness level is different; you may already notice many of the things the questionnaire asks about, or most of this may be new to you. But for almost everyone, at least a few questions will help you see yourself

Choosing a kitchen counter is just one of the major decisions that will benefit from a deeper look at your underlying wants and needs.

and your environment in a different way—a way that can play out in re-creating your home to better nourish you.

Parts of the questionnaire may seem unusual; their purpose is to stir up your not-so-linear/logical awareness. Let yourself go with these questions, and be open to pleasant surprises.

One final point: I always ask each client to fill out a separate questionnaire. This worries many couples, who fear that their unspoken or unresolved conflicts will come to the fore. Worse yet, they fear that the only possible result is deeper conflict and misery. I assure them that, in decades of helping people design or redesign their homes, I've never had a couple split up over a disagreement—or even have to adjust to being in disharmony. The reason? Through the magic of the design process, we've always been able to find solutions that meet everyone's wants and needs.

Here's how it works. People often have specific ideas about what they want or think they need. At that level, it's easy to have conflicts. But if we explore the essence of the desire—look behind the specifics to discover the underlying functional, esthetic, spiritual, or other requirements—there's almost always a solution that satisfies both people. For example, let's say Gerry wants a tile countertop, and Jude insists on laminate. Upon investigation, it turns out that Gerry wants the durability of tile, while Jude dislikes dirty grout lines. We emerge with a new set of criteria: a countertop that is durable and doesn't have grout lines. Granite, poured concrete, or composite countertops could please everyone. It can be that straightforward at every level: identify the essence of the desire, explore what really needs to be satisfied, and seek creative solutions that work for everyone.

Older wood siding and trim can be rejuvenated with caulk and a colorful paint job, as in this Portland, Oregon, home remodeled by Bloom Design.

Taking Stock: Your Home

After you know yourself better in relation to your surroundings, it's time to move out one layer and get to know your home better. This is the time to evaluate your house's strengths, as well as the features that need improvement. This is also the time to get better acquainted with the physical nature of your house; its materials and forms will suggest appropriate responses during the design and construction phases.

Making an inventory of your home's exterior materials (windows, cladding, and roof) early will help you prioritized projects later on.

In the summer when the sun is high in the sky, overhangs may keep sunlight from penetrating deeply into a room.

The House

In your Project Notebook, record answers to the following questions. If you can't determine the answers yourself, this is a good time to call on a professional.

- What are the structural materials of your home? In other words, what holds up the roof and walls? For example, your roof structure might be prefab trusses and your walls might be concrete block, with a concrete perimeter foundation.

- What are the exterior finish materials (roofing, siding, etc.)? How old are they? What condition are they in?

- Is there insulation in your roof, walls, and/or floor? If so, what kind (e.g., fiberglass, cellulose, etc.), how much (e.g., R-30, 12 inches), and in what condition?

- What kind of windows does your house have? How well do they function, mechanically and thermally? What type of glazing (single pane, double pane, low E, storm windows, etc.) and sash (wood, aluminum, etc.) do they have?

- What type of heating and cooling systems does your house have? Age? Size or rating? Location? Type and location of thermostat? Duct condition?

- What are the interior finish materials in each room (wall, floor, cabinet, etc.)? What condition are they in? How do you feel about them (love, hate, don't notice)?

The Indoor Climate

Now turn your attention to your indoor climate. For each room in your house, spend some time noticing how it relates with the natural phenomena outdoors:

- Does sunlight shine directly into the room? Is this ever a problem or an asset? How far does the sun penetrate into the room at different times of day and year?

- Is the room often too warm or too cold? Clammy? Drafty? Too bright or too dim?

- Does the interior temperature change much during a sunny day? How about on a cloudy day? Can you feel the air move in a particular pattern? Is there a draft?

- Is the room inviting? Is it more inviting in some seasons or times of day than in others?

- Does the view from the window make you smile—or not?

Check for Hazards

In addition to a basic inventory of the physical materials and systems of your home, this is also the best time to look for problem areas and potential health hazards. Lead, electromagnetic fields (EMFs), mold, toxics, pests, asbestos, or pressurization problems may already be causing problems in your house or to your health—or you may be able to deal with them before they do. You're likely to spend plenty of time and money remodeling your house, so it's best to be confident that you're not ignoring a problem that could lower the value of all your efforts (see Appendix B, page 263).

The view from this sunny window seat revitalizes the senses.

Sun streaming into a room may warm it up quickly.

Draw a Floor Plan

To know your house better, create a floor plan of your house and make notes about the rooms on the plan. This can be a simple sketch, or you can measure the whole house and draft an accurate floor plan (or hire someone to do so). Graph paper with four spaces per inch (or one-quarter inch between lines) is useful for drawing floor plans to *scale*. Let each quarter-inch space equal one foot (see figure 1). At this stage, it may not matter how accurate and detailed your plan is, but it will matter later in the process. If you decide to create measured plans (called *as-builts*), the process itself may reveal useful information about your house; until you measure it, you might not have noticed, for example, that one of your walls is thicker than the others. Such clues can tell you about hidden opportunities or about the history of the house.

Make a copy of your completed floor plan just for making notes about the rooms. Be creative. Have fun with this process. You may want to use colors: a sunny room could be yellow, and a cold one blue. Squiggly lines could indicate drafts, and hearts could show your favorite places in the house (see figure 2). Paying attention to your surroundings reaps continuing benefits. The more you pay attention, the more subtleties you will notice.

YOUR BASE FLOOR PLAN

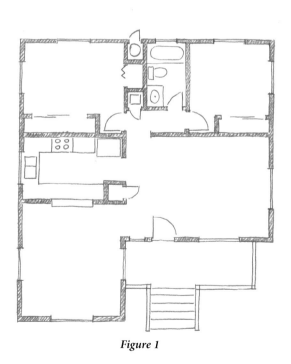

Figure 1

MARKED UP FLOOR PLAN

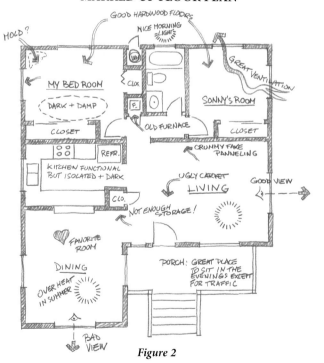

Figure 2

Taking Stock: Your Site

Now we come to one of the most important aspects of natural remodeling. This isn't just about you; it isn't just about your house; it's about how your house interacts with the world around it, and how that interaction can be used to keep you happy and comfortable without contributing to the destruction of our global life-support system. This is also one of the most fun, satisfying, enlightening parts of the process.

The information you gain here about your surroundings will help you throughout the design process. For example:

• What type and style of windows should I use?

Base your answers on how much sun, wind, and rain the windows will be exposed to, how much ultraviolet light they need to block out, whether they're needed for ventilation, whether they need to block sound, and what the views are like through them.

• Does the new entry door need a protective roof? If so, how large should it be?

Look at which directions the sun and rain come from, and in what quantities.

• What type of insulation should I use? How much do I need?

The difference between indoor and outdoor temperatures in your heating and cooling seasons will guide you to make cost-effective choices.

• What paint colors will look best in my dining room?

Consider how much sunlight the room receives and from what direction in order to find out how the natural light will affect the room's color.

You may already know more about the world around your house than you realize. You're

there morning and night, during calm weather and storms. With a little extra attention, you can quickly become an expert on your site. Take some time to sit outside your home at various times of day and night. Don't worry about recording your observations the first time; just sit and take it all in.

Sit Still and Notice

Next time you're out in your yard, use the following questions to focus your awareness. Make notes about your observations. If your life moves so quickly that you can't imagine sitting still and pondering these questions, that's okay. Just reading them and paying attention to your surroundings as you buzz through will increase your awareness. But if you can take 15 minutes or more now, and then come back to spend more time to sit and notice your world, your experience will be richer.

• What parts of the yard are sunny or shady? Where is the sun in the sky? Where did the sun come up this morning, and where will it set? Where will it rise and set in other seasons?

• What do you hear? What animals live in your yard? Is there a pond, stream, or larger body of water nearby? Do you hear traffic, machinery, or other mechanical sounds?

• Is there any breeze? If so, where is it coming from? Can you see it moving the tree branches? Does it feel moist or dry? Does it come from a specific direction during storms?

• When was the last rain? When do you anticipate rain again? Is there a rainy season? Is there any standing water on the ground? Which are the wettest parts of the site? The driest?

Warm eastern light accentuates the color of this red wall.

- Are there trees or bushes nearby? Do they cast shadows on the yard? If so, what areas are in shade at what times of day?

- Is your property flat? Sloping? Varied? Where are the lowest and highest spots? Are there any rock outcroppings? What do you observe about how ground moisture, plants, and air motion are affected by these topographic variations?

- Where are you sitting? Why did you choose this location? Is there a place in your yard where you love to be? A place you avoid? What qualities do those locations have? Do your preferences change with time of day or season?

- Is there a long view beyond your property, or just a short one within your yard? Are there things you'd rather see more of, or rather not see at all?

Once you're attuned to these features of your surroundings, you will naturally continue to observe them. Sit in different places at different times of day and continue to observe your home's surroundings.

Put up a wind sock that you can see from indoors to make the wind direction more visible; you'll soon become an expert in how the intensity and direction of your local wind varies in response to changing conditions. You can even make quick observations as you pass through your yard or look out the window. Record your observations and keep them in your Project Notebook.

Awareness of the living world can become second nature if you just take some time to sit in your yard and notice what's going on around you.

Notice the movement of sunlight and shade at different times of day. This will help you fine-tune your house to take advantage of nature's gifts.

Lightweight flags or a wind sock will heighten your awareness of even the lightest breeze. Knowing the wind's direction and intensity at different times of day and year makes it easy to design for weather protection and natural ventilation.

You'll find that you're not only amassing interesting information about your little piece of the world, you're also becoming a more refined receiver. Your curiosity has been activated, and your sensitivities are likely to remain heightened. You'll notice how the air feels, where the sun shines, and what feels good to you. You'll find yourself wanting to know what that squirrel is eating, why the wind suddenly shifted, or what will grow next spring in the boggy area. The more you notice, the more delightful and cost-effective your remodeling project will be.

After you've become more attuned to your environment, you may find that you want to know more than you can easily observe directly. This is a good time to augment your powers of observation by referring to data collected by others. Topographic maps, street maps, weather data, utility layout diagrams, watershed maps, and tables of solar radiation will deepen your understanding of your area and empower you to respond appropriately.

Creating a Base Site Plan

As you observe the microclimate around your home, you'll probably want to record your observations on a plan of your property. There are several ways to obtain such a site plan: measure and draw it yourself, acquire a copy from the person who designed your house, get a plot plan from your title documents or the assessor's office, or hire a professional to create one for you.

The site plan should be drawn to scale; the appropriate scale will depend on such factors as the size of your property and the amount of information you want to record. Some common scales for site plans are $\frac{1}{8}$ inch = 1 foot, 1 inch = 10 feet, and 1 inch = 20 feet. If your property is relatively large (over half an acre), you may want to draw two site plans: one that shows the area immediately surrounding the house, and one at a smaller scale that shows your whole property. If you will be working with an architect, building department, or design review board, they may guide your choice of scale.

WHAT'S A MICROCLIMATE?

The word *microclimate* describes the effects of sun, water, wind, topography, and vegetation on the climate in a small area—in this case, the area around your home. For example, your regional climate may be sunny and windy, but trees on your site may shade your house and deflect the wind, making your microclimate shady and calm. In fact, the microclimates on different sides of your house will differ from each other. Unless other factors intervene, the south side is likely to be drier and warmer than the north side, and in sunny climates the west side will be hotter than the east side. Ultimately, the microclimates around your home will determine the best design strategies for your remodeling project. In addition, gently modifying the existing microclimates to suit your needs can be an enjoyable way to better understand the natural world (there's more on this in chapter 6).

A patio roof made of reed mats can turn the hot western side of a house into a comfortable shade garden.

38

Your base plan should include the following elements (see figure 3):

• the property boundaries (obtained from your title description or a survey)

• a north arrow showing magnetic and true north (based on a map or direct measurement)

• your house and any other structures on the property (actual size, shape, and location)

• dominant features such as roads, driveways, walkways, trees, major landscaping, and waterways

• adjacent buildings or features that impact your house or property (a neighbor's house or tree that shades your property, a nearby well)

• planning regulations such as building *setback* lines (limitations on how close you may build to your property line) or utility easements

As with your floor plan, be creative about recording your observations on the site plan. Again, have fun with this step: use colors, symbols, and anything else that tells the story of what you observe (see figure 4).

YOUR BASE SITE PLAN

Figure 3

YOUR SITE PLAN WITH YOUR OBSERVATIONS

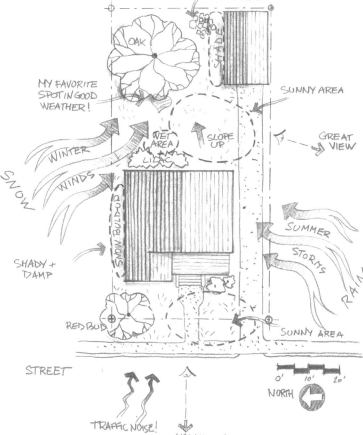

Figure 4

Carol evolved this climate rose diagram to summarize basic climate data on a site plan (see figure 5). Placing it on the plans (either drawn, or copied and pasted) through the entire design process, from site planning to final details, allows Carol and her clients to respond appropriately to basic elements of the local climate at every stage. The climate rose indicates the cardinal directions (North, South, East, and West), sun paths at the solstices, and prevailing and storm wind directions. You can create a climate rose for your own site, starting with the cardinal directions on your site plan. Add solstice sunrises and sunsets as shown (from the sun-path diagram for your latitude), and finish it off with dominant wind directions based on your observations or on weather data.

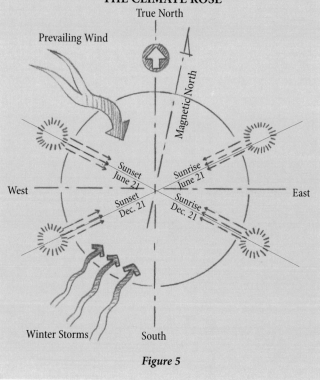

THE CLIMATE ROSE

Figure 5

Rounding Out Your Site Plan

In addition to climate, it will be helpful to plot several other features on your site plan. Some of the following items may not apply to your home, but others may be controlling factors. For instance, on a flat suburban lot, topography is not a big consideration, but the location of utility lines or building setbacks required by the local planning department might limit your options. Your material choices might be influenced by an abundant supply of stone, trees on your property that need to be thinned, or a concrete slab you want to remove. Perhaps there's a view you want to emphasize or a historic tree you want to preserve. The more relevant information you record on your site plan, the better equipped you will be when you begin to design.

TOPOGRAPHY

Topography is the direction and degree of the ground's slope. It influences the amount of sun you receive and how wind and water will flow. If you are in a hilly area, notice the variations in microclimate on slopes of various orientations. If you have (or can hire) the right skills, you can represent your topography as *contour lines*. Otherwise, just note the direction of the slope with an arrow, and the degree with a word or symbol (*gentle, steep*). The topography immediately around your house is usually the most relevant when remodeling your home.

DOMESTIC WATER AND WASTE

Locate your domestic water sources and waste lines: municipal water lines and meters, wells and supply lines, sewer lines, septic tanks, leach lines, and anything else that appears to be relevant. Your utility districts can provide information about connections to your property and any easements (limited rights to use your property by others).

If your site is rural, record wells and septic systems on neighboring properties to assure that proper clearances are maintained.

VISTA

The views from your property are an important part of your sense of place and your psychological health. On the perimeter of your site plan, make note of any visual elements that you want to enhance or minimize, near or far.

WILDLIFE

Make notes about the wildlife in your area, whether you live in a city or in the country. Record on your site plan any nesting areas, food sources, watering holes, and other signs of flying, squiggling, and four-legged creatures.

THERMAL FACTORS

When you've plotted the vegetation on your site plan, take a few minutes to consider how it affects your microclimate. Large areas of vegetation generally cool the surrounding area; they can also act as windbreaks or wind amplifiers. Exposed rock out-croppings, patios and walls of stone or concrete, and exposed

Observing patterns of sun and shade in your yard can help you decide where to place a garden bench.

gravel or soil are called "thermal mass" because they absorb and radiate solar heat. On your site plan, draw the vegetated areas and any exposed thermal mass. Make notes about how they may affect the microclimate in and around your house.

CIVIC REGULATION: PLANNING AND ZONING

If you live in or near a developed area, contact your local Planning Department and homeowner's association to determine what regulations apply to your property, including zoning restrictions, setbacks from property lines, wetlands, or wildlife corridors, and limits on building height and lot coverage. Record this information graphically on your site plan.

Near views can be enhanced with a focal point like a birdbath or statue.

You're On Your Way

Now look back at everything you've learned about yourself and your home in this chapter. Without picking up a hammer, screwdriver, or shovel, you've laid the foundation for your remodeling project. You probably knew a lot more about your site and climate than you realized, but you may not have known how to put it all in one place before. Congratulations! This information will guide you through every major decision from now on.

In the chapters to come, we'll help you understand how to make these connections between site and climate information, design decisions, and materials selections. But most important of all, by observing the ecosystems around you, you've begun to restore your awareness that you are an integral part of nature. Your body, mind, and soul have entered into a deeper relationship with the living world. And that is the most powerful, satisfying aspect of natural remodeling.

WHEN SHOULD YOU CALL IN A PRO?

Important:	What Kind of Pro?
When making structural changes (changing walls, headers, or beams; adding up or out; etc.)	Structural or civil engineer
To evaluate mold, pests, electromagnetic fields (EMFs), and/or indoor air quality problems and what to do about them	House doctor, indoor air quality (IAQ) specialist, hygienist, least-toxic pest-control operator, EMF specialist, Baubiologist
To perform an energy audit of your house and recommend options	Certified home energy analyst
For advice about using green building materials and systems with which you are unfamiliar	Qualified architect, consultant, or contractor

Not Necessary, But Helpful:	What Kind of Pro?
To draft up your site plan (including topo contours), floor plans, and other drawings	Architect, building designer, drafter, and/or surveyor
For help with your design	Architect or building designer
To fine-tune your passive solar and natural cooling schemes	Qualified consultant, architect, or building designer
To help you comply with zoning, fire codes, building codes, and energy regulations	Architect, building designer, contractor, code consultant, or energy consultant
For help with landscape/garden design	Garden designer, permaculture designer, landscape architect

NOTE: Not all professionals are experienced with ecological remodeling; you should thoroughly check out any professional's qualifications (green and otherwise). Always interview professionals, ask to see examples of their work, obtain and check references, check with appropriate licensing boards, and use a contract that explains the scope of work, each party's responsibilities, and payment arrangements.

CHAPTER 3
The Sun: Light for Life

*"Give me the splendid, silent sun,
with all his beams full-dazzling!"*

— Walt Whitman

IF YOU WANT TO BRING YOUR HOME into harmony with nature, it's a good idea to start by looking to the sun. Think of all the sun gives us: night and day, the four seasons, heat, wind, a sense of direction and time of day, and awe-inspiring sunrises and sunsets.

When you use free sunshine to heat and light your home, you get multiple benefits: greater thermal comfort and lower utility bills. Using less fossil fuel also means less pollution and less greenhouse-gas production. To top it all off, you'll be healthier and better attuned with natural cycles.

Letting sunshine in brings free light and heat, reduces fossil fuel use, and helps you tune into natural cycles.

Your Place in the Sun

Your latitude is a primary factor in your relationship with the sun and, therefore, your climate. The farther you are from the equator, the greater the seasonal variations you'll experience in air temperature and sunshine (until, of course, you reach the polar regions where cold conditions are fairly permanent). Regions that receive more solar energy generally have warmer climates, but high elevation or large bodies of water can exert a cooling effect. In the U.S., the southern states tend to be warmer all year because, on average, the sun is higher in the sky than in the northern latitudes. Northern states experience greater temperature variations in the course of a year because their part of the earth is tilted toward the sun in summer, but away from the sun in winter (see figure 1).

The sun's path is quite predictable throughout the day and year (see figure 2). This makes the process of designing for solar light and shade fairly straightforward—and empowering. The most direct way to familiarize yourself with the sun's path is through observation: Identify north, south, east, and west at your home site, and notice where the sun is as it makes its way across the sky each day.

Begin by paying attention to where the sun's light falls in your home, yard, and workplace at various times of day and notice how you use, or don't use, the light of the sun:

- How does sunshine enter the rooms where you spend most of the day?

- Do you awaken gradually in the mornings with sunlight, or does an alarm clock do the job?

- Do you spend some time outdoors every day?

- Do you notice how the color and intensity of the sun's light varies among morning, noon, and evening—and between summer and winter?

- Do you notice the sun's path being higher in summer than in winter?

- How often do you watch the sun rise or set?

Noticing how the sun shines into your home is the first step in planning for better daylighting and solar heating.

Variations in Sunlight Quality

The color, angle, and intensity of sunlight vary with the season and the time of day (see figure 3, page 45). In the morning and the evening, sunlight comes to us at a low angle, allowing it to shine directly into unobstructed east and west windows. The intensity of such solar radiation is relatively low, however, because it passes through more of the earth's atmosphere than does the midday sun, due to its low angle. On the other hand, late afternoon sunshine feels hotter than early morning sun—even though it comes from a similar angle—because, by afternoon, the sun's rays have been heating the earth and the air all day.

SUN & EARTH
(Winter in the Northern Hemisphere)

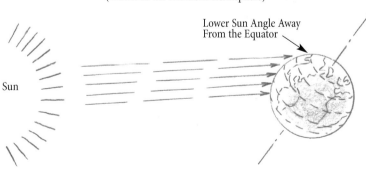

Figure 1

SUN PATH

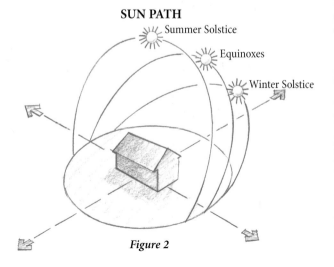

Figure 2

SUNLIGHT AND HEALTH

What's in it for you when you open your home to sunlight and spend more time outdoors in good weather? To begin with, sunlight improves your attitude and behavior. Studies have shown that students in sunlit schoolrooms perform markedly better than their peers in non-sunlit rooms. Similarly, sunlit retail stores show increased sales, lower employee absenteeism, and fewer employee mistakes than electrically lit stores. One survey of indoor workers found a strong correlation between the amount of sunlight entering the workspace and job satisfaction at every level from warehouse employees to upper management.

There's a biological basis for such findings. Not only does your body rely on the sun's daily and annual cycles to regulate its basic functions (see chapter 1), but it's important to receive the full spectrum of sunlight. When sunlight enters your eyes, it activates your endocrine system, which is connected to your immune and your nervous systems. Under fluorescent lights, you don't receive the sunlight that is vital to a proper balance of melatonin and serotonin.

According to Zane Kime, M.D., M.S.[1], the ultraviolet (UV) portion of sunlight helps your heart, blood chemistry, immune system, energy level, and sex life, while its absence weakens your body's systems and contributes to disease. A lack of sunshine sometimes brings on Seasonal Affective Disorder (appropriately known as "SAD"), a type of lethargy and depression that appears to have more in common with hibernation than with clinical depression.

As with other natural phenomena, moderation is the keyword. It's good for most of us to be exposed to direct sunlight, at least for brief periods every day; it's good for us to see sunlight often throughout the day; and it's good for us to be protected from the sun's extremes. Our homes and gardens can help us have a rich relationship with solar light and warmth, without giving us too much of a good thing.

Bringing sunlight into this formerly dark ranch house was a primary goal for this remodeling project.

Lighting Your Home with the Sun

Sunlight brings a room to life, giving it color and warmth. When people remodel, they often ask for sunnier rooms.

Using the sun to light indoor spaces—otherwise known as *daylighting*—decreases the use of electric lights that consume energy and money. Equally important, sunlight helps our bodies function well, and it provides the best color balance for a wide

QUALITIES OF SUNLIGHT FROM DIFFERENT DIRECTIONS

DIRECTION	ANGLE	INTENSITY	PERCEIVED TEMPERATURE	COLOR OF LIGHT	GLARE
NORTH	Low to absent	Low	Cool	Cool	Minimal
EAST	Low to moderate	Low to moderate	Cool to warm	Cool to warm	High in morning
SOUTH	High	High	Hot	Cool	Moderate
WEST	Moderate to low	Moderate to low	Very hot	Warm	High in afternoon

Figure 3

range of tasks. Sunlight changes constantly in color, intensity, and direction, which keeps our minds and bodies stimulated and attuned with natural rhythms.

It's best to let sunlight reflect off light-colored surfaces.

Today's window technology allows you to bring sunlight into your home while minimizing undesirable levels of heat, glare, and ultraviolet (UV) degradation. But all too often, we rely on electric lighting to make up for poor design or to extend our days well into the night. With some basic knowledge, you can unplug from dependence on electric lighting and enjoy the richer qualities of natural light from the sun.

Sunlight is very bright, so you don't need large expanses of glass to light a room. Here are some principles for bringing sunlight into your home:

• The best daylighting is usually diffuse light shining on light-colored surfaces.

• In most regions of the U.S., a glass area equal to 5% of a room's floor area will provide adequate daylight for basic vision. You may well want more window area for tasks, views, solar heat gain, and ventilation.

High windows help bring light into this cozy area.

• For adequate illumination and even sunlight distribution, the depth of a room should be less than two and a half times the height of the window head.

• Placing windows on at least two walls of a room provides balanced light distribution, reduces glare, softens contrast, and allows cross-ventilation.

• North-facing windows provide the most diffuse light and create the least glare.

• High windows throw light deeper into a space than lower windows (see figure 4).

Every latitude and climate zone presents different daylighting challenges and opportunities. For example, homes in temperate regions are often deficient in daylight, while homes in tropical regions may have an excess. In regions where the sky is generally overcast, admitting that diffuse sunlight directly into the space is usually sufficient. Where skies are clearer, reflected sunlight is easier on the eyes and minimizes overheating. You can also select window glass to balance light, solar gain, and summer shading (for more on windows, see chapter 7).

SUNSHINE THROUGH HIGH AND LOW WINDOWS

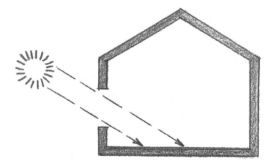

Figure 4

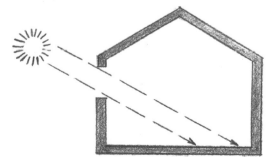

Higher windows allow deeper sunlight penetration into a room.

As you strive to improve your home's daylighting, keep the big picture in mind. If you add windows, place them to do other things as well: frame a view, admit or avoid heat, allow cross-ventilation. Keep in mind that, like your ancestors, you can make the best use of sunlight by waking up with the sun, doing most of your visual tasks during daylight, and sleeping when it's dark. You're likely to find that your body's rhythms function better this way, too.

CAROL'S EXPERIENCE *Sun-path charts are a great way to determine where the sun will be at any time of day or year, without having to make notes and measurements for a whole year (see Resources, on page 266). Using a sun-path diagram for your latitude, you can find the direction of the solstice sunrises and sunsets and plot them on a climate rose for your site (see the sidebar, Climate Rose, on page 40). Record this information on your site plan to give you an immediate picture of where sunlight comes from at various times of the year (see figure 5). This will help you decide where to put windows, how to position shading devices, where to add thermal storage, and how to design outdoor rooms (more on these later in this chapter).*

SITE PLAN WITH CLIMATE ROSE

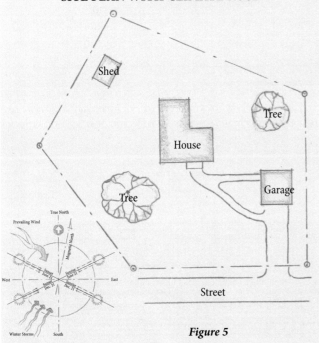

Figure 5

Low-Hanging Fruit *things you can do today*

- Get to know your sunlight. Take another look at the notes you've made about sunshine and shade on your site and floor plans. Remember that the sun's position changes seasonally; what's sunny in the summer could easily be shady in the winter. Look at a sun-path chart and imagine where the sun will be at different times of year. How will annual changes affect the sunlight in your house and yard?

- Rethink your usage. Compare the patterns of sun and shade you observe with how you actually use your home and yard. For example, if you eat breakfast in a gloomy room and use a sunny room for storage, you might want to consider changing how you use these areas. Try moving your furniture to make the best use of sunlight. For example, put reading chairs, writing desks, and grooming areas near windows and skylights; locate storage, computer and TV areas, and beds farther from windows.

- Map out the possibilities. Where you notice an excess or deficiency of sunlight, look for the causes: Are your roof overhangs too deep or too narrow? Do plants shade windows where you want light? Is a skylight too big? Make notes of these elements and consult the lists under More Advanced Moves for ideas about how to increase or temper the levels of sunlight in your home.

- Remove shade-producing obstructions where reasonable. Cut back foliage, remove poorly placed trellises, hold curtains back from windows by day, and keep the glass clean to let in sunlight.

This room's abundant sunlight could cause glare on a computer screen, but simply moving the desk away from windows will minimize the problem.

47

More Advanced Steps *things you can do tomorrow*

Once you've assessed your home's daylighting assets and liabilities, use these guidelines to make more involved improvements (see figure 6).

Light Up Notoriously Dark Areas

- Let reflection maximize the effect of incoming sunlight by making the first surface it strikes light-colored:

- Paint window casings and frames a light color. Have light-colored surfaces outside windows (paving, landscaping, adjacent house or yard walls, a pond), taking care to avoid glare.

- Use light-colored walls and ceilings to reflect incoming light; avoid dark floor coverings and furnishings. To minimize annoying reflections, use matte or eggshell paint on walls that receive direct light.

- Consider using well-placed mirrors, reflective louvers, or blinds to bounce sunlight deeper into a room.

- Paint the porch ceiling or the undersides of eaves a light (reflective) color (see figure 7).

- Add or enlarge windows or add a skylight (see sidebar, Skylights, on page 51), a light well, clerestory windows, or even an atrium. The most effective way to enlarge a window is to increase its height. If you plan to add openings in a solid wall, inside or out, check with a professional to make sure you aren't weakening the structure (see figure 8).

- Bring daylight into darker rooms from lighter adjacent rooms via interior windows (glazed or open) and reflectors (see figure 9).

- To light a basement, consider excavating a window well (see figure 10).

Sunshine reflected off the light-colored, splayed jambs of a straw-bale wall makes the opening seem larger.

DAYLIGHTING DIAGRAMS

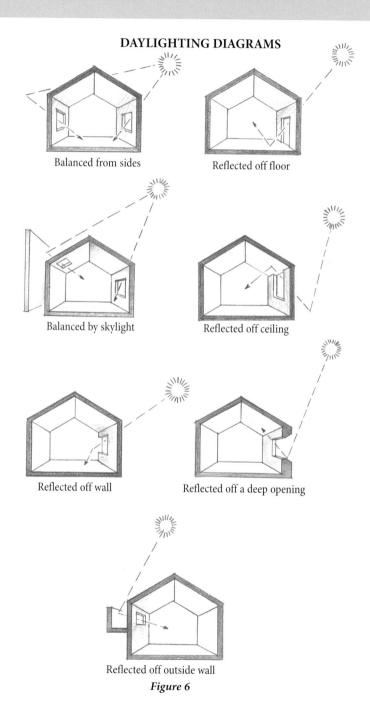

Balanced from sides

Reflected off floor

Balanced by skylight

Reflected off ceiling

Reflected off wall

Reflected off a deep opening

Reflected off outside wall

Figure 6

REFLECTIVE SOFFIT

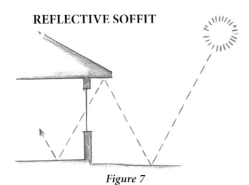

Figure 7

NEW CLERESTORY

Before

New Clerestory Windows

After

Figure 8

INTERIOR DAYLIGHTING

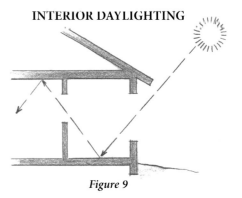

Figure 9

WINDOW WELL

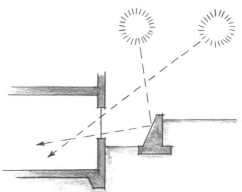

Figure 10

Adding a light monitor with clerestory windows brings reflected light deep into the living space without the liabilities of a skylight.

More Advanced Steps *things you can do tomorrow*

Reduce Glare and Balance Intensely Lit Areas

• Add shading outside windows: plantings, awnings, eyebrows, trellis/arbors, deeper eaves, a porch or other indoor/outdoor space. When planting for summer shade only, emphasize deciduous plants to admit winter sun.

• Use glazing that controls solar radiation (see chapter 7, page 124).

• Reduce contrast between the window frame and adjacent walls to lessen glare and improve vision: use light-colored window frames and casings, and splay the walls around windows when possible (see figure 11).

• Use reflection to soften incoming light. For example, a light shelf can shade the view window, reflect sunlight deep into a room, and block sky glare (see figure 12).

• Use darker colors to minimize interior reflection.

• Use translucent curtains, Venetian blinds, or shutters to lower light levels.

• Position computer screens so that they don't directly face a window or reflect electric light.

SPLAYED JAMS

Outside | Inside Outside | Inside

Thick Wall Thin Wall

Figure 11

Simply adding an awning over a window or glass door can make all the difference when the summer sun beats down.

LIGHT SHELF

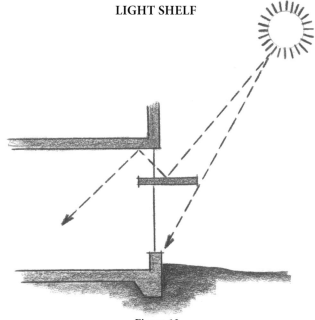

Figure 12

SKYLIGHTS

A skylight can bring magic to a darker indoor area—but it can also bring trouble if it isn't appropriately selected, located, and installed. Potential problems include condensation, winter heat loss and draftiness, summer overheating, and leaking. To maximize benefits and minimize trouble, consider the following guidelines when choosing a skylight:

- Avoid large skylights; a skylight can illuminate a room 20 times its size.

- A wide, angled skylight shaft (rather than a straight one) will provide the best reflected light. When installing a light well through an attic space, splay the walls to distribute the light; insulate the walls of the light well.

- In climates with a hot season, consider placing skylights on the north side of the roof to reduce heat gain from direct sunlight; the east side may also work well, depending on how hot the morning sun is.

- If it makes sense in your layout, install a skylight near the ridge of the roof; this minimizes the amount of rain that sheets down the roof onto the upper skylight flashing.

- Add movable shading to a skylight so that you have a choice about whether to admit all that hot summer sun.

In this converted attic, small skylights make a big difference.

Selection:
- Select skylights with the lowest U-factor you can find (see chapter 7, page 124).

- Choose skylights with a low Solar Heat Gain Coefficient (see chapter 7, see page 124).

- Avoid plastic glazing; it can't incorporate low-E coatings and gas fills, and it usually doesn't insulate well.

- Buy a skylight with a low infiltration rating and make sure it's tightly installed and caulked.

- To aid ventilation and summer cooling, use a skylight that can be opened.

- Consider installing a tubular skylight in which sunlight enters through a small dome on the roof and is reflected through the tube into the living space (see figure 13); less expensive and easier to install than standard skylights, they minimize heat loss because of their relatively small glazed area. (Be warned: the light from a tubular skylight is quite intense; you may want to select or design a light-diffusing lens for the ceiling opening.)

Well-chosen skylights can bring a special quality to a room.

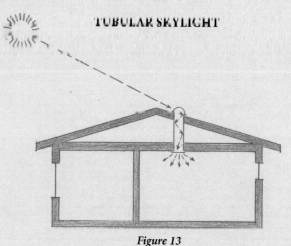

TUBULAR SKYLIGHT

Figure 13

This Pennsylvania addition was designed for passive-solar heating; note the abundant south-facing glass.

Passive-Solar Heating

The gift of sunlight is always accompanied by the sun's radiant heat—which, in most North American climates, is a winter blessing and a summer challenge. Fortunately, the predictable path of the sun allows us to make the best of both extremes. Earlier in this chapter, you learned how to determine the sun's path in your location; now you'll apply that knowledge to naturally heating and cooling your home.

PASSIVE SOLAR BASICS

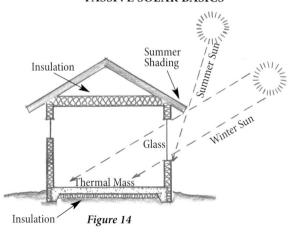

Figure 14

The simplest way to heat your home with the sun is called *passive* or *direct-gain* solar heating. The word *passive* refers to the fact that a well-designed house just sits there accepting solar heat through south-facing glass with no moving parts except planet earth itself.

By contrast, an *active* solar heating system involves collecting heat in one place (roof-mounted panels, for example) and moving it to another place (via heated air or liquid) using tubes, ducts, and possibly fans or pumps. Passive-solar heating places more demands on a house's design, but active solar systems require additional materials, technology, and energy inputs—and are more likely to break down. Your house, site, and climate will determine which type of solar heating you can employ.

The essence of passive-solar design is simplicity itself. It involves four main features (see figure 14):

- Admitting winter sunlight through south-facing glass

- Storing the solar heat in thermal mass (see Thermal Mass, page 54)

- Keeping the summer sun out of the space via shading

- Insulating the house to avoid losing the solar heat you collect

This thermal mass floor soaks up the day's solar warmth and radiates it to the room's occupants as the air cools. Large windows admit plenty of light and connect the room to the outdoors.

How Heat Gets Around

Temperature is generally more important to comfort than humidity or air movement, so it's a good idea to understand how heat travels. Heat tends to move from warmer areas to cooler areas in three ways:

- **Conduction:** heat flow through matter via molecular agitation—through air, liquid, metal, wood, or concrete, for example

- **Convection:** bulk flow of matter, such as warm air or liquid rising

- **Radiation:** energy transport via photons—visible, infrared, and ultraviolet light—for example, sunlight striking and warming our skin

Your house may or may not already incorporate these features, but in most situations you can improve your home's solar gain by following a few basic guidelines.

First, consider your climate zone. In a hot-humid climate, you may need little passive-solar heating. But if your climate is cold, you may welcome the sun's heat much of the year. By determining when you're likely to want direct solar gain, you can work with a sun-path chart for your latitude to design windows, thermal storage, shading devices, and insulation.

Next, evaluate your site. If your house is in a deep east-west canyon, on a steep north-facing slope, or in a dense forest, you may be unable to heat your house with direct sunshine. But if the sun has a clear shot at your property from 10:00 a.m. to 2:00 p.m., it's worth looking at ways to use that solar gain. On your site plan, mark hills, trees, shrubs, vines, outbuildings, or other features that can block winter sunlight, noting whether plants are deciduous.

Finally, look at your house itself. On your floor plan, note where your house has good passive-solar design features (a south-facing living room with a picture window, a good overhang, sunlight falling on a concrete slab floor). Then make notes about which areas could be improved (a north-facing breakfast nook, a roofed porch that shades the living room in winter, a narrow overhang that lets in summer sunshine). Assess the fit with your climate, how you use your home, and how the sun shines into your home, then look for ways to improve the situation.

Of these three, radiant heat transfer can be the most crucial to our comfort. Though many people don't realize this, the temperature of the surfaces around you often plays as great a role in your comfort as the air temperature. Imagine, for example, that it's winter and you're in an uninsulated house heated by a furnace. Let's say the indoor air temperature is 70°F, and the outdoor air temperature is 40°. The indoor warmth quickly passes through the walls to the cold outdoors, so the interior surface of the exterior wall might be at 55°. It doesn't take an engineering degree to see that your body will radiate heat toward that wall at a pretty good pace. Though a 70-degree air temperature should be comfortable, you *feel cold* because your body heat is radiating to the cold walls (see figure 15).

SURFACE TEMPERATURE VS. AIR TEMPERATURE

Figure 15

In summer, such an uninsulated house would create the same problem in reverse: The summer heat travels inward, through the roof and walls of the house, until the indoor surfaces are too warm to let you cool off by radiating body heat to them.

Now let's put you in a well-designed passive-solar home. In winter, sunlight comes into the space and warms the floor and walls, which are made of a material that soaks up heat—perhaps stone, earth, or concrete. Insulation slows the heat's escape to the outdoors, so although the indoor air may be cool, the surfaces around you are warm. You feel comfortable because you aren't losing body heat to the interior surfaces. In summer, the roof overhang keeps out direct sunlight, so the interior surfaces tend to stay cool. Your body can radiate heat to those surfaces, helping you feel comfortable even if the air warms up. At night, you'll flush the house with cool air to carry away any heat that has built up during the day, and start the next day with cool surfaces again (for more on this, see chapter 4).

Thermal Mass

One of the crucial players in the scenario just described is *thermal mass*, a term that indicates a class of dense materials that conduct heat slowly. Thermal mass materials are neither good insulators nor excellent conductors, but their quality of slow conduction makes them useful for natural heating and cooling. Stone, brick, earth (adobe, cob, rammed earth), concrete, ceramic tile, and water are commonly used to provide thermal mass. The beauty of thermal mass is that we can use its slow heat transfer to *store* heat energy and release it when we need it. This lessens the extreme temperature swings that would otherwise occur from day to night.

Here's an example of how thermal mass functions. Sunshine falling on thermal mass warms the mass. The heat passes slowly through the mass, which in effect stores the heat. At night, when the surrounding air cools

down, the thermal mass gives back the heat as long as the mass is warmer than the air.

Thick thermal mass that receives direct sunlight, such as a concrete slab or an earthen wall, is called *concentrated mass*. *Distributed mass*, or *thin mass*, functions slightly differently; it can be especially appropriate for remodeling because it's relatively easy to add to an existing home. It could take the form of plaster walls, a stone countertop, or a tile floor. Distributed mass should be about 2 inches thick, and it is generally spread over a greater area than concentrated mass. It works best when it receives heat indirectly, such as from warm air or by radiation from concentrated mass. Like concentrated mass, distributed mass is an important component in reducing indoor temperature swings.

Slate tile on a concrete slab is a good example of thermal mass.

Distributed mass, like this earth-plastered wall, can play an import role in a passive-solar heating strategy.

The art of using thermal mass in passive-solar heating involves several factors:

- Placing the mass where the sun falls on it (or using distributed mass)

- Selecting a thermal-mass material that transfers heat at a desirable rate

- Providing enough thickness of mass to store heat without overdoing it (too much thickness means the mass stays too cool). In most North American climates, 4 to 6 inches is typically a good thickness.

- Insulating the outside of the mass so that heat isn't lost to the ground or the outdoor air

For example, in many climates a 4-inch-thick concrete slab floor with perimeter insulation in a room with south-facing glass is appropriate. If your house has a concrete slab floor, or if your walls are made of adobe or concrete, you may already have all the thermal mass you need.

There is much more to know about how thermal mass works. In particular, it's important that the amount of mass be appropriate for your climate and for the amount of sun that enters your home. If you want to use thermal mass with passive-solar heating in your home, we suggest that you turn to the resources at the end of this book or hire a qualified professional.

CAROL'S EXPERIENCE *Understanding thermal mass not only helps you tune up your home, but it makes you a smarter consumer. I've heard salespeople say, "This product has the insulation value of a foot of adobe." Well, that's not a very good thing because adobe isn't a good insulator; it conducts heat well enough to function as thermal mass, but that is more conduction than we want in our insulation. You might also sometimes hear, "This product is both insulation and thermal mass." Buyer beware! What they're telling you is that the product does neither job particularly well. You'd be better off having a good thermal mass material on the interior surface to soak up heat and a good insulating material on the exterior side of the mass to keep your house from losing that heat.*

Low-Hanging Fruit *things you can do today*

Before you start altering your home in big ways, try some easy things to improve your solar heating situation.

- **Landscape for comfort.** If you have plants shading the winter sun from rooms that need more warmth, consider transplanting, removing, or pruning the plants. If too much sun gets into your home in summer, try planting deciduous trees, vines, or shrubs to provide seasonal shade.

- **Add shading devices.** If the sun shines into your windows too harshly (especially in summer), you can add awnings (retractable fabric ones give you more options), trellises above windows, or roofed outdoor rooms (see Smart Shading, page 57).

- **Change your window treatment.** If your home loses a lot of heat on winter nights, install insulating shades on your windows. If your windows let in too much solar heat, add a film to cut down on radiant heat gain. (Note: if sunlight enters a window, it will heat the room even if there are interior shades; the best way to keep a room cool is to keep sunlight from striking the glass.)

- **Add easy (distributed) thermal mass.** If your home could use some more thermal mass, add a layer or two of plaster to the interior walls—especially in rooms that tend to have big temperature swings. Even a new tile floor or some large plants in heavy pots can have an impact.

Deciduous vines provide shade in summer and admit sun in the winter after the leaves drop.

For every architectural style, there's a fitting way to bring shade to vulnerable windows.

More Advanced Steps *things you can do tomorrow*

Once you have a good picture of your home's assets and liabilities in relation to solar heating, you can proceed to make more serious changes. At this point, you might want to add a qualified design professional to your team.

- **Add or change windows.** If you have a south-facing wall with small windows, it might be a good idea to add more windows or replace your current windows with larger ones. Conversely, you might want to remove some north-facing windows (and even west-facing windows where afternoons are hot) or replace them with smaller windows. Be sure to select new windows carefully for your conditions (see chapter 7). A rule of thumb for passive solar gain is to have the south-facing glass area of your home equal to 7 to 12 percent of the floor area of your home.

The addition to this house was oriented specifically for passive- solar heating.

- **Add a sunspace to the south side of your house.** If you have a good south-facing wall, but it's not practical to increase the window area there, you might want to add a sunspace to collect heat that you can then bring into the house via an open door, a fan, or ducts.

- **Add concentrated thermal mass to south-facing rooms.** If you have plenty of south-facing glass, you'll need enough thermal mass to avoid overheating. The appropriate way to add thermal mass depends on your home's structure and materials. You might be able to add a mortar-set tile floor over wood joists if they're sized to handle the load—or if you're willing to beef them up. Or perhaps you will want to add a low masonry wall as a room divider and pour a new chunk of foundation to support it.

- **Take advantage of existing thermal mass.** If you have rugs covering a concrete slab floor or wood paneling over a concrete-block wall, you may be hiding one of your house's greatest assets. Consider removing these barriers and replacing them with a finish that allows radiant heat to pass through, such as paint, tile, or plaster. For a concrete slab, you may also want to add perimeter insulation to keep your slab from losing solar heat to the cold winter air. If you have a real brick or stone fireplace, consider adding a window that will let direct sunlight hit it. (You should also make the fireplace as energy-efficient as possible; add a damper or replace with an EPA-approved wood-burning insert or stove.)

- **Alter your overhangs.** As part of the solar-massaging package, you may need to extend or cut back your roof overhangs, particularly on the south side. Be sure to consult a sun-path chart or a professional to size your shading devices correctly.

- **Heat your water with the sun.** Even if your windows don't face south, you can use the sun's energy to heat water for bathing and cooking. You need an unobstructed patch of roof or yard that is sunny most of the day. Using the sun's radiant energy to heat water for your home is one of the most cost-effective and energy-efficient uses of solar energy, reducing water-heating costs by 50 to 80 percent. For more on this, see chapter 8.

Smart Shading

Sunshine streaming in across the floor is a blessing in winter and spring, but a curse in the heat of summer. Shading windows is your primary tool for fending off unwanted solar warmth. You can use your eaves, a trellis, retractable awnings, a canvas canopy, a porch roof, well-placed plantings, or even a tunnel of woven mats to provide that shade (see figures 16, 17, and 18).

- If your climate has hot summers, aim to completely shade south-facing windows from 9:00 a.m. until 3:00 p.m. on June 21 (summer solstice). You can determine the sun angle for any time of day or year for your latitude at www.susdesign.com/sunangle, and see an animated model of your overhang design at www.susdesign.com/overhang/index.html.

- For windows that face east and west, roof overhangs can't block the morning or late afternoon sunlight that comes in at a low angle. Here you'll need to provide shading from the side, such as with vertical fins, roll-down exterior blinds, or a vertical trellis. Or consider planting a deciduous bush or tree—a good solution that doesn't change the architectural style of your home.

- The sun's path is the same on March 21 and September 21 (the equinoxes), but March is much cooler than September at most latitudes because heat has been building up all summer. So how can one create a shading device that admits sunlight in early spring but blocks it through late summer and early fall? The answer is movable shading, such as retractable awnings or removable canopies. Or, for a really natural solution, install a trellis with a deciduous vine that leafs out in mid-summer to provide late summer shade.

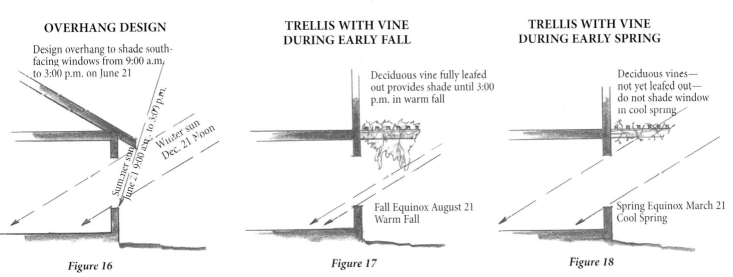

OVERHANG DESIGN

Design overhang to shade south-facing windows from 9:00 a.m. to 3:00 p.m. on June 21

Summer sun June 21 9:00 a.m. to 3:00 p.m.

Winter sun Dec. 21 Noon

Figure 16

TRELLIS WITH VINE DURING EARLY FALL

Deciduous vine fully leafed out provides shade until 3:00 p.m. in warm fall

Fall Equinox August 21 Warm Fall

Figure 17

TRELLIS WITH VINE DURING EARLY SPRING

Deciduous vines—not yet leafed out—do not shade window in cool spring

Spring Equinox March 21 Cool Spring

Figure 18

PROFILE IN DESIGN: BUILDING A SOLAR ADDITION
The Flint Residence *Silver Spring, Maryland*

The Flint family lived in a modest WWII-era, three-bedroom house in Silver Spring, Maryland, that had one-and-a-half baths, a tiny kitchen, a narrow living room, and a dark, leaky, low-ceilinged basement. In order to create more flowing, comfortable, sustainable living spaces, Alan Abrams of Abrams Design Build removed a small, deteriorating addition, reconfigured the existing living areas, and constructed a solar addition.

The original house was not well oriented to receive sunlight, but "The addition is dramatically rotated in relation to the existing house," says Abrams, "with sunshine pouring in through many large south-facing windows on all three levels, slashing winter heating and lighting bills." In the living area, a dark slate floor set on a thick cementitious bed absorbs solar heat by day and radiates warmth by night. In

Engineered beams like these can support typical household loads, and help lighten the demand on our forests.

This space uses large south-facing windows and thermal mass to achieve solar heating and daylighting.

Roof overhangs on the first and second floors provide shade to help keep the addition cool in summer.

58

summer, roof overhangs on the first and second floors provide shade to help keep the house cool.

Abrams chose building materials with an eye to their environmental impact. The exposed roof framing is of Parallam beams, made of wood fiber from branches and trees too small for use as conventional lumber (www.trusjoist.com). The floor underlayment at the second floor is Dow Woodstalk—rigid panels manufactured from wheat straw (www.dow.com/bioprod).

Energy efficiency was also a primary consideration. The walls and roof are insulated with Icynene (www.icynene.com), and white-colored roofing materials reduce cooling loads (www.mulehide.com/products.html). New windows meet the U.S. EPA's Energy Star efficiency requirements.

The Flint project received the 2005 Honor Award of Excellence from the American Institute of Building Design.

Windows all around the addition allow light to pour into the living space throughout the day, slashing bills for heating and lighting.

Integrating Passive-Solar Heating with Daylighting

For daylighting, you generally want diffuse light, reflected off light-colored surfaces. But to take advantage of solar warmth, it's a good idea to let in plenty of sunlight and have it strike dark-colored, thermally absorptive surfaces. Fortunately, if you admit enough sunlight for passive-solar heating, you'll welcome some dark surfaces; otherwisethe ambient light might be too bright. In your quest for solar heating, don't forget to balance the interior lighting with some small windows from another direction, or with a skylight.

Here are some general rules to help you choose surface colors to balance daylighting and passive-solar heating[2]:

- Lightweight objects should be light in color; because they have a low thermal storage capacity, they function best as reflectors.

- In a space that receives direct solar gain, if the sun first strikes a wall or ceiling, that surface should be light-colored to reflect the light and heat.

- Thermal-mass floors in direct-gain spaces should be dark-colored to store solar heat.

- If more than half the walls in a direct-gain space are thermally massive, they should be light-colored. If only one wall is thermally massive, it should be dark-colored (except as in second item, above).

- Clerestory windows should be located so that the winter sun strikes low in the space. Otherwise, the surface where the sun first strikes should be very light colored to reflect the light down into the room.

ELECTRICITY FROM THE SUN
by Johnny Weiss

Solar electricity, or photovoltaics (PV), is a remarkable technology that's ready for homeowners to use today. These seemingly magical systems convert invisible photons of sunlight into practical electricity. They have no moving parts, will never run out of energy, and are typically warranted for 20+ years.

PV solar electric systems (not to be confused with solar water-heating systems) generate, store, and/or distribute household electricity. PV panels can be mounted on existing roofs, installed as ground-mounted systems, placed on sturdy steel poles, or integrated into the structural roof or wall envelope.

There are three basic ways for homeowners to utilize photovoltaic systems:

This northern California home integrates photovoltaic panels with a ridge skylight.

Stand-Alone Systems.

These systems allow independence from any electric utility company. They require a battery storage component in order to operate home appliances at night and during cloudy weather. Stand-alone systems are generally appropriate for remote homes that are not served by utility power, and for homeowners determined to provide their own electricity.

Utility-Interactive (Grid-Tied) Systems. These solar electric systems connect to the local electric power grid, and seamlessly buy and "sell" electricity with the utility company, which acts as a "storage battery." When a PV system generates more electricity than the home is consuming, the utility company is required to buy the excess electricity. If the local utility company allows net-metering (which tracks the net quantity of electricity you've purchased from the utility company after selling them your PV power), the PV system will automatically spin the utility meter in the homeowner's favor, registering solar "credit" whenever the sun shines. Your local utility must be willing to cooperate in such an installation. Note that these systems provide no electricity independence in the event of utility-grid failure.

Utility-Interactive with Battery Back-up Systems. This most recently available option can give homeowners the best of both worlds. Adding a battery storage component to a grid-tied system allows homeowners to receive utility power when needed, "sell" solar electricity to the utility company when extra sunshine is available, and store solar-charged battery power for use in the event of utility failure.

The size, and therefore the cost, of a home-sized solar electric system is determined mostly by lifestyle. The critical determinant is how wisely and efficiently homeowners use electricity. It's important to evaluate your electrical needs and design goals so that a solar professional can design the best system for your household. It's helpful that solar electric systems are modular, allowing owners to expand their PV systems as needs change and budgets permit.

A complete PV system can cost anywhere from $10,000 to $50,000. A growing number of states, utility companies, and community environmental organizations offer significant financial incentives to encourage this green-building option. Visit www.dsireusa.org to learn about financial incentives available in your area. To learn more about residential PV systems, hands-on workshops, online courses, and educational programs see Resources on page 267. When you are ready to learn more about specific options for your home, interview and select an experienced local PV installing dealer.

Johnny Weiss is the founder and Executive Director of Solar Energy International (SEI), a nonprofit educational organization that provides education and technical assistance.

The Sun-Tempered Home

Sunshine is the main organizing principle for an ecologically responsive home. If it isn't easy to tweak your present home into the realm of passive-solar heating, you can still benefit from the sun's gifts. Any amount of sunlight that enters a room will warm and light it. If you can add some thermal mass to minimize overheating and store a bit of solar warmth for a cool evening, all the better. Whatever heat or light you get directly from the sun will reduce your need for nonrenewable energy sources, and that's all good.

You might also consider using the sun to provide electricity (see the sidebar, Electricity from the Sun, page 60) and heat your water (see chapter 8). You'll also want to know more about the flip side of solar heating: natural cooling with breezes (see chapter 4, page 64). And you'll want your landscaping to support your strategies for sunlight and ventilation (see chapter 6). Once you work out your relationship with the sun, other pieces of the puzzle can fall into place.

KELLY'S EXPERIENCE *Passive-solar homes got a bad reputation in the 1970s when they often overheated badly. The problem? Too much south glazing and not enough thermal mass. If the ratio of your house's south-facing glass to floor area exceeds 7 percent, you'll need thermal mass to absorb the heat. Plan on at least six square feet of exposed thermal mass for each square foot of south-facing glass. In any case, don't overdo the glass; south-facing glazing should never exceed 25 percent of the floor area.*

A 4-inch thickness of thermal mass is perfect for absorbing and releasing heat on a daily cycle. While sunlight shining directly onto thermal mass is especially effective, any exposed thermal mass can absorb heat—and besides, it's better to distribute mass throughout the room rather than concentrate it in a single area.

Air: The Breath of Vitality

"Now I see the secret of the making of the best persons. It is to grow in the open air, and to eat and sleep with the earth."

— Walt Whitman

THE WARM, DRY, MESQUITE-SCENTED AIR in the desert, the hot muggy summers of the south, the cool damp feel and earthy smell of a coastal forest—each is a distinct, evocative experience. The characteristics of the surrounding air can make the difference between a place where we love to linger and one we can't wait to leave. When the air feels too hot, too cold, too moist, or too dry—or when it moves too quickly or slowly for our comfort—we want something to change. This chapter will give you some tools for making those changes.

Air circulates unceasingly around the world, driven by warmth from the sun and the earth's rotation. The prevailing winds in a given area are fairly predictable, but many regional characteristics affect air movement, such as mountains, plains, oceans, lakes, and rivers. The time of day or of season also has an impact. For example, air tends to rise up canyons in the morning as the temperature increases, then move back down in the evening as the land and air cool. The direction of your local wind probably changes seasonally, and storms may approach from a different direction than the prevailing winds.

Air can bring us scents, moisture, warmth, or coolness. It can soothe us as a gentle breeze, or threaten us in a storm. Industrial processes pollute our air, and biological processes can help cleanse it. It's easy to take air for granted unless it becomes a problem. But in this chapter we'll look at ways to consciously make your experience of air at home refreshing and delightful. Getting to know how this abundant natural element moves in and around your home can be an empowering experience.

A simple open door can connect you with the smells, sounds, and breezes outside.

Contact with fresh air was a high priority in this addition.

The Air at Home

The air inside your home may be stuffy or fresh, moist or dry, warm or cool. It enters and leaves through windows and doors, your heating or cooling system, and unseen holes in your home's shell. Driven by pressure differences, air can leak into wall cavities and attics, causing moisture buildup and consequent mold and structural damage. Your indoor air can become polluted by toxic household products, combustion products from cooking and heating, and volatile organic compounds (VOCs) released by finishes and furnishings.

As with the sun's warmth, your demand for the movement of air in, through, and around your house depends on your climate zone, the season, and the time of day. However, air movement isn't predictable in the way that the sun's path is. In order to work with air in your home, you need to observe its local ways, be prepared to respond to its whims, and coax it as best you can.

Take some time to think about the breezes and winds around your home:

• At what time of day and year are the winds strongest?

• From which direction does your prevailing wind come (the one that blows most of the time, when there are no storms)?

• What direction do storms come from?

• Is there a noticeable breeze or wind most of the year? Does it vary much from season to season?

• Is there a daily shift in your local breezes?

• Is local air movement influenced by geographic features or landscape elements?

There are several ways to learn about local wind direction and intensity: observing for yourself (at different times of day and year), asking local farmers and other people who work outdoors what they observe, and accessing collected weather data (see Resources, page 266). Understanding your seasonal wind patterns will help you adjust your window openings, outdoor spaces, and windbreaks to increase your comfort without relying on nonrenewable fuels.

On the site plan you developed back in chapter 2, record the basic seasonal wind direction and intensity with arrows. Use heavier, darker arrowheads to indicate stronger winds. Plot the intensity and direction of storm and other significant winds if they differ from prevailing winds.

Now look at your house to assess how air moves through it. You can make basic observations on your own, but you may want to bring in a professional for more technical assessments.

• What kind of windows does your house have: casements, double-hung, fixed, other?

A combination of high and low windows makes it easy to exhaust hot air and draw in cooler air.

Double French doors open through this breezeway onto a courtyard.

- Does your house have other ventilation openings (i.e., screened or louvered vents, exhaust fans or turbine ventilators, cupola, thermal chimney)?

- Are there operable windows or other vents on opposite ends of your house? Are some high and some low?

- Can you open enough windows to provide good ventilation in hot weather?

- Does your landscaping funnel breezes to your house in summer and protect it from cold winter winds?

- Does your house's enclosure have cracks that admit cold air in winter?

- How high are your ceilings? Do they allow warm air to collect high in the room (a blessing in summer and a problem in winter)?

- Do vents or fans exhaust unwanted air (unpleasant smells, excess moisture)?

- Even with windows open, are there *dead air* zones in your house?

Be sure to indicate these features on your floor plan. Use colors, notes, icons, and diagrams to fully capture your feelings.

Cooling with Air

Natural ventilation makes the most of air motion to cool you and your home. This is the primary passive cooling strategy in all climate zones, but the nuances of its application vary by region. In hot humid climates, for example, maximum airflow combined with shading is the dominant natural comfort strategy. In hot dry climates, ventilation is welcome in the hot seasons, and night cooling of thermal mass (see chapter 3, page 54) is particularly useful due to cool nighttime temperatures. In cold climates with cool summers, there may be little need for enhanced natural ventilation. Many temperate and mixed climates will require a variety of tricks as the seasons move from one extreme to another. As you read on, think about your own climate zone and your experiences living there; focus on the approaches that feel most relevant to your situation, and see how you might improve the existing relationship between your home and the breezes (see Climate Zone Map, page 16).

Once you've observed and mapped your local wind patterns and your home's airflow characteristics, you can use a host of tricks to improve ventilation for cooling. If your home has appreciable thermal mass, or if you choose to add some, you will especially want to use these ventilation techniques to cool

A cupola allows warm air to escape. A wind-driven turbine ads an extra boost.

the mass at night in the hot season so that during the day it can absorb unwanted heat from the air and from your body.

The openings that allow air to pass through your home needn't always be windows. We ask windows to do many things: admit light, welcome solar heat, frame views, and provide ventilation. But these functions often have conflicting requirements. In hot dry climates, for example, breezes are more desirable than sunlight. Sometimes the best solution—particularly in a retrofit situation—is to provide vents that are separate from windows. Adding sun protection, insect screens, louvers, insulated doors, or a combination of these will allow you to fine-tune your new vents. A good example from historical buildings is the cupola, which has louvered vents all around that allow warm air to escape as it rises, inducing air movement through the whole house.

Cross-ventilation

Cross-ventilation is the most common, straightforward ventilation strategy. When air flows into a room from one side and out the other, you've got cross-ventilation. As with any air movement, cross-ventilation can cool your body by speeding up the evaporation of sweat, and it can cool your home by removing hot air from indoors—especially at night, if the incoming outdoor air is cool.

KELLY'S EXPERIENCE *We can learn a lot from vernacular buildings that were designed to make the best use of nature's cooling ventilation in their particular climate. In the South, shuttered verandas, high ceilings, operable transoms, two-story porches, and dogtrot houses maximized both cross-ventilation and shade to counter the humid heat. In the Midwest, summer kitchens kept the heat of cooking out of the home, while screened sleeping porches put warm human bodies in the path of nighttime breezes. In desert regions, the thick earthen walls of adobe homes protected the interior from harsh sun during the day; at night the cool breezes swept away any lingering warm air.*

This Louisiana addition stays true to the southern vernacular: shaded porch and high transom windows to let out warm air collected at the ceiling.

Any room with openings on opposite sides can be cross-ventilated if the openings are large enough (see figure 1). But most homes are at least two rooms deep in many places, so you also need to look at airflow through the whole house in order to effectively ventilate the rooms. Think of your house as a system of corridors and doorways that can channel air from one end to the other (see figure 2).

Looking at the air-motion notes you've made on your site plan and floor plan, see if the combination of prevailing breezes, house orientation, room layout, and openings (windows and other vents) could be improved to make the best use of those breezes. Are there air inlets on the windward side and outlets on the leeward side? Ideally, you would have large inlets and outlets perpendicular to the prevailing summer wind direction, but openings up to 40 degrees off perpendicular can still provide good indoor airflow. If your home isn't oriented to face the prevailing breeze, you can use landscaping or wing walls (see figure 3) on the windward side of your house to encourage the wind to approach your inlets head-on.

CROSS VENTILATION

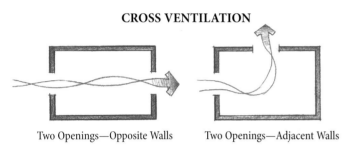

Two Openings—Opposite Walls   Two Openings—Adjacent Walls

Figure 1

INTERIOR VENTILATION

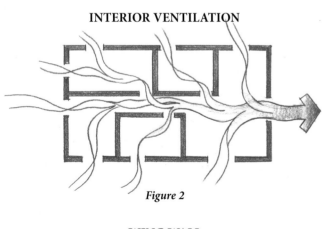

Figure 2

WING WALL

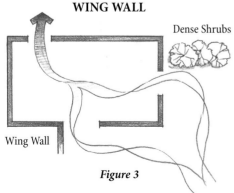

Dense Shrubs

Wing Wall

Figure 3

OPENING HEIGHTS

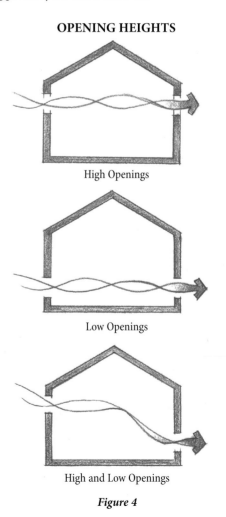

High Openings

Low Openings

High and Low Openings

Figure 4

Prevailing breezes pass over this swimming pool, cooling the air before it reaches the patio and the living room.

PRE-COOLING AIR

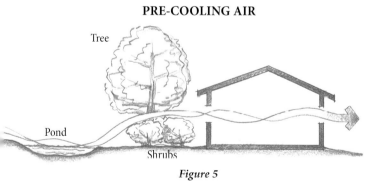

Figure 5

As you plan to make changes in your house's air inlets and outlets, consider these rules of thumb:

- Openings in opposite walls allow maximum air movement through a space.

- Openings in adjacent walls create air turbulence, increasing the cooling effect.

- A combination of low inlets and high outlets can achieve the greatest scouring of room air; this strategy is especially useful for night cooling of thermal-mass floors (see figure 4, page 66).

- Wherever you locate openings, make sure the air moves around the people in the room in order to best cool them; having either some low and some high openings or all openings at a mid-height should achieve the desired effect.

Finally, you can enhance the effectiveness of cross-ventilation by naturally cooling the air before it enters your home (see figure 5). Shade, plantings, or water (in dry climates) in the form of a pond, fountain, or mister can all remove heat from the air. When located on the windward side of your home, these features can increase your indoor comfort in hot weather (see chapter 6, page 93 for more landscaping information).

This cupola takes advantage the chimney effect, naturally ventilating the living space below.

The Chimney Effect

If you live where breezes are rare, or just a bit too gentle, you can use the *chimney* or *stack* effect to enhance air movement. The chimney effect is driven by the rising of warm air; when air is heated, it expands, becomes lighter, and rises. If that rising warm air is allowed to escape high in a structure, it will be replaced by cooler (heavier) air entering lower in the structure. You can immediately see the advantages of this.

The rate of air movement is affected by the vertical distance between inlets and outlets, the size of the openings, and the difference in air temperature from the bottom to the top of the "chimney"; the greater each of these features, the faster the air movement. One advantage of this strategy is that it doesn't require any particular orientation to the prevailing breezes; it drives itself.

If you have a tall house—one with multiple levels or high ceilings or both—you may already have the necessary components for taking advantage of the chimney effect. You can use an existing stairwell, atrium, clerestory, or other vertical air passage to increase airflow in your house. If you already have the necessary openings at the top and bottom of this airspace, your only task may be to open and close them as needed. Or

This California home owner added operable windows to draw out hot air in summer.

perhaps you have the needed airspace, and the addition of vents will allow it to function as a thermal chimney.

However, if your house doesn't have any such features, you can add a chimney or atrium to pull hot air out in summer. You can further enhance the airflow by adding south-facing glass at the top of the chimney (see figure 6) to increase the temperature difference from top to bottom, or even by adding a fan to increase airflow when necessary. Placing the outlet on the leeward side of the building will further enhance airflow; as wind blows around the chimney, it will essentially suck air up the chimney. The rate of airflow will be greatest when the cross-sectional area of the chimney remains the same from inlet to outlet.

THERMAL CHIMNEY WITH DIRECT SOLAR ASSISTANCE

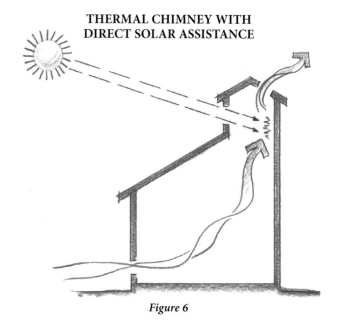

Figure 6

Wind Catchers

If there are breezes in your area, but buildings, vegetation, or landforms keep them from getting to your house, there's another way to bring those breezes indoors. Wind catchers (also known as wind scoops) have been used for centuries in the Middle East, where temperatures are high and buildings are often packed close together. A wind catcher is a tower that rises from the house into the airspace above the rooflines. Its opening faces into the prevailing wind, *scooping* the breeze down into the rooms below (see figure 7). Capturing air higher up has additional benefits: the air is cooler, the breeze moves faster (unimpeded by the ground), and the air carries less dust. When the air is still, well-designed wind catchers can work in reverse, with the chimney effect drawing air upward and out of the house.

A wind catcher can also be an elegant solution where windows aren't oriented well for capturing breezes. The windows may face any which way, but the wind catcher can be precisely oriented to the prevailing breeze. Based on knowledge of wind patterns in your area, you can design a wind catcher with openings in as many directions as you need. For best results, inlets should be at least eight feet above surrounding obstructions, so take care to integrate this feature with your overall design. If your climate is not hot all year, you may want to add insulated doors to your wind catcher to avoid winter heat loss.

WIND CATCHERS

Iranian, 2-sided

Egyptian

Iranian, 4-sided

Figure 7

Vegetation shades this porch and directs air flow for additional cooling.

Turbine Ventilators

The little whirling globes you may have seen on rooftops of older industrial buildings are turbine ventilators. Now making a comeback in naturally cooled homes, these vents use air motion at the roof level to pull air out of the house. While they act somewhat like a fan, they are entirely run by the breeze, which catches the fins of the turbine ventilator and makes it spin, pulling air upward and out through its openings. Cooler air can then enter at a lower level to replace the exhausted air.

Vegetation and Other Landscaping

You can use garden plantings and landscape walls to direct and even cool a breeze before it enters your home. Rows of leafy trees or tall, dense shrubs can funnel air to open windows, their shade and transpiration cooling the air as it moves through (see figure 8).

LANDSCAPING CHANNELING AIRFLOW

Figure 8

Low-Hanging Fruit *things you can do today*

- **Experiment with your existing windows to improve airflow** (see figure 9). If your house has casement windows, not only can you get the maximum ventilation area for a given glass area, but you can also use the windows to catch and direct airflow . For double-hung windows, you might want to try opening both sashes partway; this can let cooler air in at the bottom and warmer air out at the top. If you have operable transoms above doors and windows (interior or exterior), use them to exhaust hot air that collects near the ceiling; you might want to add transoms if you don't already have them. If your house has more than one level, try opening high and low windows to pull air through the house vertically.

- **Get to know the wind patterns around your home.** Hang a wind sock in your yard. A friend who lives near the ocean has done this; she and her family enjoy being aware of changes in the wind's direction and force, making them feel more like part of their natural surroundings: "Our prevailing wind comes from the northwest, so most of the time the wind sock points to the southeast. But sometimes that sock suddenly turns and points north, and then we know there's a storm coming in." A weather vane would provide the same information, as long as you can see it from indoors.

The sound of bamboo rustling in the breeze can enhance a sense of cooling for people sitting nearby.

- **Set up a home weather station.** This will help you learn the most about the wind direction and speed, temperature, humidity, and barometric pressure around your home. Keep your own records for a year or more, and you'll be loaded with useful data that you can apply to make your remodeling project weather-responsive.

- **Tune in to the breeze.** When it's hot, anything that amplifies your awareness of the breeze can have a psychological cooling effect. Hang a wind chime or bell, or plant bamboo or another "rustly" plant in the path of summer breezes, and enjoy the sense of wind amplification.

WINDOWS AND AIRFLOW

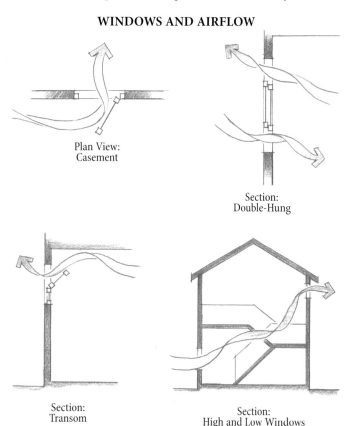

Plan View:
Casement

Section:
Double-Hung

Section:
Transom

Section:
High and Low Windows

Figure 9

More Advanced Steps *things you can do tomorrow*

When you're ready to take on more substantial projects, consider the following possibilities:

• Add new openings in your home's walls for natural ventilation

• Create a thermal chimney

• Seal the cracks around the perimeter of your house (see chapter 7)

• Landscape to redirect the wind (see chapter 6)

• Create outdoor rooms; depending on where it's located and how it's designed, an outdoor room can be an island of calm when it's too breezy, or it can put you in the path of cooling breezes when it's hot (see chapter 6)

A Breath of Fresh Air

The physical structure of a home encloses a volume of air. The materials, products, appliances, processes, people, and other features of the home can fill that air with smells, volatile organic compounds (VOCs), combustion products, dust, mold spores, and even toxic chemicals. While remodeling, you have the opportunity to make your indoor air clean and wholesome.

The first step is to detect and deal with any air-quality problems you may already have in your home. Appendix B: Hazards, on page 263, will guide you through a process to identify and minimize existing lead paint, mold, toxic substances, pests, pesticide residues, or asbestos.

The next step is to avoid introducing new indoor air quality (IAQ) problems. If you aren't careful about the products and systems you choose, remodeling can be dangerous. Many healthy people have become chemically sensitive during the

AUGMENT NATURAL VENTILATION WITH CEILING FANS

People tolerate higher temperatures when air is in motion, and ceiling fans are a relatively energy-efficient, affordable way to enhance your house's natural airflow. Check for the most efficient ceiling fans at the Energy Star website: www.energystar.gov/index.cfm?c=ceiling_fans.pr_ceiling_fans.

Here are some pointers to maximize your comfort and minimize your energy usage:

• **Turn the fan off when nobody's in the room.** Air movement cools people, not rooms.

• **Adjust the ceiling fan controls seasonally.** In summer, use the ceiling fan in the downward airflow direction and position yourself in the path of the moving air; the higher the air speed, the greater the cooling effect. In winter, operate the ceiling fan at low speed to bring warm air from near the ceiling down into the occupied space.

Ceiling fans are an energy-efficient way to keep air in motion, keeping occupants cooler in summer and pulling warm air down from the ceiling in winter.

course of a home remodeling project; standard paints, flooring, cabinetry, sealants, solvents, and other building materials can quickly create a debilitating toxic soup. Furthermore, remodeling almost always changes the air-pressure balance in a home, which can lead to backdrafting of combustion by-products and other air-pressure-related problems (see chapter 7).

Natural ventilation, both during and after remodeling, is one way to handle indoor air pollution; diluting and exhausting the indoor air makes any pollutants less hazardous. But what about wintertime, when you want to keep your warm air inside? And what about indoor air hazards that are too highly concentrated for ventilation to dilute them significantly? A trio of strategies can help you minimize indoor air pollution:

- **Eliminate:** Become aware of the nastiest pollutants, and don't use them. Many standard building materials off-gas, or release, toxic substances, but with some education you can avoid the worst offenders and cope with the rest (see chapter 12).

- **Separate:** Some sources of air pollutants are difficult to eliminate (e.g., a gas-fired water heater or a home-office copier). In such cases, you may be able to separate the polluter from your main living space. You can do this in one of two ways: physically move it to an isolated space (for example, put a copy machine out in the screened porch), or seal it to decrease the rate of off-gassing (for instance, you might apply several coats of a specially formulated sealer to formaldehyde-laden particle-board cabinets).

- **Ventilate:** Whatever undesirables are left in your indoor air may be removed or diluted by ventilation. You can ventilate the whole house, individual rooms, and even special areas (for example, we've seen chemically sensitive people vent glass-doored bookcases to the outdoors to avoid breathing the gases given off by printing ink). Even in winter, it's important to get fresh air into your home. A heat-recovery ventilator (HRV) can keep you from throwing out all of your heat along with the exhaust air (see chapter 7, page 117).

Finally, if there's unwanted junk in your air that's hard to control—smog, pollen, dust, woodstove emissions—you might want to use an air filter. There's a lot of misinformation available these days about air filtration, so we recommend that you look to the EPA or American Lung Association for guidance (see Resources, page 268).

Clay plasters and no-VOC paints on the walls, and water-based sealer on the wood floors, can help set the stage for healthy indoor air quality.

Air Flows Everywhere

Air is involved with every aspect of your home. Be sure to design your remodeling project to account for how air relates to:

- Winter drafts and air infiltration (see chapter 7)

- Moisture and thermal comfort (see chapter 1 and chapter 7)

- Solar heating strategy (see chapter 3)

- Landscaping (see chapter 6)

- Indoor air quality (see chapter 7, chapter 12, and Hazards, page 263)

Water: Your Place in the Flow

Instead of thinking of [water] as a physical substance, I began to perceive it as a flow of life-giving aware-ness, constantly cycling through the world.

— Starhawk

HOW OFTEN DO WE THINK about where the water we use daily comes from, or where it will go after we use it? Except in desert regions and in times of drought, we tend to take water's presence for granted. But living in harmony with nature means understanding how much we need water, recognizing the deep joy it brings us, identifying the sources of our water, and using it with care (see figure 1).

Free water falls from the sky regularly, and nutrient-rich water leaves our homes every day. By welcoming water, enjoying it, not wasting it, and using it more than once before letting it pass into the earth to recharge the aquifer, you can restore your healthy relationship with this vital substance.

HYDROLOGIC CYCLE

Glaciers

Evaporation

Precipitation

Evaporation from land

Evaporation from ocean

Runoff

Underground flow

River flow

Ocean

Figure 1

Where Does Your Water Come From?

Let's explore your place in the hydrologic cycle. Dig out your Project Notebook and jot down some observations:

• If your water comes from a municipal water service, where do they get it—wells, a river, a reservoir? If you get water from a well, what sources does it tap?

• Does your water source replenish itself faster than you draw water out, individually or as a community? (In many areas, the underground water table is getting lower, while the concentration of solids in the water is increasing to an unhealthy degree.) How extensive is the watershed that feeds your water system (see figure 2)?

Now let's look at your water quality:

• How is the water treated before it arrives at your faucet?

• Do you currently add your own water treatment?

• How often is your water tested, and by whom? Is it tested at the faucet in addition to where it leaves the well or water company?

You may not know all the answers to these questions, but enlightenment can be yours. If you have a municipal water supply, your water company can supply information. If you use well water, check with your county government, local agricultural extension, or other regional services.

Now consider the water you get from the sky:

• How much rain or snow falls on your property annually? (Estimate based on experience for now; you can check climate records later if you like.) What are the wettest and driest

WATERSHED

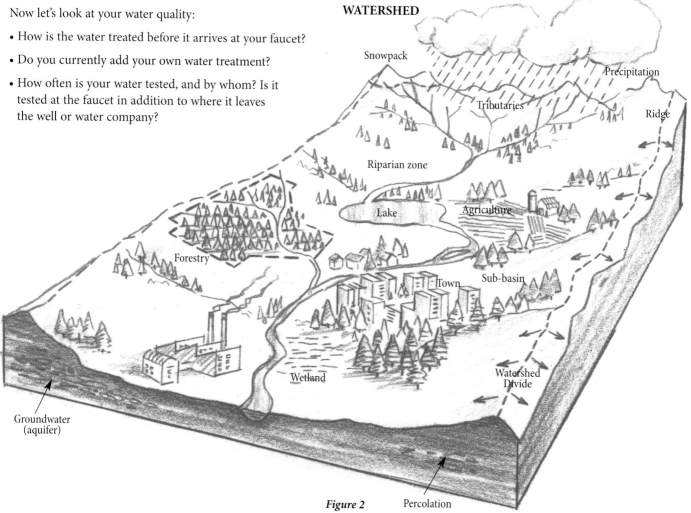

Figure 2

months? When there is precipitation, is it light and steady or sudden and heavy? Are there ever floods?

- What is the pH of your rainwater? (Some hobby shops that sell chemistry sets and other scientific equipment have inexpensive pH-measuring devices, as do aquarium supply stores and some drug stores; you can also check online.)

- In your memory, what was the longest rainy or snowy period?

- Do you get local precipitation effects: heavy snows near large lakes, ocean fog, mountain-induced rainshadow (see figure 3)?

Also consider the water in or on the earth around you, recording important items on your site plan:

- Is there a body of water on or near your property? Are there wet or dry areas in your landscape? Are you in a flood zone? (Check your local municipal maps for this information.)

- How high or low is the water table in your vicinity? What is the nature of the aquifers beneath you (check with county or other regional services)?

- Can rain and surface water percolate into the soil in your yard? Does it run off paving and into a storm sewer?

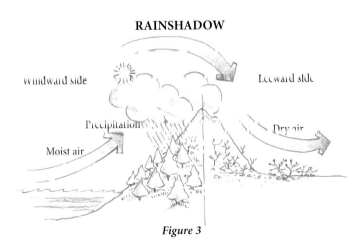

RAINSHADOW

Windward side   Leeward side

Precipitation   Dry air

Moist air

Figure 3

CAROL'S EXPERIENCE *Seventy percent of the earth's surface is covered with water, and further vast quantities reside in underground aquifers. No problem, right? Not quite. Most of that water is either saline or frozen, leaving less than one percent suitable for human use. For all practical purposes, the amount of water on, in, and around the earth doesn't change; what matters is how we use it—and the way we're using it is leading us toward a crisis.*

We're currently polluting our water faster than natural processes can clean it, effectively reducing the quantity of water available to us while damaging living systems. On top of that, population is growing and per-capita water consumption rates are increasing. With growing demand for a shrinking supply of usable water, a collective wake-up call is upon us.

Industry and agriculture account for much of global water consumption and pollution, so how much impact can you have at home? First, becoming more aware of water issues makes you a more effective world citizen; home is a good place to develop that awareness. Second, even if it seems like a drop in the bucket, there's no point in wasting water at home. Using water to clean, cook, drink, and keep your plants alive is a good thing; let's cut back on sending water down the drain without using it well.

You can reduce your contribution to water pollution both at home and in the arena of commerce: replace toxic household products that end up in your wastewater with more benign products, and cut back on purchasing goods from companies that pollute (check Environmental Defense's Scorecard Website, www.scorecard.org, for starters).

And did you know that your food choices have a big impact on water usage? Sixty-five to seventy percent of the water used in the U.S. goes to water-intensive industrial farming. You can do your part to improve that picture by growing your own food using wise water practices, buying from farmers who use water responsibly, and getting involved in local agricultural issues.

How Do You Use Water?

According to the American Water Works Association Research Foundation, the average American household uses 146,000 gallons of water each year; 42 percent of that water is used indoors, and 58 percent outdoors. Roughly one-third of that water is wasted—by leaving the water running when not in use, watering the sidewalk, and other thoughtless activities. The accompanying pie chart shows average household water usage (see figure 4).

You can get a pretty good idea of how much water you actually use—and where, when, and how you use it. This will give you a clear picture of the opportunities to change your patterns for the better. If you have a municipal water system, get out your water bills and make a chart that shows your household water use on a month-by-month basis. Then total your monthly water usage to arrive at an annual water figure; divide that by 365 to come up with an average daily usage. How do your numbers compare with the national average?

With some extra observation, you can figure out your usage patterns. Look at your major water-using appliances and fixtures, and determine their flow rate (you may have to make general guesses, or you can actually make some measurements if they don't indicate their rating). Then note how much you use each of these items in a day. The difference between your winter and summer water usage probably represents the water you use to irrigate your landscape or garden. Filling in the accompanying chart, you can figure out where your water is going (see figure 5). Or you may want to go to www.h2ouse.org and click on Water Budget Calculator.

INDOOR HOUSEHOLD WATER USAGE

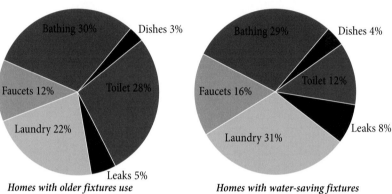

Homes with older fixtures use about 75 gal/person/day

Homes with water-saving fixtures use about 55 gal/person/day

Figure 4

WATER DEMAND				
FIXTURE	**USE**	**FLOW RATE**	**NUMBER OF USERS**	**TOTAL**
Toilets	flushes per person per day (new toilet)*	1.6 gallons per flush* (if new toilet)		
Shower	minutes per person per day (5 minutes suggested max.)	2.75 gallons per minute* (restricted flow head)		
Bath	baths per person per day	50 gallons per bath (average)		
Faucets	kitchen sinks and bathrooms (excluding cleaning)	10 gallons per day	n/a	
Washing Machine	loads per day	50 gallons per load (average)	n/a	
Dishwasher	loads per day	9.5 gallons per load	n/a	
			Total	gallons/day
			multiply (x) 365	gallons/year

Figure 5

* All flow rates shown are for new fixtures. Older toilets use 3.5 to 7 gallons per flush. Older shower heads my use up to 10 gallons per minute.

Where Does Your Water Go?

The final stage in understanding your place in the flow is to identify where your water goes after you use it. In America, we tend to do one thing with water; after we wash, cook, drink, or water plants, we discard it. You can begin by asking yourself if water serves more than one function for your household before it returns to the earth.

Explore where your water goes after you use it:

• Does all of your household water go into one waste pipe? Where does it go next—into a cesspool, a septic system, a municipal sewer system, a body of water? What kind of treatment does your "waste" water receive—percolation through soil, digestion by microorganisms, chemical treatment, aeration, none at all?

• Where does that treated "waste" water go—to irrigate landscapes, into a body of water?

Next time you water your garden, notice whether the water hits the mark:

• Do you give your garden more water than it needs? Are you watering the plant leaves, or the root zone (the root zone is typically more effective)?

• Does the water evaporate before the soil and plants can take it in (in other words, are you watering during the hottest, sunniest part of the day)?

• Does all the water fall onto the plants you're aiming for? Does any of the water fall onto pavement? Does any of the water run down slope, not sinking into the soil and perhaps carrying topsoil with it?

Now check out where the free water from the sky ends up:

• When it rains (or when snow melts), where does the water that lands on your roof flow to?

• Does any rainwater or snow fall onto impervious paved surfaces? If so, where does that water flow?

This unique downspout guides roof water to a splash bowl, which protects against soil erosion and overflows, watering nearby plants.

• Does water flow off your property into a storm sewer? If so, does that water get processed in a treatment plant? Where does that water then go?

If you don't have answers to some of these questions, a call to your health department or waste treatment facility will expand your world.

Low-Hanging Fruit *things you can do today*

Reworking your home's water system needn't be intimidating. You can jump-start your water awareness and conservation practices with the following easy projects.

- **Use less water:** Install low-flow devices at easy points like shower-heads and faucets. Check for and repair leaks; even small leaks can cause staggering water loss, especially within toilets.

- **Catch rainwater:** Place a rain barrel at a roof downspout to collect water for your garden (be sure to keep it covered or otherwise discourage mosquitoes), or run a sleeve from your downspout to direct rainwater to a moisture-loving part of the garden.

- **Start new habits:** Look for easy ways to not waste water, such as turning off the faucet while soaping up or brushing your teeth, or taking shorter showers. Before you shower, you can catch the "warming-up" water in a bucket and carry it out to your garden.

- **Revise your landscape watering practices:** Water your plants more efficiently (see chapter 6, page 100).

- **Take notes:** Watch how water flows in and around your house. Where does the water go? Are you getting the most from it? Make notes in your Project Notebook, then let your observations sink in; see if they inspire solutions that boost your household's water conservation efforts.

More Advanced Steps *things you can do tomorrow*

In order to use water optimally, indoors and out, it's best to employ a combination of strategies. Here are a few of the more detailed options you may want to consider as you develop the total strategy for your home:

- **Install better equipment:** Evaluate your water-using appliances (washing machine, dishwasher, etc.) and plumbing fixtures (toilets, faucets, etc.), and replace the guzzlers with more efficient models.

With new dual flush toilets you have a choice of flushes: 0.8 gallons for liquid waste or 1.6 gallons for solids.

- **Reuse water:** Install a greywater system (see sidebar, "Use That Water Again!," page 82 for more).

- **Catch rainwater:** install a comprehensive rainwater collection system (see page 79).

- **Increase your contribution to the local water table:** Allow more water to percolate into the ground—and less to run off into storm sewers—by replacing impervious paving with water-permeable surfaces, terracing steep slopes, mulching planting beds, and covering bare ground with vegetation.

Pavers allow water to percolate into the soil and refresh the aquifer.

Less Is More

Using less is always a great first step any time we're talking about a precious, finite resource. It's easy, it saves money, and it makes any additional resource-saving steps more effective. For example, installing a good-quality low-flow showerhead allows you all the pleasure of a hearty shower with about half the water use.

Installing water-conserving appliances is a no-brainer. If you pay for water or water-heating, more efficient appliances and fixtures will soon pay for themselves. According to the American Water Works Association Research Foundation, a family of four can save over 8,000 gallons a year by installing a high-efficiency clothes washer; a household that replaces a 12-gallon-per-load dishwasher with a 6-gallon-per-load machine can save 1,250 gallons of water a year.

Many communities have incentive programs for replacing high-volume flush toilets with low-volume models. The sponsors of these programs recognize that reducing water waste reduces the financial and environmental costs of operating and expanding their treatment and supply facilities. The same programs often supply faucet aerators at little or no charge; these simple devices give you the water pressure you want at a fraction of the water usage. By the way, if you've heard that low-flow toilets and faucet aerators function poorly, check again; more recent, higher-quality models can do an excellent job.

Try to select appliances that use both water and energy efficiently, keeping your clothes and the environment clean.

Collect Rainwater

Capturing and using rainwater can be an enjoyable way to reconnect with nature's water cycle. If your area receives plenty of rain, you have an abundant resource that you can collect for household use or for landscape use in the dry seasons. If you live in a dry area, the little rain that falls is especially precious; you will want to make the best use of what water you get from the sky.

Rainwater is free and usually of high quality—the primary exception being in areas with acid rain or other industrial emissions. You can collect rainwater to augment or even replace other sources of water, saving money and lessening the drain on your area's water reserves. You can use anything from a rain barrel at a downspout to a system that includes pipes, a cistern, a pump, and filters.

Rainwater catchment systems fall into two general categories: those for direct landscape use and those for domestic uses, including drinking. Obviously, the former type is simpler and cheaper. Rainwater collection for drinking requires an investment of money, equipment, and time in order to avoid health hazards. Check with your local authorities before undertaking any significant projects.

Basic Components

Whether simple or complex, rainwater catchment systems have five basic components (see figure 8):

1. The catchment area: the surface upon which the rain first falls, often a roof (possibly gullies, swales, or other surfaces)

2. The collection and conveying system: gutters, downspouts, and pipes, as well as the leaf screens and "roofwashers" that remove contaminants and debris

3. Cisterns or storage tanks

4. A treatment system, possibly including filters and additives, to settle, filter, and disinfect the stored water

5. A delivery system, involving gravity or a pump, to get the treated rainwater to its place of use

The first thing to consider is the surface the rain falls on. Rain can wash bacteria, molds, algae, protozoa, and other contaminants from a roof into a storage tank. For landscape use, these may be of little or no concern; for bathing, drinking, cooking, and other uses, they may be critical. Metal roofing without lead flashing or solder is the preferred material for rainwater harvesting. If your roof has lead, is painted, or is covered with asphalt composition, asbestos, or treated wood shingles, you can still collect rainwater, but you should use it only on your landscape—and not on food crops. The same goes for water collected in gullies or swales.

MAJOR COMPONENTS OF A RAINWATER CATCHMENT & DISTRIBUTION SYSTEM

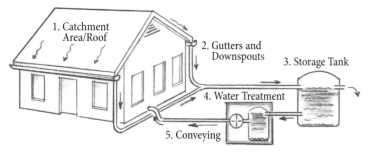

Figure 8

How Much Water?

The next step is to calculate how much rainwater will fall on your collection surfaces. Then you can compare that figure with your household water usage to get a sense of how much of your water needs you can meet with the rain.

First, calculate the horizontal area of your roof, counting only guttered portions that will flow into your collection tank (see figure 9); your answer should be in square feet. Then look up precipitation data for your area; annual figures are useful for yearly projections, and monthly figures will allow you to compare rainwater availability to your monthly water demand.

Now you can convert inches of rain per month or year to a volume of water that will fall on your roof (or other collection surface). One inch of water falling on one square foot of collection surface (in other words, 144 cubic inches of water) is equal to 0.623 gallons. Therefore, the following formula will yield a total estimated volume of available rainwater:

Area of collection surface (square foot) x rainfall (inches per month or year) x 0.623 (gallons per inch of rain per square foot of roof) = gallons of rainwater available (per month or year, depending on which calculation you're doing)

In short:

Area x rainfall x 0.623 = gallons of rainwater

You may be surprised at how much water is available from your roof. You may lose about one-fourth of that volume to system inefficiencies, but it's still a lot of water. Compare your household water usage to the available rainwater on a month-by-month basis, and you'll get a sense of when and how much water it would be worth collecting. If you live in an area where most of the rain falls during one season, you may not find it practical to store all the rain that falls on your roof. Balance the available rainwater, your water needs, and the space and money available for storage tanks, and come up with a system that works for you.

CALCULATING CATCHMENT AREA

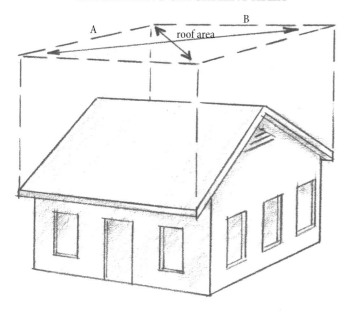

Figure 9

This cistern stores rainwater runoff from the roof until it is needed for landscape irrigation during dry Austin, Texas summers.

CAROL'S EXPERIENCE *Along with behaving responsibly toward water, don't forget to keep some of it around just to love it. Every time I look at the birdbath or the small pond in my yard, something in me feels good. Seeing that small body of water brings peace to my soul. The fact that I'm doing the local wildlife a favor by providing a watering hole is a bonus.*

And then there's the delight of having little fountains indoors and out. That lazy sound of drizzling water, or water gurgling over rocks, is soothing—and it helps mask the ubiquitous traffic noise. If you're shopping for a fountain, though, check out how it sounds. Avoid the ones that sound like rushing rivers, adding to the noise and frenzied feeling!

This small backyard pond was created especially to attract wildlife. Its three-foot depth keeps it cool in summer, and its vertical sides discourage raccoons.

USE THAT WATER AGAIN!
by Art Ludwig

It's a waste to irrigate with great quantities of drinking water when plants thrive on used water containing small bits of compost. Any wastewater used in the home, except water from toilets, is called *greywater*. Dishwashing, shower, sink, and laundry water comprise 50-80 percent of residential *wastewater*, and may be reused for other purposes. Toilet flush water is called *blackwater* because it contains organisms that can cause disease. Contaminated or difficult-to-handle greywater, such as solids-laden kitchen sink water or water used to launder diapers, I call *dark greywater*; some regulators consider these blackwater.

Greywater systems are more site- and user-specific than almost any other home-scale appropriate technology. Each system must be designed and operated in response to the particular circumstances involved, including climate, rainfall, property size, soil types, lifestyle, and landscaping.

Greywater use has many benefits. It reduces your use of freshwater and the strain on your septic tank or treatment plant, with accompanying reduction in energy usage (for pumping) and chemicals (for treatment). It returns nutrients to the soil. And it saves money while increasing your awareness of natural cycles.

However, greywater use may be inappropriate if you have insufficient space, extremely permeable or impermeable soil, an unsuitable climate, not enough time to operate the system, or a highly visible site in a location where laws don't permit greywater use.

Keep it Simple

Some greywater treatment systems aren't worth building. If a greywater system costs more than a few hundred dollars, you might be better off paying for the extra water, and the earth would be less impacted by the wasted water than by the wasted pumps, valves, piping, filters, and electricity used by an overbuilt system. Furthermore, the maintenance on a complicated system may cause you to abandon it.

For a home, any system that uses a pump or filter, involves disinfection, or costs more than you spend on water in a year is suspect. The state of California's mini-leachfield system, which involves burying truckloads of gravel in your garden, is also missing the point.

The majority of successful greywater recycling systems are so simple and inexpensive that they are beneath recognition by regulators, manufacturers, consultants, and salespeople. If you have the energy and the garden bed, no system can equal the efficiency attainable by bucketing—carrying greywater to the garden in a bucket. If you just want to get greywater out of your septic system, no system is simpler than a "drain to mulch basins."

MATCHING GREYWATER SOURCES TO IRRIGATION NEEDS

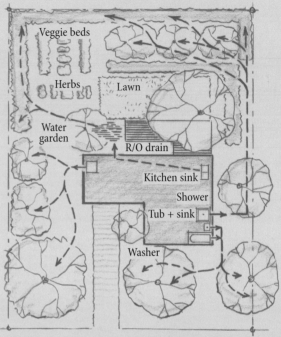

GREYWATER SYSTEMS USED

Washer: "Laundry system" to downhill and slight uphill plants.

Tub plus Bathroom Sink: "Branched drain to mulch basins" around large trees.

Shower: "Movable drain to mulch basins," plumbed to opposite side of house where irrigation need is greatest.

Kitchen Sink: "Drain to mulch basin" around one big tree.

Reverse Osmosis Water Purifier Wastewater (Clearwater): Through 1/2-inch drip irrigation tubing to water garden. (Note: This small line would clog with greywater.)

Figure 6

Watch What Goes Down the Drain

When you use greywater for irrigation, you have to think more about what you put down the drain. Most of the substances in household greywater biodegrade into plant nutrients—lint from natural fabrics, dead skin, sweat, hair, food particles, dirt, grime, and the like. Household cleaners are the main exception; they vary in their toxicity to plants and soil.

Health Issues

In overdeveloped countries, greywater use poses little health risk. Nonetheless, follow these two basic principles:

• allow greywater to pass slowly through healthy topsoil to allow natural purification;

• avoid direct human contact with greywater before purification.

Don't store greywater for more than twenty-four hours; stored greywater rapidly turns into blackwater as bacteria multiply.

To avoid contact with undesirable microorganisms, follow these guidelines:

• Don't recycle greywater via a sprinkler

• Don't apply greywater directly to foliage or aerially to lawns

• Don't apply greywater to saturated soils

• Don't irrigate with greywater near a water well

• Don't water vegetables with greywater (use it on ornamentals, then fruit trees)

• Don't use products that will pollute groundwater or plants

• Don't discharge greywater directly into bodies of water or onto pavement

• Carefully label greywater components, and wear gloves when handling them

Greywater Basics

On your house plan, note the number of gallons per week available from each group of fixtures and the path of the plumbing. Then look at where in the yard this greywater could go, and note this on your site plan (see figure 6).

Consider the following simple, direct ways to reuse greywater: dump dishpan water into a flower bed; siphon tub water to the garden with a hose; shower outdoors under a fruit tree; direct a drain pipe outside to a mulch-filled basin; install a branched drain greywater system.

The Household Water Cascade (see figure 7) provides an image of one set of possibilities for managing your household water as a whole system.

*Greywater Guru **Art Ludwig** has written the authoritative books on greywater and water storage. He invented the first cleaners that biodegrade into plant nutrients. For more detailed information, visit www.greywater.net.*

HOUSEHOLD WATER CASCADE

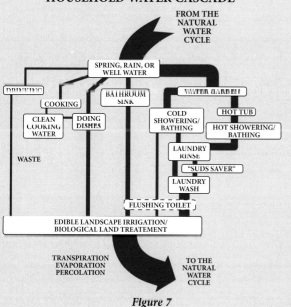

Figure 7

How Water Flows with Other Aspects of Your Home

Water will flow anywhere it can, and our use of it is closely related to our health and comfort, our use of solar energy and fossil fuels, our garden and landscaping practices, and our concerns about mold and structural damage. To round out your water picture, be sure to refer to the information on human comfort (see page 12), solar water heating (see page 136), energy efficiency (see page 138), gardens and landscaping (see page 100), building science (see page 109), and mold (see page 264).

DESIGN SPOTLIGHT
Paul Lusk

When Paul Lusk, Associate Professor of Architecture and Planning at the University of New Mexico, added on to his house near Albuquerque, he made it a living experiment in ecological design. With a failing septic system and shallow groundwater, his goals were to reduce household water consumption and to purify greywater for use in the landscape and garden. His 800-square-foot *green room* addition houses a waterless composting toilet and a constructed wetland that flows into an exterior rock marsh and evaporative pond. A passive evaporative cooling tower cools the green room in the summer. In random tests by local authorities, water flowing out of the exterior wetland was judged "suitable for discharge into a potable stream."

For more details, see www.unm.edu/~plusk/ecodesign/index.html.

This addition houses a new constructed wetland that processes and cleanses the home's greywater.

After flowing through an aerated settling tank (not shown), greywater enters a constructed wetland in the greenhouse, where the nutrients feed native and tropical aquatic plants.

Exiting the interior constructed wetland, the water flows into an exterior rock marsh, where it is further cleansed by cattails, river reed, bulrushes, and other aquatic plants before entering the adjacent evaporative pond.

An updraft solar chimney tower is coupled with a downdraft evaporative cooling tower to passively cool the greenhouse during the summer.

Breezes are cooled by passing through the damp pads of the evaporative cooler at the top of the tower, then drop down into the greenhouse, cooling it by an average of 12 to 15 degrees.

Roof water from the addition is channeled down a tiled downspout next to the cooling tower and into a pumice-filled planting bed.

Lerner Residence
El Cerrito, California

Visitors to Kelly Lerner's home are greeted by a lush garden and a meandering stone path that leads to a bamboo gate. Beyond the gateway and through the sunny patio, the front door opens onto a sensory feast of expansive views, sunlight, and natural finishes. But it wasn't always this way.

When Kelly and her family bought their northern California home in 1996, they chose it with an eye to remodeling. They found a fixer-upper's dream: a homely 1940 bungalow in need of repair, on a large sunny lot with great views. They settled in with the idea that they'd rehab the house in stages while living there—not everyone's idea of a good time, but they coped by being creative.

Being at Home

The house is in the East Bay hills across from San Francisco, where the temperate Mediterranean climate is defined by San Pablo Bay. In the hot dry summer, fog rolls in off the bay in the late afternoon and often doesn't burn off

Kelly started her remodeling project by landscaping the front yard.

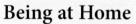
A neglected rental home for many years, Kelly saw the home's potential.

until mid-morning the following day. Most of the rainfall is in winter, and there's rarely a hard frost. September and October are the hottest months, with long sunny days, but temperatures are mild enough that most homes don't need air-conditioning.

Perched at the top of a sloping lot, the house appears to have one story from the street (on the uphill side of the property). A daylight basement adds living space, but also some headaches. During their first winter in the house, water ran across the downstairs slab floor in a small stream. Furthermore, the stairway to the basement was steep, the basement ceilings were less than 7 feet high, and it was always cold and damp.

The main level of the house had its own problems. The southwest-facing living room overheated in the afternoon, and the single-pane windows fogged up when they cooked. The living room was large, but doors on three walls and picture windows on the fourth made furniture arrangement difficult. There was no dining room. The kitchen had the best location for views and sunlight, but its small corner windows allowed for neither. A single floor furnace provided heat. The electrical wiring was ancient. In Kelly's mind, the house was pure potential.

The patio is a perfect spot; the house blocks cool winds, and the flagstone and brick are warmed by the sun.

Fortunately, Kelly had some construction skills. She also wanted to use her own home to try out materials and techniques that interested her; it was better to be her own guinea pig than to learn at the expense of her clients.

First Things First

By living in the house and making changes gradually, Kelly was able to observe what worked well and what needed improvement. As she remodeled in stages, she was also able to adjust to the changes and then notice what still needed attention.

The house itself set the agenda for how to begin; the day after moving in, the sewer plugged up. While replacing the sewer line, Kelly decided that, as long as she was digging up the front yard, it was a good time to replace the original galvanized water line (now corroded) with copper pipe and install a French drain to intercept the groundwater that was running into the basement. It also seemed like a good time to install a drip irrigation system for the yard and to lay a solid pipe in the French-drain trench to carry rainwater from the downspouts to the future orchard in the backyard.

With emergencies addressed and the irrigation system installed, Kelly turned to landscaping. "I didn't start with the inside," she said, "because the landscape takes the longest to mature—and if the yard looks good right away, the neighbors are happy; they'll be more understanding of future construction projects." Looking ahead, she didn't plant anything close to the house in areas where they expected to remodel.

Kelly began by planting drought-tolerant native plants in the front yard; an orchard, herbs, and a vegetable garden in the backyard; and bamboo (with root barriers) front and back. "I knew I would want to use bamboo for later building projects," she said, "so I planted my building materials first." She also integrated two of the evolving landscape features: she had some thirsty plants, so she directed the groundwater and rainwater she was collecting via her newly laid pipes to water the bamboo groves and the orchard.

The next winter, some water still got into the basement. Because the house had a U-shape, with the "courtyard" facing uphill, it funneled water into the basement. But Kelly took the opportunity to turn a lemon into lemonade: In the entry courtyard, she

The flagstone entry courtyard, shielded from the street, extends the interior living area.

The new office opens onto the entry courtyard through salvaged French doors. Built-in bookshelves and bamboo work surfaces make the most of a small room.

poured a concrete slab that sloped gently toward the French drain, then paved it with flagstone. "I generally don't like patios that keep water from soaking into the ground, but I needed this courtyard to help keep water out of the basement. Once we started using the front patio, I became viscerally aware of how well semi-enclosed spaces function." The house blocks the prevailing northwest wind, and the patio faces northeast and gets lots of morning sun. The thermal mass of the flagstone and the brick chimney store the solar heat, and in cool weather the patio stays comfortably warm into the evening.

The transformed single-car garage opens onto the new entry courtyard. The salvaged French doors match the pair on the other side of the courtyard.

By then, there was also a good crop of bamboo. Kelly crafted a lacy bamboo fence and gateway to enclose the street side of the patio; it became an outdoor room that made the house feel larger and more gracious—and a wonderful spot for enjoying breakfast.

One Room at a Time

Two years after moving in, Kelly turned the front bedroom into an eco-friendly office. It was a good place to start remodeling because it could be isolated from the house. She upgraded the electrical system to support computers and printers. She also built in bamboo desktops and bookcases of Medite (formaldehyde-free fiberboard), refinished the existing white-oak floor, and installed salvaged French doors that open onto the front patio, bringing in more sunlight.

Next, the attached garage warranted attention. Kelly wanted to claim the space for a family room and dining area. She gutted the garage, insulated the walls and ceiling, and poured an insulated slab with in-floor hydronic (fluid-based) radiant heating, connected via a heat exchanger to the domestic water heater. As with the office, she installed salvaged French doors that open onto the front patio. "It makes the room so much more useful and comfortable to open it up and have that indoor/outdoor experience."

Kelly also built storage cabinets along one long wall to compensate for the loss of garage storage. Because the wall faced the neighboring house, the storage wall also increased the sense of privacy in the new room.

A decorative border impressed in the earth plaster acts as trim. Ply-boo (laminated bamboo) cabinets match the work surface in the office.

Kelly laid Mexican tile on the floor, covered the ceiling with woven bamboo mats, and applied earth plaster to the walls, with a decorative border. "People just love it," she says. "The room has a feeling of solidity and the craftsmanship of earlier times. Because of the insulation and the earth materials, it's also the quietest, coziest room in the house. Most people don't experience rooms like this in stick-framed houses."

The old kitchen had charm, but was too small. Upper cabinets blocked the view of the Golden Gate Bridge.

Going for It

Finally it was time to remodel the rest of the house. Not wanting to overbuild, Kelly explored several scenarios and decided that a small addition (5½ feet by 13 feet) would significantly improve the house at a reasonable cost. "Besides, we have so much indoor/outdoor living space that the house didn't need to be much bigger," she said. "And a big addition would have messed up the backyard and shaded the rest of the house, leaving it too cold in winter."

The first step was to tear out the basement slab to lower the floor. Rather than sending the broken-up slab to the landfill, it was used to make retaining walls to terrace the sloping backyard. Kelly installed hydronic heating in the new, insulated basement slab and extended the system to add wall radiators to the upstairs rooms, eliminating the floor furnace and vastly increasing the comfort level.

Kelly widened the kitchen only enough to add a sunny built-in dining nook.

Then, with the help of a cooperative contractor, Kelly tore out and remodeled the kitchen, adding a dining nook surrounded by windows that overlook the bay. The kitchen cabinets are made of wheat-straw board, with doors and drawer fronts of beautiful reclaimed Douglas Fir, its iron-nail-stains adding character. The flooring is prefinished cork tiles. Countertops are Richlite, a solid-surface composite of wood fiber and resin, chosen largely for its durability: "Durability is green."

The kitchen walls are finished with gypsum plaster, over which a homemade casein (milk-protein-based) glaze tinted with mineral pigments was applied. The ceiling was finished with a lime wash and a glaze; the opalescent off-white color improves light distribution and provides a feeling of spaciousness.

The built-in corner dining nook is surrounded by windows, and opens onto the new deck.

Salvaged Douglas Fir was re-milled to build the doors and drawer fronts of these wheat strawboard cabinets.

"I love natural finishes," says Kelly. "You can literally go into your kitchen, get your materials together, and mix your paint. And if you don't like it, you just try something different and go over it again. It takes a little time, but it's easier than going to the paint store, looking at all the paint chips, and paying a lot of money for some stuff that's generally toxic."

Off the dining nook, a new deck adds outdoor cooking and eating space with sweeping views of the bay and hills. The deck allowed Kelly to keep the kitchen/dining addition small by extending the living space at a reasonable cost. The deck's structural members are custom-milled salvaged cypress, and the decking is a composite material of recycled plastic and wood fibers.

During this stage of remodeling, Kelly added cotton batt insulation to the roof and exterior walls of the house, and replaced most of the single-pane windows with double-pane wood windows. The difference in comfort—and utility bills— is palpable. She selected the window glazing on a room-by-room basis. For example, the living room, located in the upper, southwest-facing part of the house, tended to overheat in summer; Kelly used low-e glazing there to cut down on solar heat gain. But downstairs, where there was now plenty of thermal mass in the slab floor and earth-plastered walls to modulate temperature swings, she used plain double-glazing to let in the sun's radiant warmth.

Around the living room, chest-height bookcases topped with beautiful reclaimed wood were added to gently define the spaces while adding storage and display space. To increase the feeling of depth, the living-room walls were plastered, painted with a light-colored micaceous clay (clay with shiny natural mica in it), and glazed with casein paint.

Naturally pigmented stains on the plaster walls and ceiling complement the colors of the cork floors, Douglas Fir cabinets, and Richlite countertops.

The deck framing is custom-milled cypress, salvaged from trees cut down to clear a construction site in the area.

The open living room and kitchen share light and views, but are defined by a lowered beam and half-height bookcases.

89

Downstairs, the walls are earth-plastered over sheetrock, with a micaceous clay finish and a tinted casein glaze. "Thanks to the insulation, the double-pane windows, the radiant heating, and the thermal mass of the earth plaster and the tiled floors, it's really quiet and cozy down here," says Kelly.

Living in a Construction Zone

Though it's generally not a good idea to live in a house that's undergoing construction, the phased nature of this project made living in it possible—eliminating the cost of renting elsewhere for several months. Having already remodeled the office and family room (previously the garage), Kelly and her family moved into those rooms and stored most of their furniture in a neighbor's garage. The upstairs bathroom was intact and accessible. Because the construction was planned for summer, they were able to create a temporary outdoor kitchen and dining area in the courtyard, which was conveniently adjacent to both the completed office and family room.

The system worked well until construction stretched into November and December, when rain and evening darkness forced the family to eat in restaurants frequently. "Everything was dark, wet, and cold," says Kelly. "We were so tired from the constant disruption of construction that we couldn't face cooking in the rain, although we did consider putting up a tarp over the whole patio and toughing it out."

Eden in the Backyard

Off the downstairs bedroom is a flagstone patio that invites dining al fresco. The flagstones soak up daytime sun and give back evening heat, allowing warmth-loving plants to inhabit the area, too. Under the new deck is a shady place to lie in a hammock and catch a breeze on hot days. Nearby, tucked under the bamboo grove, is a quiet spot for rest and reflection: a bench overlooking a pool with a little waterfall.

Rustling bamboo, the gentle splash of water into the pool, and warm sunshine create an outdoor room for peaceful contemplation.

The space below the new deck is beautifully sheltered for dining alfresco.

On the next level down, the gardens are now mature. The orchard produces raspberries, blackberries, apples, apricots, peaches, nectarines, cherries, lemons, oranges, limes, and guavas. The next terrace contains vegetables and herbs. Looking upslope, the revived house presides proudly over them all. It's a fine place to contemplate the fruits of one's labor.

CHAPTER 6

The Garden: Growing Green

"No occupation is so delightful to me as the culture of the Earth."
—Thomas Jefferson

THE WORLD OUTSIDE YOUR HOUSE is an integral part of your natural dwelling. The soil, plants, animals, sun, water, and wind all interact with you and your house. In fact, they're the next layer outward in a continuum that ranges from your body to the universe.

The way you garden affects the rest of the world. Equally important, your garden can be a place for personal rejuvenation. In other words, your garden is one place where doing good things for the world is also delightfully good for you.

In front of this remodeled northern California home, drought-tolerant trees provide habitat, food, and shade.

Your Garden, Your Home

Treating your garden, landscape, and outdoor spaces as part of your home has many benefits:

- Plantings can improve the energy efficiency and comfort of your home.

- You can grow your own food, in garden rows or edible landscaping.

- You can restore the web of life by providing habitat for local fauna.

- A garden humming with life will feed and stimulate your senses.

- Planting native species restores the landscape that's best adapted to your area.

- A well-designed organic garden can improve air, soil, and water.

- Outdoor rooms extend your living space affordably and delightfully.

- Thoughtful landscaping can lessen noise pollution in your garden.

- Your garden becomes part of a water and nutrient cycle that makes the best use of resources and reconnects you with how life works.

In addition, studies by real estate agents and professional foresters indicate that the presence of trees raises a home's resale value 7 to 20 percent.[1] What other form of remodeling investment provides visual delight, food, *and* cleaner air and water? Here's another way to look at this: Buildings—even "green" ones—almost always consume natural resources, but gardens can be highly productive, enhancing both biodiversity and resources.

Gardening for an Energy-Efficient Home

Plants are more responsive to seasonal changes than any fixed device, such as an overhang for shading. Deciduous trees and shrubs leaf out in summer, just when you need the shade. And in winter, they lose their leaves to admit solar warmth. Because their leafing cycles are triggered by outdoor temperatures, they even adapt to differences from year to year: in a cool spring, leaves arrive later; in a warm autumn, they drop later. Plants also provide a dappled, animated shade that lends vitality to the landscape.

Virginia Creeper is especially well suited to seasonal shading, leafing out late in the spring and keeping its leaves through late fall.

Vines growing up the trellis on this tall, exposed wall will soon shield it from sun and rain.

Summer Cooling

Vegetation can help cool your home and yard:

• By providing shade

• Through transpiration

• By directing breezes

The amount of shade that a plant provides depends on the density of its foliage. As a plant matures, its leaf density increases, with vine-like plants offering shade sooner than slower growing trees. It's a good idea to have a shading plan that accounts for your immediate and long-term needs. Reference books (see Resources, page 269) can help you select plants with the desired leaf density, shape, and maturation period.

As you begin to plan for shading, take a look at your home's orientation. Tall trees can block the midday sun at its higher angle, and shorter vegetation on the east and west will intercept lower-angle sunrays (see figures 1 and 2).

PLANTED SUNSCREEN

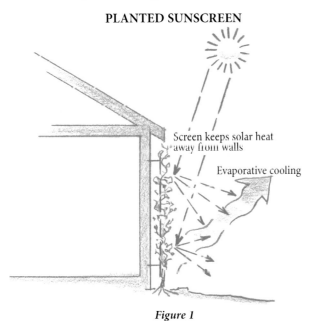

Figure 1

SHADE FROM PLANTS OF VARIOUS HEIGHTS

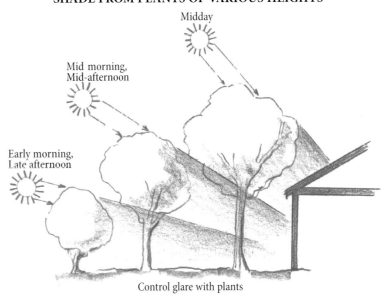

Figure 2

Don't overlook sunlight that's reflected off nearby light paving and bodies of water. Vegetation can help block that unwanted light, too, as can replacing paving with groundcover or other less reflective surfaces (see figure 3).

Transpiration is somewhat like our perspiration. It's the process by which plants protect themselves from overheating by using excess solar heat to evaporate water. Because the change from liquid to vapor requires heat, this process of transpiration removes heat from the air. Thus, plants can lower the surrounding air temperature while increasing humidity.

You can also use plantings to sculpt the wind (see figure 4), slowing it to a gentle breeze at an outdoor room or directing it toward a patio or your windows to enhance your natural ventilation scheme (see chapter 4, page 64).

REFLECTED LIGHT

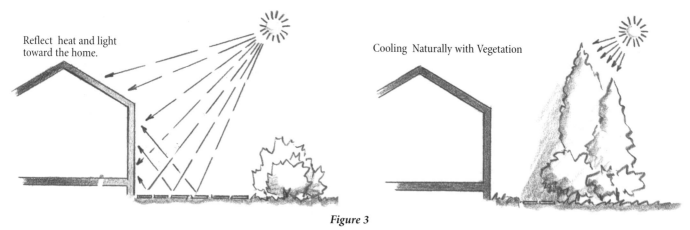

Reflect heat and light toward the home.

Cooling Naturally with Vegetation

Figure 3

MODIFYING WIND FLOW

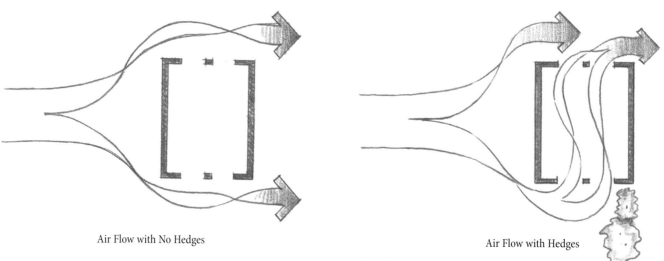

Air Flow with No Hedges

Air Flow with Hedges

Figure 4

Winter Warming

Carefully selecting and placing plants can help keep you warm in winter by:

• letting in sun

• providing a windbreak

• maintaining an air pocket next to the house

Those same deciduous trees that bring you summer shade have to get out of the way to admit solar warmth in winter. If you're employing this natural heating/cooling strategy, select plants that have an open branching structure. Otherwise, even the bare branches will block a significant amount of solar radiation. If you have solar panels, be especially careful that they're not shaded.

When cold winds whip around your house, they carry away the warm layer of air that insulates your outer walls (see figure 5). By looking at your site plan and the wind information you've collected, you can create a planted windbreak that will slow or redirect those chilling winds. On the north and northwest sides of your house, evergreens might be a good choice; they keep their dense foliage all year (see figures 6 and 7).

WINDBREAKS AND AIRFLOW

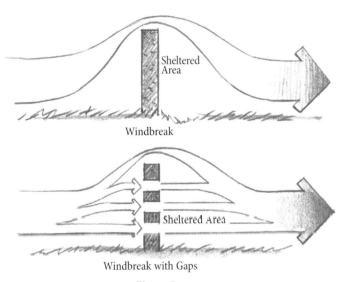

Figure 5

WINDBREAKS

Windbreak on South Side

Windbreak on North Side

Figure 7

WIND SPEED REDUCTION

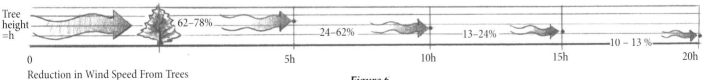

Reduction in Wind Speed From Trees

Figure 6

95

Closer to the house, you can plant shrubs to hold a layer of still air against your outside walls for insulation. Don't plant too close, or you might create new problems of moisture buildup and plants growing under your siding (see figure 8).

These advantages don't come without thought. Arbitrary landscaping can actually increase your energy bills. When you plan your garden, take into account all the information you collected in chapter 2 about yourself and your site and climate, as well as the many possible gardening strategies we'll discuss in this chapter.

INSULATING AIR SPACE

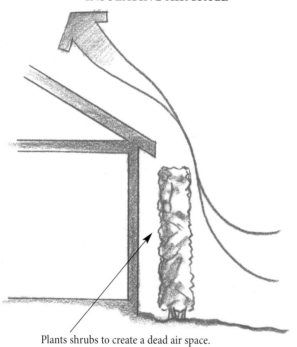

Plants shrubs to create a dead air space.

Figure 8

Use Table 1 (bottom, page 97) to help you design an appropriate landscape for your climate zone, and refer to *Energy-Efficient and Environmental Landscaping* (see Resources, page 269) for more detailed suggestions. But always let your own observations about your particular site and microclimate guide your decisions.

SOME COMPELLING STATISTICS ABOUT PLANTS AND ENERGY

It's in our blood to love plants, but knowing a few facts can make us appreciate them even more. If you had any doubts about the power of your garden, check out these stats:

• Carefully positioned trees can cut a household's total energy consumption by 20 to 25 percent, according to the USDA.[2]

When you use plantings to keep you cool in summer:

• Planting trees is 10 times more cost-effective than building new power plants for summer cooling.[3]

• Through evaporation alone, one tree can produce cooling effects approximately equal to 10 room-size air conditioners working 20 hours a day.[4]

• A well-planned landscaping program can reduce an un-shaded home's summer air-conditioning costs by 15 to 50 percent.[5]

• A single tree, located to provide shade during the afternoon, may reduce wall and roof temperatures as much as 20-40°. Shading your air conditioner could increase its efficiency up to 10 percent.[6]

And don't forget that planted windbreaks can protect you from winter winds:

• A South Dakota study found that windbreaks to the north, west, and east of houses cut winter fuel consumption by an average of 40 percent. With a windbreak on only the windward side, the homes still consumed 25 percent less fuel than similar unprotected homes.[7]

• An Oklahoma study found that a tall evergreen hedge on a home's north side reduced fuel consumption by 10 percent during light winds and by 34 percent during high winds.[8]

Poison-Me-Not

Before we say more about the delightful and practical aspects of gardening, it's important to address the potential to blow it all by loading your landscape with toxic chemicals—pesticides, herbicides, and synthetic fertilizers. A study in the San Francisco Bay Area found gardening to be the largest single source of pollutants.[9]

Fertilizers

Fertilizing may sound like plant nutrition, but pick your nutrients well. Highly refined synthetic fertilizers can disturb natural growth processes, weaken plants, encourage weed growth, introduce hazardous chemicals to soil and waterways, and discourage growth of native species. Furthermore, their production and application needlessly consumes energy resources.

If your garden needs feeding, look to organic fertilizers, manures, and composts. Not only are they more likely to make

TABLE 1:
ENERGY-CONSERVING LANDSCAPING BY CLIMATE ZONE[10]

CLIMATE ZONE	SUMMER	WINTER	OTHER
Temperate (including Mixed and Marine Mediterranean)	Maximize shade; allow air circulation; guide cooling breezes to the house	Maximize solar access; reduce cold winds near house	Thermal mass in the landscape can help reduce temperature swings
Hot Dry	Shade walls and windows on east, south, and west; shade roof (consider palm trees for tall, drought-resistant shade); allow transpiration to cool air around the home; funnel cooling breezes to the home but discourage hot winds; use drought-resistant trees to maximize shade	Block winter winds	Avoid paved areas directly to the south of the house; balance the desire for evaporation and transpiration with water-conservation practices
Hot Humid	Allow full wind access; maximize roof shading with tall trees; shade windows, walls, air conditioners, and walkways; avoid heavy plantings that generate excess moisture and block breezes	Block or filter storm winds	Avoid plants near house that require frequent watering; avoid water features that increase humidity
Cold	Shade all windows from direct sun, especially south-facing	Protect from winds with dense windbreaks; admit sun via south-facing windows	Consider using pavement on the south side of the house to absorb solar heat and radiate it at night; a berm to the north might also be helpful

plants healthier, but they complete cycles by putting nutrient-rich substances into the soil that would otherwise be considered waste. What could be more satisfying?

Managing Garden Pests

Pesticides typically create more problems than they solve. In the United States, more pesticide is applied per acre to home gardens than to farms.[11] Pollution of air, water, and soil is one obvious hazard of this practice, but pesticides also cause horticultural problems. Killing its natural enemies helps a pest thrive, and repeated pesticide use results in resistant strains, feeding a vicious cycle. Furthermore, production and application of many pesticides consumes nonrenewable resources and energy.

The natural solution to pest problems is called Integrated Pest Management (IPM). IPM isn't just something you *do* to a garden; it's a relationship with your garden. Like many other aspects of natural living, this relationship is not only less harmful to you and the ecosphere, but it can be personally enriching. As you come to understand how all the living organisms—plants and animals—in your garden interact with each other and with the soil, climate, and other influences, you'll probably find yourself more deeply involved with life itself.

There is no single IPM strategy. You create a plan based on your locale, your plants, your preferences, and local pests and other challenges. Your goal is to plant a garden that's so healthy that it resists most pests and attracts beneficial insects that dine on pests. You'll need to stay involved and keep a close eye on the balance and flow of life in your garden. If things don't take care of themselves, you can employ natural management strategies and less-toxic controls to aid the natural process (see Resources, page 269).

The best news is that a healthy, balanced garden needs little intervention to keep it humming along. And we mean "humming" literally; a well-functioning garden is abuzz with birds, bees, butterflies, and other beneficial creatures, all on their pollinating and feeding rounds that contribute to the garden's vitality.

Welcome the Wildlife

The next step in making your garden more eco-friendly is to provide habitat for many of the creatures that are native to your region. Once again, here's an activity that can bring you delight while healing Mother Earth. With backyard wildlife habitat gardening, you can increase biodiversity, help reverse species extinction trends, build soil, improve your neighborhood, provide sensory richness, teach people how ecosystems function, and provide soul-satisfying fun all at the same time.

In fact, when you create a habitat garden, you're likely to get back more than you put in. Hearing birds sing by day and crickets chirp by night, watching bees and butterflies on their pollinating rounds, seeing sunlight glint off trickling water, and catching the scent of flowers and rich earth will nourish you in profound ways. Anything less rich-textured than this natural complexity, with which you evolved, is unsatisfying to your body and soul.

It's ironic, then, how often we humans unwittingly create homes for ourselves while destroying the habitat of countless other species. Globally, habitat loss is the greatest threat to biodiversity and a major factor in species extinction. As human settlements grow, natural areas become smaller and more fragmented.

CAROL'S EXPERIENCE *Backyard wildlife habitat gardens don't just attract wild critters, they attract people, too. When I created a habitat garden in the front yard of an urban apartment building I once lived in, I made lots of new friends. People I never saw before stopped to spend time in the little oasis. They talked about how good it felt to come in off the street and relax in its lushness. One of them donated a birdbath to the garden; others contributed plants.*

Whenever people stopped by the garden, I took advantage of the opportunity to educate them by pointing out its habitat features and my organic gardening practices. Then one day all my efforts were rewarded: I looked out the window and saw one of my neighbors giving her anti-environmentalist father a tour of the garden, explaining all the features that were helping bring beneficial critters back downtown.

The addition of a simple birdbath can increase your backyard bird population and even encourage nearby nesting.

Migratory birds lose their stopovers, pollinators must travel farther to find food, and amphibians become deformed by contaminated air and water. Urban areas have become the true deserts; natural deserts support far more richness and diversity of flora and fauna than do most backyards. But it doesn't have to be this way! Whether you have acreage, a backyard, or a balcony, you can do something to provide wildlife habitat.

Basic Elements of Habitat Gardening

At first glance, it might seem that any garden is good for biodiversity. But in terms of supporting a complex, species-rich ecosystem, there is a big difference between a garden of exotics (non-native species), managed with pesticides and fertilizers, and a garden of native plants that relies on soil-building and natural pest controls. In fact, the three Eurasian grass species that constitute the bulk of lawns are of little use to most beneficial insects and animals.

In order to provide wildlife habitat, think in terms of four basic elements:

• Food

• Water

• Shelter

• Territory in which to reproduce and raise young

Vegetation can provide food in the form of acorns, nuts, berries, seeds, buds, catkins, nectar, and pollen; birdfeeders can fill in while plants are maturing and during winter. Water can be supplied in a birdbath, small pond, recirculating fountain, or shallow dish. Shelter can be found in dense shrubs, hollow logs, rock or brush piles, stone walls, evergreens, patches of meadow,

In this northern California backyard, the owner included a shallow "bog" that attracts frogs, salamanders, and even butterflies.

and ponds. Territory can include safe areas for bird nests; larval plants for butterflies; bodies of water for tadpoles, salamanders, and insects; and nesting boxes for birds, bats, or squirrels.

Native plants—the ones that grew in your region before people imported exotic plants—are a central element of habitat gardening. Because they are adapted to your soils and climate, they generally require less water, care, and maintenance. And because local fauna are adapted to them, they provide the best food sources, often supporting 10 to 50 times more species of wildlife than nonnatives. Even when exotic plants provide food for wildlife, they generally can't supply the range of seasonal habitat features that well-chosen natives can. Nearly 500 native plant species are currently on the verge of extinction in North America; natural landscaping can help reverse that trend.

Though it begins locally, habitat gardening isn't just a personal solution. When you nurture pollinators and migratory birds, your reach may extend thousands of miles. When neighbors alter their fences to create wildlife corridors, they counteract the trend toward habitat islands.

Backyard wildlife habitat gardening can also weave you into a nationwide web of other gardens, gardeners, support, and information. The National Wildlife Federation (NWF) has operated its Backyard Wildlife Habitat™ program since 1973 and has certified over 27,000 habitat gardens in five countries (see Resources, page 269).

Indigenous and drought-tolerant plants both play a role in making the desert garden a water-responsible paradise.

Become a Better Water Manager

It's easy to feel conflicted about using water in the garden. On one hand, we need to conserve water; on the other, water is a vital, sensuous, nourishing element. We like to view water as a precious gift, a valuable resource, something to be appreciated and used with respect. Don't waste it or pollute it, but do enjoy it and use it well. Here are some tips that will help you enjoy water without wasting it.

Plan your garden thoughtfully:

• Consider the characteristics of various parts of your site and climate—slopes, soil types, wet and dry areas—when planning your garden.

• Select drought-tolerant and locally native plants; they'll need little or no watering after they're established.

• Group plants with similar water needs together, and locate water-loving plants near the house to take advantage of greywater, roof rainwater, and pavement runoff.

• Water thoughtfully (if you need to at all!).

• Water in the early morning or evening to minimize waste by evaporation.

This lush planting bed next to a house in Portland, Oregon is watered by the downspout from the porch gutter.

• Don't water pavement or overwater your plants (excess water may run off into storm drains, encourage molds and fungi, and weaken plants).

• Use mulch (a protective layer of nonliving material that covers the soil surface around plants) to reduce weeds and conserve moisture while cooling and enriching the soil; organic mulch (wood chips, grass clippings, straw, sawdust) improves soil texture and fertility.

If you're ready to make some changes in your landscape, consider:

• Contouring the ground to direct rainwater where plants need it.

• Allowing water to percolate into soil; for example, use pavers rather than a concrete slab for a patio.

When you're ready to plant your garden:

- Place water-loving plants in naturally moist areas of your property.
- Locate shade plants to minimize the water needs of lower-growing plants.
- Limit the size of irrigated lawn, or plant native grasses or a mixture of drought-tolerant species (typical lawns consume excessive water, are heavily fertilized, and provide no habitat).

For some smart upgrades to your watering system:

- Use a soaker hose or drip system for trees, shrubs, flowers, and ground covers; they use 50 percent less water than sprinklers, deliver water directly to the root zone, water slowly so little is lost to runoff, and reduce insect problems (insects and disease like wet foliage).
- Maintain and adjust your watering system regularly.
- Use rainwater and greywater if appropriate (see chapter 5).

Outdoor Rooms

Once your garden is vibrant, you're naturally going to want to spend more time taking in the fresh air, the warming sun, the gentle breeze, the fragrance of earth and plants, and the sounds of birdsong, moving water, and rustling leaves. An outdoor room is the natural place to enjoy all of this. Whether you're dining on a patio, having tea in a solarium, rocking on a front porch, or meditating in a gazebo, your senses and your biological rhythms will be revived by the vitality of the outdoor world.

This lawn is kept small intentionally to reduce the need for water.

With soft moveable cushions and a roof overhead, this outdoor room in Portland, Oregon can be a cozy spot year-round.

How to Begin

Planning an outdoor living space is a good way to practice ecological design by shaping the microclimates around your home. Using your marked-up site and house plans—or just sitting in your yard at various times of day and year—will suggest ways to take advantage of nature's gifts while fending off some of its less comfortable extremes. This is an opportunity to relearn skills that were instinctive to our ancestors: watching the path of the sun, noticing the direction and force of the wind, observing seasonal precipitation, and taking note of landmarks, topography, flora, fauna, and water flow.

Look around your home for indoor/outdoor living opportunities. If you have enough space, you might choose more than one spot, developing each for different uses or climate conditions. You might want a solarium on the southeast side for winter breakfasts, a screened sleeping porch on the west side that also shades the house in summer, and a vine-covered trellis on the north side with a lazily dribbling

A simple porch extends the living area of this small Portland, Oregon house and is a favorite gathering place for meals and conversation.

Isn't it nice to know that the planet benefits from all this bliss, too? A well-conceived outdoor living space is warmed by the sun and cooled by shade, breeze, and moisture, extending your living space without using fossil fuels. Furthermore, attached outdoor rooms can improve the energy efficiency of your home: a porch can shade a south or west wall in summer, a semi-enclosed patio can keep a layer of still air near the house in winter, a sunspace can collect solar heat. But perhaps most important is the experience itself. Moving your activities outward reunites you with the community of living things.

The living area of this small house was nearly doubled with porches that also protect the new straw-bale walls.

102

Before you build a trellis and plant vines, investigate sun patterns and your need for shade by using a movable umbrella.

fountain, where you sip mint juleps on a hot summer day.

The key is to notice what the elements give you—sun, wind, humidity, precipitation, vista—then marry that microclimate to your needs by choosing among some simple climate modifiers:

- Plants (for shade and beauty, to attract wildlife)

- Water (a fountain, birdbath, pond)

- Fabric (awning, umbrella)

- Screens (to keep out bugs or calm the wind)

- Structure (a solid roof or wall, trellises, arbors)

- Glazing (glass, plastic)

- Thermal mass (stone, concrete, or earth that absorbs heat and reradiates it when air temperatures drop)

You can use movable climate modifiers to extend the range of your indoor/outdoor room. For example:

- Retractable blinds or deciduous vines can shade a sun room in hot weather

- Operable or removable windows make a screened porch more comfortable in cool weather

- An umbrella or awning can bring temporary shade to an open patio

An outdoor living area need not be expensive or elaborate. A bench, some potted plants, a bird feeder, and a small fountain can transform a place. No matter what your budget, it's a good idea to start with a few simple changes, spend some time in the space, and make other modifications as the need and inspiration arise.

PROFILE IN DESIGN
The Rapaport Residence Washington, D.C.

The Rapaport family lives outside Washington, D.C., in a modified farmhouse that features a wonderful sunny kitchen and eating area. But even with this delightful room, they felt the steps down to the backyard made them feel disconnected from the outdoors. Because their summers are humid and bug-ridden, they wanted to add a screened porch off the kitchen, with a deck beyond. But architect Rick Harlan Schneider of Inscape Studio pointed out that an attached covered porch would block the sunlight that made the kitchen so cheery.

Instead, Schneider and project architect Petros Zouzoulas proposed building a screened porch away from the house, with a deck in between. The result is a playful cube with wood slats applied over the wall screening to provide privacy and welcome the breezes, and a "butterfly" roof that shades the space

The Rapaports' outdoor room is open to sunshine and breezes, and screened to keep out insects. It stands away from the house so as not to shade the indoor rooms.

Pier footings minimize damage to the roots of the old nearby tree, and the butterfly roof allows rainwater collection for garden watering.

These slats are narrower and the spaces between them wider, allowing more air and light to pass through where privacy isn't needed.

Once inside, the screened porch feels both cozy and open. Decking and wall slats are of sustainably forested cedar.

and collects rainwater for the garden. The porch and deck are built on pier footings to minimize impact on the beautiful old shade tree.

Shade and breeze are the best natural cooling strategies for a hot, humid summer. In addition to shade from the roof, an adjacent tree, and the wall slats, having four open walls allows maximal cross-ventilation. When a cooling boost is needed, the ceiling fan increases air movement.

Each wall of the cube responds to the unique needs of its exposure. Facing the neighbor's house, the slats are wider and the spaces between them smaller. Toward the yard, the slats are narrow and the spaces wide for greater visual transparency.

Rick and Petros also specified environmentally friendly materials: sustainably forested cedar for the deck and slats; ACQ-treated framing lumber; metal tubing for the roof structure; and an acrylic canvas roof, rather than environmentally harmful vinyl.

A screened window folds up awning-style above a counter, facilitating outdoor eating on the new deck.

Grow Your Own Food

Finally, what better way to enjoy your garden than to eat it? You can grow your own pesticide-free food in a garden plot, or you can distribute it around your yard as edible landscaping. The beneficial insects you attract by your good gardening practices will help pollinate your crops and keep the garden fauna in balance. Feeding your garden with compost made from kitchen scraps makes natural nutrient cycles very real. Meanwhile, you're not buying food that's traveled halfway around the world, burning fossil fuels on its way. And there's no fresher and more nutritious produce than the fruit and vegetables you pick right outside your kitchen door. Being green can be delicious!

The Integrated Garden

Some of the most satisfying opportunities in natural remodeling come from redesigning your house in conjunction with your garden. Look for ways to relate your garden to your strategies for:

- Solar heating (see chapter 3)
- Natural cooling (see chapter 4)
- Water use (see chapter 5)
- Your kitchen (see chapter 11)

WHAT IS PERMACULTURE?

by Penny Livingston-Stark

If you're interested in natural living, you'll want to look into permaculture—a set of ecological design principles and practices for providing food, energy, and shelter via highly productive environments. These principals are rooted in careful observations of natural patterns and can be applied anywhere.

The concept of permaculture was developed in the 1970s by Bill Mollison, a forest ecologist, and David Holmgren, an environmental design student. They coined the term to articulate the notion of *permanent agriculture*, and it has now expanded to denote *permanent culture*—a way to provide for our needs and the health of the environment indefinitely.

A permaculture designer gradually discerns optimal methods for integrating water catchment, human shelter, and energy systems with tree crops, edible and useful perennials, self-seeding annuals, domestic and wild animals, and aquaculture. Waste products from plants, animals, and human activities are used as nutrients to benefit other elements in the system. Plantings are arranged in patterns that can catch water, filter toxins, absorb nutrients and sunlight, and block the wind. Particular associations of trees, perennial vines, shrubs, and ground covers are clustered together to nourish and protect each another. Ponds and other elements are constructed in patterns that increase biological activity at the intersection of two ecosystems.

Creating a permaculture environment is a gradual, long-range process. Proper sequencing and flexibility allow changes to be made as observation and experience bring new understanding. Techniques and principles from many traditions are incorporated, such as indigenous land-use and food systems, natural building materials (earth, straw, stone, and bamboo), and renewable energy systems.

Since 1981, thousands of people have attended permaculture design courses, forming a loose global network. Their work fosters a growing understanding of nature's patterns and generates models of sustainable living that aim to achieve maximum productivity with minimal inputs.

Penny Livingston-Stark is internationally recognized as a prominent permaculture teacher, designer, and speaker. For more information about Penny and about permaculture, see www.permacultureinstitute.com.

CHAPTER 7

Natural Forces within Your Home: Managing Moisture, Air, and Heat

Nothing happens in living nature that is not in relation to the whole.

—Goethe

Y OU'VE BEEN LEARNING ABOUT THE NATURAL FORCES outside your home. Now it's time to study the natural processes at work inside your home. Moisture, air, and heat move constantly throughout your house. When that migration works to your benefit, your home is comfortable, healthy, durable, and energy-efficient. But when things go wrong, they can go wrong in big ways. The problems may include the following:

- Mold growth leading to possible structural damage and health problems

- Compromised comfort and indoor air quality due to leaky windows, doors, and ducts (which also waste valuable heating and cooling energy)

- Lowered interior air pressure, causing *backdrafting* through flues and chimneys and leaving high levels of unhealthy combustion byproducts, such as carbon monoxide

The Building Envelope

The key to creating a healthy, happy house is to understand and improve its enclosure—the *building envelope* formed by the roof, floor, and exterior walls. This envelope acts like a negotiator between the indoors and the outside world. Air, moisture, and heat all travel across this boundary seeking to balance any differences in air pressure, moisture level, and temperature. Your goal is to control that migration so that you let in the good stuff, like fresh air and sunlight, and exhaust or exclude what you don't want—air pollutants, excessive moisture, extreme heat or cold.

Stated differently, the main job of the building envelope is to *temper* the interior environment to enhance your health and comfort. To do that, the envelope is made up of a *thermal boundary* (insulation) and an *air boundary* (air barrier). The envelope also needs to allow unwanted moisture—which always finds its way in eventually—to leave the enclosure. You could liken this combination to wearing a sweater (the thermal boundary, that stops heat flow) and a windbreaker with underarm vents (the air boundary, that controls air movement and exhausts moisture buildup as needed). All three—the thermal boundary, the air boundary, and a way to let moisture get out—are needed because most insulation doesn't stop air flow, an air barrier typically doesn't slow the passage of heat, and either one may or may not allow moisture to escape.

In order to effectively control the passage of moisture, air, and heat, your home's envelope needs to be continuous. In other

An attic can be converted into a delightful study or guest room.

words, it can't have significant gaps or holes (windows and doors don't count as holes if they can be tightly sealed). If your home's envelope is not continuous, problems can occur: drafts, uncomfortably high or low humidity, condensation on windows and walls, termites, dust mites, and mold growth.

Defining Your Home's Envelope

The first steps toward improving your home's envelope are to identify its current position, locate any gaps or flaws, and decide whether to modify it.

Throughout most of your house, the exterior walls generally define the envelope. But determining where that boundary is located may get tricky at the top and bottom of the house. For example (see figure 1), are your attic and your basement or crawlspace within or outside the envelope?

THERMAL BOUNDARY DECISIONS

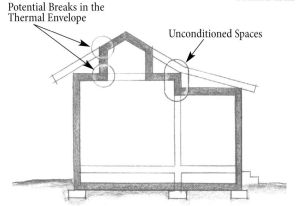

Potential Breaks in the Thermal Envelope

Unconditioned Spaces

Porch, Attic and Crawlspace Excluded

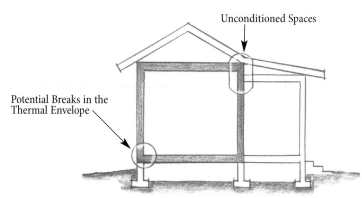

Unconditioned Spaces

Potential Breaks in the Thermal Envelope

Porch, Attic and Crawlspace Included

Figure 1

108

In general, it's best to have heating equipment and ducts inside your envelope; if this isn't the case, you may want to either move the equipment or ducts, or redefine the envelope to bring them within it. (To avoid indoor air-quality problems, any combustion equipment—such as fuel-burning furnaces, boilers, or water heaters—located inside your envelope should have sealed-combustion venting; see page 134.)

Managing Moisture

Moisture buildup is the number-one troublemaker in homes, potentially causing rot, mold, and fungus—which can, in turn, result in structural failure and indoor air-quality problems. Damp building materials provide a comfortable environment for pests such as dust mites and termites. Moist basements and attics can ruin the furnishings and keepsakes stored in them. Before tightening your home's envelope, you'll want to control potential sources of moisture in and around the home.

Whether you're insulating your house for the first time, beefing up existing insulation, or reinsulating your house, it pays to deal with moisture issues *before* you insulate. Wherever water vapor finds its way into a wall, ceiling, or floor cavity, if part of that cavity is cool, the vapor may condense on the cool surfaces, compromise your insulation, and encourage growth of molds and fungi. (If you already have mold problems, refer to Hazards, page 264.)

These are two key rules of moisture control:

• Don't let the building materials in your house get wet.

• Because the materials will get wet despite your best efforts, help them dry out.

Most people understand the importance of keeping materials inside the building's "skin" from getting wet. But few realize that it's equally important for these materials to be able to dry out. Perhaps we want to believe that moisture never finds its way inside our roof, walls, and floors, but it often does so nevertheless. And when building materials get wet, they need to dry out. In fact, many techniques employed by builders to keep water out of building cavities (e.g., installing a polyethylene vapor barrier or vinyl wallpaper) may actually trap moisture inside walls because they restrict drying, but it all depends on your climate. Look at Let Your Framing Cavities Dry Out, page 111, for more.

Low-Hanging Fruit *things you can do today*

In your Project Notebook, sketch a cutaway view of your house (also called a section) and draw in your proposed, uninterrupted envelope. Don't worry about details at this point; just identify the envelope's location so that you can assess its continuity and identify potential problem areas.

• **Find the gaps.** Make notes about which areas are already insulated and which may need insulation. Note any gaps in the air barrier, such as fireplace flues, attic hatches, holes in gypsum board walls or ceilings for plumbing runs, or recessed light fixtures.

• **Redefine the envelope.** If you are adding to your house or expanding into a porch or garage, you will need to redefine the envelope to include all the new mechanically heated and/or cooled living space. In some cases, this task may go beyond the simple; if so, call in a professional to help with this assessment.

KELLY'S EXPERIENCE *The building envelope is most important when the differences between indoor and outdoor conditions are greatest—in the dog days of August or the depths of a cold winter. In a mild climate or when conditions outside are pleasant, you'll probably have your windows open and your home's envelope won't matter a lick. In fact, if the outdoor temperatures in your climate are comfortable all the time, you could forget improving your envelope and just live in a tent. That said, few of us are fortunate enough to live in such benign climates—and even in those exceptional climates, our homes usually need to be tempered at some point. The better your envelope, the more comfortable your home will be.*

Humidity Is Relative

In order to understand how moisture operates in your house, it may help to review some basic principles of humidity. Humidity is a measure of the amount of water vapor present in the air. *Relative humidity* (RH) is the ratio of the amount of water vapor present to the maximum that could be present at a given temperature. In other words, 100 percent RH represents the maximum amount of water vapor you can have in a given volume. *Absolute humidity*, by contrast, is the *quantity* of water vapor present in a given volume of air—in other words, an absolute amount, as opposed to a relative amount or ratio.

Warm air can hold more water vapor than cold air, therefore 70 percent RH at 70°F represents much more water vapor than 70 percent RH at 40°F. As the temperature drops, the amount of moisture that can remain in the vapor state goes down, and the vapor condenses into liquid water or ice. When water vapor condenses outdoors, we call it fog, rain, or snow. If water vapor condenses on the walls of your house or inside a building cavity, you could be ripe for moisture damage.

Keep Water Out: Source Control

The best way to control moisture in your home will depend largely on your climate and your lifestyle (see figure 2). If you live in a dry climate and don't cook on your stovetop much or take long showers in the morning, you needn't be as concerned as someone in a moister climate—or someone who cooks pasta frequently and takes long showers every morning.

Minimize moisture buildup by dealing with its major sources:

- **Rainwater:** This is potentially the most damaging source of moisture. You can discourage its entry with a few basic techniques: Layer exterior building materials like scales on a fish to direct water downward, outward, and away from your house and from openings; slope the roof and provide deep overhangs to shed water away from the building; slope the ground away from the house; divert downspouts away from the foundation and toward plantings or into a cistern (see chapter 5); and avoid foundation plantings that need to be irrigated—don't water near your house!

- **Groundwater:** If you have a damp basement, stop the water before it gets in with an exterior waterproofing and drainage

SOURCES OF MOISTURE

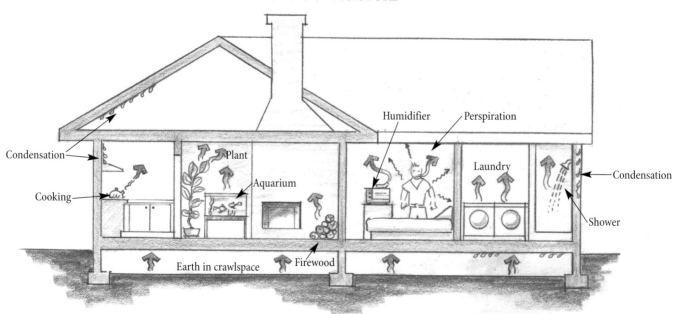

Figure 2

system (French drain). If you can't work from the outside, install an interior drainage system with a perimeter drain (generally not recommended for rubble masonry, brick, or concrete block foundations). In crawlspaces, installing a polyethylene vapor barrier on top of the soil helps keep moisture from migrating into your home. You might also consider insulating and conditioning (heating or cooling) the crawlspace (see page 124).

- **Plumbing leaks:** Install a drain pan and water-resistant floor coverings wherever you have a water heater or clothes washer (unless they are in a garage or in a basement with a floor drain). If you are rearranging spaces, keep water lines out of exterior walls and ceilings adjacent to unconditioned attics, where they are subject to extreme temperature swings. Install a shutoff valve for your clothes washer, and use it between washing sessions to avoid indoor floods from burst hoses, leaky washers, or broken equipment.

- **Water vapor from indoors:** The greatest sources of indoor moisture are steamy showers and boiling water. Equip bathrooms and kitchens with high-quality, quiet, energy-efficient exhaust fans ducted to the outdoors. An automatic timer can keep a bathroom fan running to exhaust steam after you leave—especially helpful in moist climates. It may also be advisable to run one or more of these fans continuously, or on timed cycles throughout the day, to ensure adequate ventilation around the clock (see page 116).

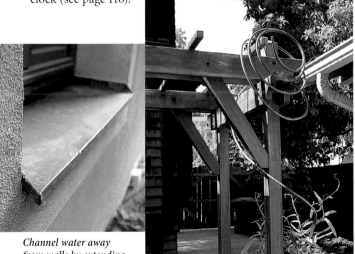

Channel water away from walls by extending windowsills beyond the face of the building.

Gutters and downspouts can funnel water away from the building and toward plants.

Let Your Framing Cavities Dry Out

There will always be moisture in your environment, indoors or out, but excessive moisture buildup in your wall cavities or attic can shorten the life of your home. Water vapor migrates into the cavities behind your home's interior surfaces in two ways: being carried by moving air, and passing through building materials. Of these two, the first is the most critical; air can carry a surprising amount of water (see figure 3).

DIFFUSION THROUGH GYPSUM BOARD VS. AIR LEAKAGE THROUGH SMALL HOLE

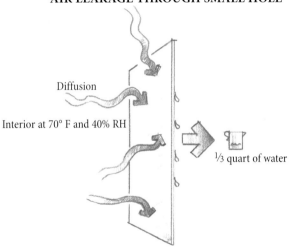

Diffusion

Interior at 70° F and 40% RH

⅓ quart of water

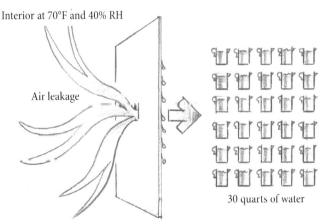

Interior at 70°F and 40% RH

Air leakage

30 quarts of water

Over an entire winter in a cold climate, only one third of a quart of water diffuses through a 4x8-foot sheet of gypsum board, while as much as 30 quarts of water can easily move into walls through a one-inch-square hole.

Figure 3

111

Manage the flow of airborne moisture into the wall cavities and attic by air-sealing your house (which we discuss in the next section) and providing adequate exhaust ventilation. If you're building an addition, you can also minimize the passage of water vapor through building materials by installing an exterior and/or interior air barrier and a vapor retarder.

Air Barriers

Every house needs an air barrier as part of its envelope. An air barrier stops the flow of air—from the conditioned interior of the house into framing cavities, and from the outdoors to the indoors. Air barriers don't keep moisture from migrating through building materials, but they do stop the passage of air that carries water vapor.

An air barrier can be behind the siding (like a house wrap) or behind the interior finish. It's great to have both, but for an existing house it makes sense to concentrate on improving the interior air barrier, unless you are replacing siding or building an addition. The air barrier is usually made up of a system of materials. For example, an interior air barrier system in most existing houses would consist of a plywood subfloor, gypsumboard walls and ceiling, wood trim, windows, electrical boxes, doors, and caulking or foam insulation where different materials come together (this is the missing piece in most houses; see pages 114 and 116 for more).

The most important factor for an air barrier is continuity; even small gaps in the air barrier are an open invitation for moisture-laden air to enter. People often confuse air barriers with vapor barriers; a vapor barrier can act as an air barrier, but an air barrier is not always a vapor barrier.

Vapor Barriers

A vapor barrier—such as vinyl wall covering, or polyethylene film installed behind gypsum board—blocks the passage of water vapor through building materials. Common building wisdom used to be "Put a vapor barrier on the warm side of the wall." But in most climates (except very cold ones), the "warm side of the wall" changes seasonally (see figure 4); the indoors is warm in winter, but cool in summer, especially in air-conditioned houses. Because of this, polyethylene vapor barriers have caused moisture buildup and subsequent mold

growth in many houses. *In mixed-humid, marine, hot-dry, and hot-humid climates, it's a bad idea to install a vapor barrier (such as polyethylene film) on the interior side of your walls, floors, or ceilings.* In these climates, water vapor may migrate either from indoors to outdoors, or from outdoors to indoors, depending on the season, so it's best to allow it to migrate out of the wall in either direction. Vapor barriers *can* be successfully installed in buildings in cold and very cold climates, but only if there's no mechanical air-conditioning.

MOVEMENT OF MOISTURE, AIR & HEAT

Interior Conditioned Space
68°–85°F 30%–60% RH

Exterior Variable Conditions

Uninsulated Wall or Attic;
No Air-Sealing Measures

Moisture Higher — Moisture Lower
Air Warmer — Air Cooler
Surface Warmer — Surface Cooler
Warm | Cool
• Condensation in walls
• Rampant movement of air, heat & moisture

Cold Winter

Moisture Higher — Moisture Lower
Air Cooler — Air Warmer
Surface Cooler — Surface Warmer
Cool | Warm
• Rampant movement of air, heat & moisture

Hot Dry Summer

Moisture Lower — Moisture Higher
Air Cooler — Air Warmer
Surface Cooler — Surface Warmer
Cool | Warm
• Condensation in walls
• Rampant movement of air, heat & moisture

Hot Humid Summer

Figure 4

112

Vapor Retarders

A vapor retarder slows the passage of water vapor through walls, ceilings, and floors. Paper-faced batt insulation, semi-permeable rigid insulation, or even latex paint can act as a vapor retarder. Building codes in cool and cold climates often require installation of a vapor retarder on the warm side of the wall, but never a vapor barrier. Avoid the use of polyethylene, vinyl, or sheet foil (which are all vapor barriers) if all you need is a vapor retarder.

Deciding which materials will best control air flow and moisture in your framing cavities, in your particular house and climate can be challenging; even professional building scientists are still conducting research to determine which materials work best in each climate. For recommendations on the use of vapor barriers or vapor retarders in your climate, see Resources, page 267.

MOLD LOVES DRYWALL

You've probably heard a lot about mold in homes. Mold spores are always present in the air, but they thrive only where there's moisture, food, and warmth. Much of the problem has to do with common building materials. Some materials are almost immune to the effects of water, but others—such as paper-faced gypsum board (also known as drywall)—are havens for mold.

To avoid housing and feeding mold, use paper-faced gypsum board only in locations where it will stay warm and dry. Never use paper-faced gypsum board under exterior siding materials. When hanging gypsum board on walls in basements or other moist areas with concrete slab floors, make sure there is a ½-inch gap between the bottom of the gypsum board and the slab to prevent water from wicking up. Never use "greenboard" behind tile in a shower or around a bathtub; instead use cement backer board made from portland cement and fiberglass mesh or a similar material without paper facing.

Managing Air Flow

There are two aspects of managing air flow: air sealing and ventilation. Because moisture, heat, and pollutants are all carried by air, managing air flow can:

• Keep airborne moisture (vapor) from going where you don't want it

• Keep heat from going where you don't want it

• Help damp materials dry out

• Remove stale air and bring in fresh air

Though many people think the greatest heat losses and gains in a home result from lack of insulation, air leakage can account for more than 50 percent of the energy wasted by an unsealed house.

Cellulose insulation, bound with water-based glue, can be blown into wall cavities. Excess insulation is scraped off, leaving a flat layer that fits snugly around the studs, electrical cables, and box.

Create an Air Barrier at the Envelope

To take charge of how air flows through your home, begin by stopping air leaks. Get the biggest bang for your buck by sealing the largest holes first. If your house has large holes—attic hatches, chimneys without dampers—the air escaping through them may pull air into your house through smaller cracks at windows and doors (see figures 5 and 6).

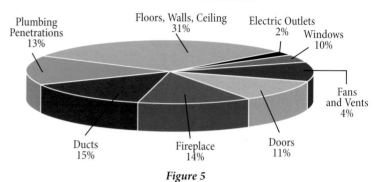

AIR LEAKS IN A HOME

Floors, Walls, Ceiling 31%
Electric Outlets 2%
Windows 10%
Plumbing Penetrations 13%
Fans and Vents 4%
Doors 11%
Fireplace 14%
Ducts 15%

Figure 5

COMMON AIR LEAKS

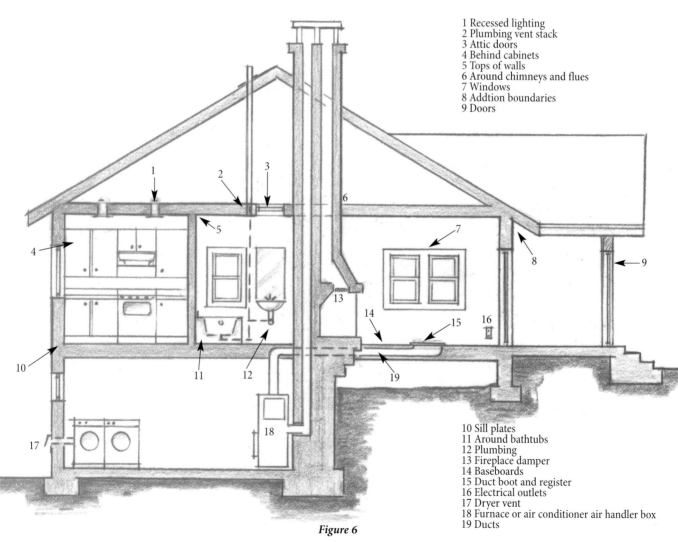

1 Recessed lighting
2 Plumbing vent stack
3 Attic doors
4 Behind cabinets
5 Tops of walls
6 Around chimneys and flues
7 Windows
8 Addtion boundaries
9 Doors

10 Sill plates
11 Around bathtubs
12 Plumbing
13 Fireplace damper
14 Baseboards
15 Duct boot and register
16 Electrical outlets
17 Dryer vent
18 Furnace or air conditioner air handler box
19 Ducts

Figure 6

Low-Hanging Fruit *things you can do today*

There are many ways to find the air leaks in your home:

- **The easy leak detector.** Shut each door or window on a piece of paper. If you can pull the paper out without tearing it, the seal is poor and air is leaking through.

- **Smoke it out.** Accentuate air flows and make them easier to detect by depressurizing your home: Turn on all your exhaust fans or open the windows on the leeward side of the house, then walk around inside your home with a smoking stick of incense or a piece of cellophane taped to a coat hanger. In each room, hold it close to the perimeter of windows, doors, baseboards, crown molding, electrical boxes, and any other wall penetrations. If the smoke stream or cellophane moves horizontally, being sucked out of or blown into the room, you have located an air leak that may need caulking or weather stripping. Note this on your floor plan.

- **Call in a pro.** For a more thorough and accurate measurement of how leaky your house is, hire a certified Residential Energy Services Network (RESNET) contractor to conduct a blower-door test (see Resources, page 267).

MAKE IT TIGHT
by Carl Seville

Not too wet, not too dry, just right; if only Goldilocks knew what to look for in a house.

Air infiltration affects indoor humidity, contributing significantly to our comfort (or discomfort) and the durability (or vulnerability) of our homes. The more leaks there are in a building's envelope, the more readily moisture travels between the indoors and outdoors.

When outdoor temperature and absolute humidity are high (in other words, the air is moist), we want to keep our homes at a lower relative humidity (RH) to maintain comfort—typically below 50 per cent RH (see figure 7). But leaks in the building envelope allow water vapor to enter from outside. The resulting higher RH makes occupants feel sticky and requires the air-conditioning system to work harder to remove excess moisture from the air.

Conversely, when outdoor temperature and absolute humidity are low (the air is dry), high levels of air leakage can leave the house feeling too dry (as often occurs in the Northeast in winter, for example). When indoor RH drops below about 30 per cent, occupants typically experience static electricity and sinus problems, and interior finishes can crack as woodwork shrinks.

Many homeowners install humidifiers to replace this lost moisture when they should be sealing air leaks instead. We generate enough humidity by breathing, bathing, and cooking to keep almost any house comfortable—provided we don't allow that moisture to leak out of the house. When a house requires mechanical humidification it is often an indication of a poorly sealed building envelope. In this situation, it is usually a better investment to air-seal the house than to install a humidifier.

"Build it tight, ventilate right" is more than just a catch phrase. It is the key to making a house comfortable and efficient year-round.

Carl Seville founded and served for 25 years as vice president of SawHorse, Inc., an Atlanta, Georgia, design/build firm that pioneered green home renovation.

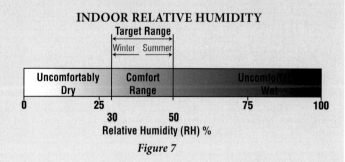

INDOOR RELATIVE HUMIDITY

Figure 7

More Advanced Steps *things you can do tomorrow*

Once you find the holes in your home's enclosure, seal them using one or a combination of these:

- **Caulking:** for cracks, gaps, or joints less than 1/4 inch wide (cracks 3/8 inch or more need a backer rod with caulking applied over it)

- **Expanding foam sealant:** for larger holes around pipes, at rim joists, and around windows and doors frames (if and when walls are open during renovation)

- **Weather stripping:** for windows, doors, and attic hatches

- **Foam gasket seals:** for electrical outlets and switches

CHOOSING A CAULK OR FOAM SEALANT

It's important to select a type of caulking appropriate for the material and location to be caulked. Some are flexible, permitting them to stretch or compress. Some shrink upon application. Some don't adhere to metal or can't be painted over. Many caulks contain toxic solvents (toluene, xylene, acetone), so look for water-based caulking compounds such as silicone or polyurethane, particularly for applications inside the envelope. Polyurethane foam sealants are commonly available in high-expanding and low-expanding formulations. Low-expanding foam is better for most renovation projects because it won't put too much pressure on existing finishes (see Resources, page 268).

Get the Fresh Air You Need

Once you've sealed the gaps around your house, you'll need some way to get rid of stale, humid, or polluted air and bring in fresh air. Every tight, energy-efficient house requires a ventilation system to keep pollutants, moisture, and odors from building up.

- **Exhaust-only** systems use a fan to pull air out of one room (e.g., a bathroom fan) or several rooms (e.g., a centralized exhaust fan with ducting to several rooms). Makeup air from outside comes through the small cracks and gaps that exist even after air sealing (see figure 8). The fan should be outfitted with a programmable timer and run on a regular schedule. Exhaust-only systems are easy and inexpensive to install, but if placed inappropriately, they may draw in makeup air

EXHAUST-ONLY SYSTEM

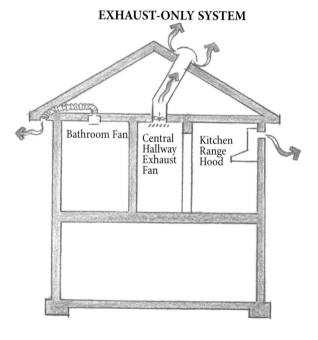

Figure 8

from polluted sources, such as attached garages. They can also cause combustion gas spillage if you have a heating device vented by a chimney. Use an exhaust system only if you have sealed or direct-vent combustion appliances (see page 134), and install a carbon monoxide alarm.

- **Supply-only** systems pull fresh air into the house whenever the air handler is turned on (if integrated with the HVAC system) or when activated by a timer or occupancy sensor (if a separate venting appliance). In colder climates, they are usually integrated with a ducted HVAC system (see figure 9). A supply-only system offers better overall ventilation than an exhaust-only system and draws air from a known source, but it can be more expensive to operate if it uses a large blower motor.

- **Balanced systems** supply fresh air and remove exhaust air in equal quantities (see figure 10). This balance can be achieved with a combination of exhaust fans and supply-air ventilation or by using a Heat Recovery Ventilator or Energy Recovery Ventilator.

Heat Recovery Ventilation (HRV) systems draw warm, moist air from kitchens and bathrooms, exhaust it through a heat-exchanger to preheat incoming air, and distribute the fresh air

SUPPLY ONLY SYSTEM

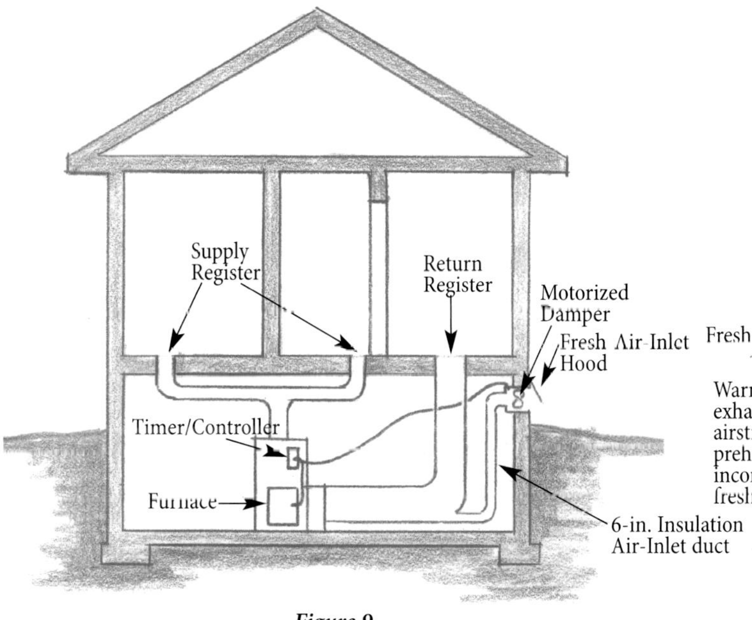

Supply Register

Return Register

Motorized Damper

Fresh Air-Inlet Hood

Timer/Controller

Furnace

6-in. Insulation Air-Inlet duct

Figure 9

BALANCED SYSTEM

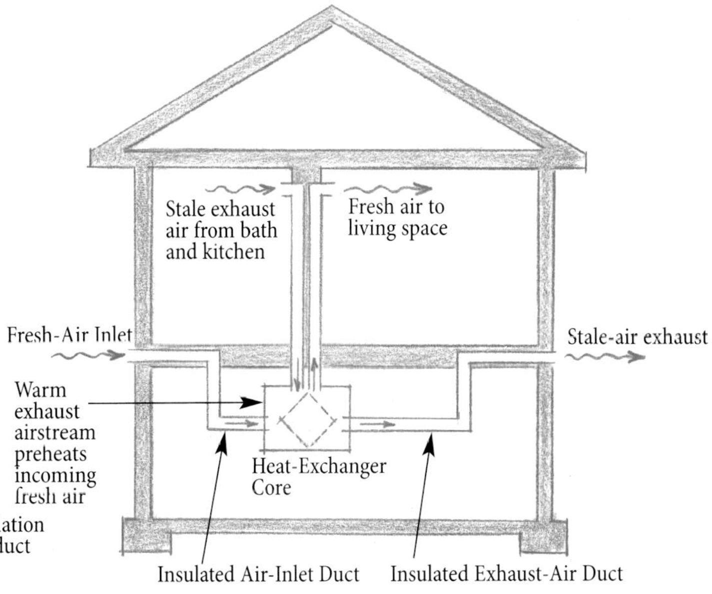

Stale exhaust air from bath and kitchen

Fresh air to living space

Fresh-Air Inlet

Stale-air exhaust

Warm exhaust airstream preheats incoming fresh air

Heat-Exchanger Core

Insulated Air-Inlet Duct

Insulated Exhaust-Air Duct

Figure 10

to living areas and bedrooms. Energy Recovery Ventilators (ERVs) transfer both heat and moisture between the incoming and outgoing air. Both systems provide good mechanical ventilation for your home while keeping heat loss and gain to a minimum. In new construction, HRVs and ERVs are installed with their own separate ductwork, but they can also be retrofitted onto existing ductwork for remodeling projects. HRVs are most cost-effective in cold climates.

Even if your ventilation system provides plenty of fresh air, you won't have good indoor air quality if that air can't circulate throughout your home. You can improve air circulation by keeping interior doors open, trimming the bottoms of interior doors to create about a 1-inch gap, or installing air-transfer grilles between closed rooms (particularly sleeping rooms) and hallways. However, these techniques will also reduce acoustic separation. If you want to increase airflow while keeping rooms acoustically isolated, you'll need to provide ventilation ducts to each room.

Balance Your Home's Air Pressure

Many things can cause air pressure differences within a home. Forced-air heating and cooling systems are notorious for introducing pressure differences between rooms and between indoors and outdoors (see figure 11). Exhaust fans and combustion equipment with flues (fireplaces, gas- and oil-fired heaters and water heaters, clothes dryers, and stoves) may lower indoor air pressure by removing air faster than it can be replaced.

If the air pressure inside your home becomes significantly lower than outdoor air pressure, exhaust air from combustion equipment can be sucked down the flues and into your home; this is called backdrafting (see figure 12). Bath and kitchen exhaust fans are usually small enough (under 120 cfm) to not cause backdrafting by themselves, but the larger fans (300 cfm or more) found in clothes dryers, central vacuums, or commercial kitchen exhaust fans may cause air-pressure problems. To avoid backdrafting, seal your house's ducts, relocate the house's envelope to include all air ducts, and make sure that all fuel-burning appliances have sealed combustion or have power-vents that exhaust directly to the outdoors.

HOW DEPRESSURIZATION OCCURS

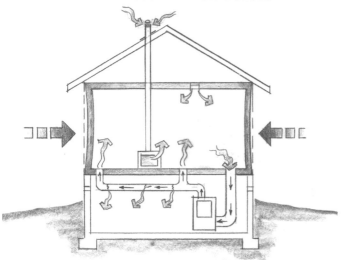

Return ducts exhaust more air from conditioned areas than leaky ducts can supply. Air is sucked into the house through holes in the air barrier.

HOW PRESSURIZATION OCCURS

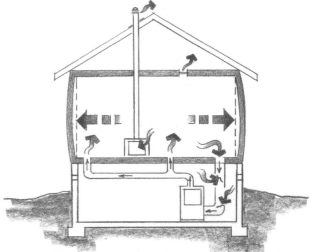

Ducts supply more air to conditioned areas than leaky return ducts can exhaust. Air leaks out of the conditioned area through holes in the barrier.

Figure 11

Seal Leaky Ducts

If you have a ducted heating/cooling system and your ducts are outside your envelope, sealing the ducts will keep hot or cold air from escaping on the way to its destination. Duct sealing may also improve indoor air quality, increase your comfort, and keep your house from becoming pressurized or depressurized. (An effective fix is to relocate either the ducts or the envelope so that all ducts are within the envelope; then it won't matter if they leak. However, this can be both tricky and costly.)

To seal ducts, use water-based duct mastic at all seams and joints; for larger holes, use fiberglass tape and mastic. (Ironically, though duct tape may be handy for just about everything else, it's not durable enough for sealing ducts.) Also seal joints between the supply/return boots and the floor, wall, or ceiling where they terminate (at grilles) with mastic or caulk. You can hire a duct sealer to pressure-test the system after sealing, in order to ensure that the job was done correctly.

Managing Heat Flow

About 40 percent of the energy used in the average home is spent on maintaining a comfortable temperature. Whether you're using "free" energy from the sun or buying energy in the form of electricity, natural gas, oil, or wood, you'll want to make the most of it. Insulating your ceiling, walls, and floor, and improving the thermal performance of your windows, will help your envelope keep heat where you want it—inside or out.

Insulate Your Envelope

Insulation slows the passage of heat, usually by means of many tiny air pockets. The appropriate insulation levels for your roof, walls, and floor are determined by climate; more extreme climates call for higher levels of insulation. R-value is a measure of how well a material resists the flow of heat ("R" stands for "resistance"); the higher the R-value, the more effective the insulation. Many experts believe that insulation is the cheapest, most effective way to improve your home's energy performance, and that you should install as much insulation as your home will accommodate.

WHERE DEPRESSURIZATION CAN OCCUR

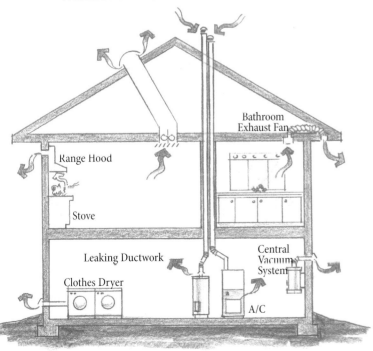

Range Hood

Stove

Bathroom Exhaust Fan

Leaking Ductwork

Central Vacuum System

Clothes Dryer

A/C

Figure 12

Insulation comes in many forms, and the quality of the installation job is important. No matter how high its R-value, insulation won't perform well if it doesn't fill the whole space without gaps. Loose, fibrous insulation (such as cellulose or loose fiberglass) can be blown into attics and wall cavities and fills well around irregular surfaces. Batts of fibrous insulation (such as fiberglass or cotton) must be installed carefully so that they fit tightly around wires, pipes, and electrical boxes.

Rigid insulation is a good choice when you need a high R-value, but there isn't a lot of space for insulation. Rigid insulation may also be appropriate where there's no cavity to fill—at concrete walls, for example—or as a continuous wrap around framed buildings, which lose and gain heat through the framing itself. Air-impermeable spray-foam insulation can act as both insulation and air barrier. Insulations that incorporate a radiant barrier reflect heat; they must be installed with the shiny radiant surface next to air space in order to work properly (one half inch of air space is optimal).

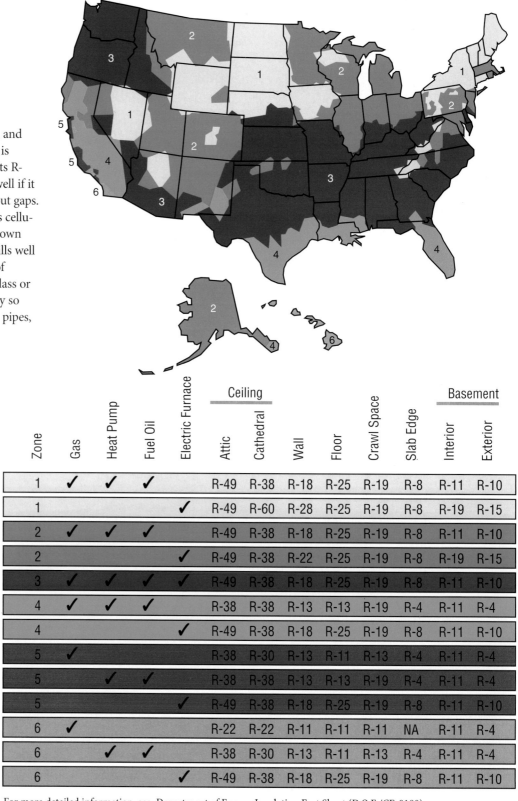

RECOMMENDED INSULATION LEVELS

Zone	Gas	Heat Pump	Fuel Oil	Electric Furnace	Ceiling Attic	Ceiling Cathedral	Wall	Floor	Crawl Space	Slab Edge	Basement Interior	Basement Exterior
1	✓	✓	✓		R-49	R-38	R-18	R-25	R-19	R-8	R-11	R-10
1				✓	R-49	R-60	R-28	R-25	R-19	R-8	R-19	R-15
2	✓	✓	✓		R-49	R-38	R-18	R-25	R-19	R-8	R-11	R-10
2				✓	R-49	R-38	R-22	R-25	R-19	R-8	R-19	R-15
3	✓	✓	✓	✓	R-49	R-38	R-18	R-25	R-19	R-8	R-11	R-10
4	✓	✓	✓		R-38	R-38	R-13	R-13	R-19	R-4	R-11	R-4
4				✓	R-49	R-38	R-18	R-25	R-19	R-8	R-11	R-10
5	✓				R-38	R-30	R-13	R-11	R-13	R-4	R-11	R-4
5		✓	✓		R-38	R-38	R-13	R-13	R-13	R-4	R-11	R-4
5				✓	R-49	R-38	R-18	R-25	R-19	R-8	R-11	R-10
6	✓				R-22	R-22	R-11	R-11	R-11	NA	R-11	R-4
6		✓	✓		R-38	R-30	R-13	R-11	R-13	R-4	R-11	R-4
6				✓	R-49	R-38	R-18	R-25	R-19	R-8	R-11	R-10

For more detailed information, see: Department of Energy Insulation Fact Sheet (D.O.E./CE-0180); or visit www.energy.gov.

Figure 13

Low-Hanging Fruit *things you can do today*

Blown-in attic insulation is fast and cost-effective but doesn't allow the attic to be used as living space.

• **Investigate and insulate.** Check the insulation level in each element of your envelope. If the insulation isn't up to snuff, consider how you might add more. Note that the depth of framing is typically the limiting factor as to how much insulation you can install.

• **Get R-rated.** To maximize the R-value of your insulation, consider upgrading to a material that has a high R-value per inch, such as a rigid insulating foam board (e.g., extruded polystyrene or polyiso-cyanurate). Where the framing is open on one side, such as under the floor or in an attic, you may also be able to install a layer of continuous insulation below or on top of the framing.

Take It from the Top: Insulation Guidelines for Everyone

Roof: The roof is the most important part of your house to insulate; in winter, rising warm air encourages heat loss through the ceiling, and in summer the sun's rays beat down on the roof. Insulation either in the attic floor or along the roof slope can be effective. Take care to allow for ventilation.

GOING UP?

Have you been thinking about turning your attic into living space? Or maybe you'd like to transform a flat ceiling into a cathedral ceiling? In either case, it's time to think about how to insulate that sloped ceiling—and then how to ventilate the insulation space. In most climates, insulated roofs must be ventilated to prevent condensation on the underside of your roof sheathing; you don't want water dripping into your insulation, or your rafters rotting. Make sure you have enough room for adequate roof insulation (see page 120 for recommended roof R-values, and page 219 for R-value per inch for different insulation types). In addition, allow 2 inches of space above the insulation for ventilation—and then make sure there's a way for the air to enter and leave that ventilation space without letting the rain or insects enter.

If attic headroom is at a premium, you have a few options for creating an unvented roof. The International Residential Code (IRC) currently allows unvented roof assemblies under a 2004 code supplement if two conditions are met:

• The interior surface of the ceiling has no vapor retarder that would prevent drying to the interior.

• The underside of the roof deck is insulated with enough spray-foam insulation (vapor- and air-impermeable) to keep its monthly average temperature above 45°F.

In hot dry climates, a roof's monthly average temperature is usually above 45°F, so venting wouldn't be required, but you'll still want insulation to keep summer heat out and winter heat in. You can also create an unvented roof with structural insulated panels (SIPS) or by insulating on top of your current roof with enough rigid foam insulation to keep the interior surface of the roof sheathing above 45°F. For construction details for both vented and unvented roofs, look online at www.buildingscience.com/resources/roofs/Roofs_Design.pdf.

With proper insulation, ventilation, and lighting, an attic can become a delightful living space.

Installing spray-foam insulation in wall cavities through holes in the interior plaster.

Walls: Unless you live in a mild climate, it's worth insulating your walls. Existing exterior walls may be best insulated by hiring a professional to blow loose-fill or spray-foam insulation into the walls through drilled holes (which are sealed after insulating). If your home has wooden clapboard siding, shingles, or vinyl siding, it's probably least disruptive to insulate from the exterior. If your house has vertical tongue-and-groove, exterior-grade plywood, or board-and-batten siding, the holes on the interior walls will be easier to patch. It's also important to insulate the rim joist areas (where the floor meets the wall); use spray foam or tight-fitting rigid insulation and caulking.

Floor or crawlspace: If you decide to keep a basement or crawlspace outside your house's envelope, be sure to insulate the floor between the conditioned and unconditioned spaces.

Rigid foam insulation is cut carefully around floor joists to insulate the rim joist and basement walls.

Also insulate floors that extend beyond the foundation, such as cantilevered bays.

Basement: Basements require extra care when converting them to living space. Before you insulate a basement, make sure it is well drained. If you are digging down to add exterior drainage, you can waterproof and insulate basement walls from the exterior. However, most basement renovations involve interior insulation. You can avoid some moisture problems by installing expanded polystyrene insulation directly against the basement wall, then framing in walls and adding finish materials to the interior side of the rigid insulation. Avoid installing a vapor barrier at insulated basement walls; the walls must be able to release moisture to the interior. You can insulate a basement slab with a layer of polystyrene insulation covered by 1x3 sleepers and a plywood subfloor (see figures 14 and 15). Avoid installing carpet on an uninsulated slab; moisture may condense on the cool surface, inviting mold and dust mites. See Resources, page 267, for more on insulating a basement.

HAZARDS OF OLD INSULATION

Old insulation materials rarely pose a significant danger as long as they are isolated from living spaces (another good argument for air sealing), but they can be dangerous if they're disturbed. Asbestos insulation is often found on forced-air ducts and hot water pipes; it should never be disturbed or moved, except by a licensed asbestos remediation specialist. Vermiculite insulation, which was used in walls and attics in the '60s, '70s, and '80s, also may contain asbestos; it's best to leave it undisturbed and cover it with another insulation.

Urea-formaldehyde foam insulation (UFFI) was used as retrofit insulation prior to 1980; it was subsequently banned because of toxic formaldehyde gas emissions, but don't be alarmed if you find it in your walls; the formaldehyde has probably all outgassed by now. And existing fiberglass insulation may harbor rodents and their excreta; consider removing it if it's damaged or gross.

VAPOR CONTROL OPTIONS FOR FLOORS OVER CONCRETE SLABS

INSULATED BASEMENT WALL AND BASEMENT FLOOR

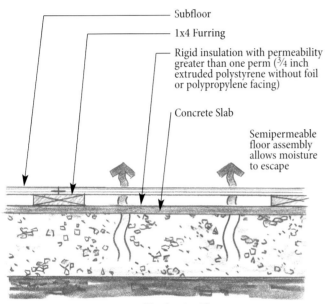

- Subfloor
- 1x4 Furring
- Rigid insulation with permeability greater than one perm (¾ inch extruded polystyrene without foil or polypropylene facing)
- Concrete Slab

Semipermeable floor assembly allows moisture to escape

Semipermeable Floating Floor

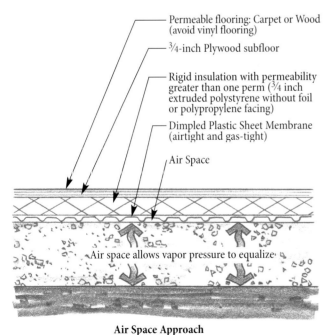

- Permeable flooring: Carpet or Wood (avoid vinyl flooring)
- ¾-inch Plywood subfloor
- Rigid insulation with permeability greater than one perm (¾ inch extruded polystyrene without foil or polypropylene facing)
- Dimpled Plastic Sheet Membrane (airtight and gas-tight)
- Air Space

Air space allows vapor pressure to equalize

Air Space Approach

Figure 14

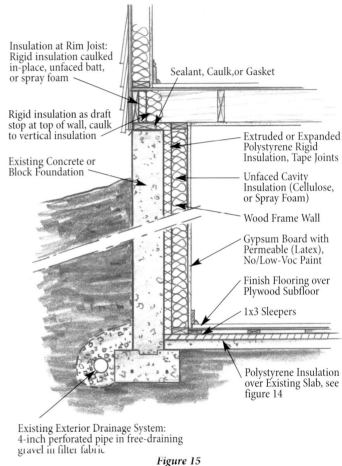

- Insulation at Rim Joist: Rigid insulation caulked in-place, unfaced batt, or spray foam
- Sealant, Caulk, or Gasket
- Rigid insulation as draft stop at top of wall, caulk to vertical insulation
- Existing Concrete or Block Foundation
- Extruded or Expanded Polystyrene Rigid Insulation, Tape Joints
- Unfaced Cavity Insulation (Cellulose, or Spray Foam)
- Wood Frame Wall
- Gypsum Board with Permeable (Latex), No/Low-Voc Paint
- Finish Flooring over Plywood Subfloor
- 1x3 Sleepers
- Polystyrene Insulation over Existing Slab, see figure 14
- Existing Exterior Drainage System: 4-inch perforated pipe in free-draining gravel in filter fabric

Figure 15

123

Including a Crawlspace within Your Envelope

For years, it has been common practice to ventilate crawlspaces, but it's becoming apparent that this can cause serious moisture problems. In hot humid climates, moist outside air enters the crawlspace and condenses on cool foundation walls. In cold climates, cold air from the crawlspace seeps indoors through cracks and gaps in the floor and framing. Ducts running through a crawlspace sacrifice heating or cooling energy to the outdoors.

If you are changing exterior wall finishes, it's relatively easy to replace the whole window, rather than just the sash.

Building codes prohibit construction of *unvented* crawlspaces, but they generally allow construction of *conditioned* (heated or cooled) crawlspaces. In other words, a crawlspace can be treated as a minibasement that's within the conditioned space of the house (see figures 16 and 17, page 125).

To bring a crawlspace into the envelope, install perimeter insulation (rigid or blown foam) and a continuous, sealed groundcover, such as taped polyethylene sheeting. If the level of the earth in the crawlspace is below the surrounding ground level, install perimeter drainage as you would with a basement. If you live in an area at risk for radon, install a soil-gas ventilation system under the ground cover. You'll also need to make sure your crawlspace stays dry by conditioning it with air from your home's interior.

Before you insulate and air-seal your crawlspace, discuss the issue with your local building official. If you meet with resistance, provide your building official with a copy of "Conditioned Crawlspace Construction, Performance and Codes," available from Building Science Corporation (see Resources, page 267).

Better Windows

Depending on your climate and your house, windows may account for 15 to 30 percent of your home's total winter heat loss; in warm climates they can account for over half the summer heat gain. Replacing or reconditioning your windows can also improve thermal comfort while reducing noise transmission, condensation on glass, and fading of drapes and upholstery.

Nevertheless, window replacement is expensive compared to other energy-efficiency upgrades. If you live in a mild climate or you are renovating with a limited budget, consider reconditioning your windows rather than replacing them. You can improve the thermal performance of your windows by adding weather stripping, installing an interior or exterior storm sash (preferably with low-E glass), or even hanging insulating shades.

Window Replacement

High-performance windows, now widely available and moderately priced (depending on frame material and options), use double or triple glazing, low-E coatings, gas-fills, and insulating spacers and frames that reduce both winter heat loss and summer heat gain.

There are two basic approaches to window replacement: replace just the sash (the frame that holds the glass) or replace the whole window, including the outer frame. Sash-replacement kits require little trim work and are the less expensive option, but they reduce the glass area slightly and are limited to double-hung and sliding styles. If you are replacing exterior siding and trim anyway, you might want to install new windows. In either case, be sure to seal and insulate all cracks and gaps with a low-expanding type of soft spray foam.

If you're interested in energy efficiency and comfort, double-pane, low-E glass is a boon in any climate. Low-conductance frames (of wood or fiberglass) and warm-edge spacers will also reduce heat conduction. Beyond that, the most important features are the U-factor (a measure of heat conductance) and the SHGC (Solar Heat Gain Coefficient).

AIR SUPPLY FROM HOUSE TO CRAWLSPACE

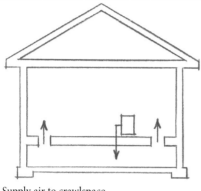

Supply air to crawlspace

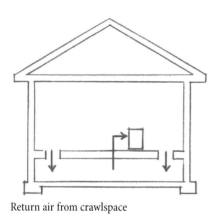

Return air from crawlspace

Figure 16

CRAWL SPACE INSULATION

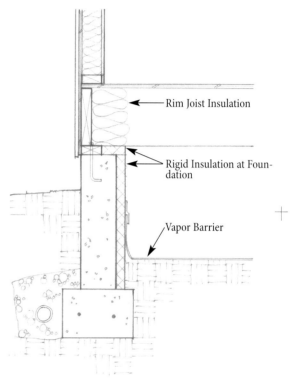

Rim Joist Insulation

Rigid Insulation at Foundation

Vapor Barrier

Figure 17

125

In hot climates, where most of your energy budget is spent on cooling, the SHGC is the most important attribute. Select windows with an SHGC rating below 0.40 and a Visible Transmittance (VT) of 0.5 or more (to avoid reducing night visibility through your windows too much). In cold climates, where heating is the main concern, select windows with the lowest U-factor you can afford (0.35 maximum). In mixed climates, look for both a low U-factor and a low SHGC. But if you want passive solar heating, make sure your south-facing windows have a high SHGC (above 0.50 at a minimum).

For help in choosing the best replacement windows, see Resources, page 267.

Proceed with Care

This study of how moisture, air, and heat move through your home is called "building science." It's an emerging field, and new information is always coming to light. We've introduced you to some of the basic principles and cautions of building science to help you avoid the most obvious problems. However, every home is different and each climate demands its own best practices. We recommend that you consult up-to-date building science resources (see Resources, page 267) or engage the services of a qualified professional when making decisions that affect the flow of moisture, air, and heat in your home.

HOW TO READ NFRC WINDOW LABELS

The National Fenestration Rating Council (NFRC) is a non-profit, public/private organization created by the window, door, and skylight industry. The NFRC has established a voluntary national energy-performance rating and labeling system that reports values for the entire window unit, including glass, sash, and frame. The NFRC label, which can be found on most new windows, is the best way to compare true energy performance. The NFRC product directory is available online at www.nfrc.org.

U-Factor: The U-Factor represents conductive heat loss—smaller is better (U is the inverse of R: U=1/R).

Solar Heat Gain Coefficient: The SHGC is a measure of the amount of direct solar radiant heat that gets in through the windows. Lower SHGC reduces summer cooling loads, but higher SHGC increases solar heat gain in winter.

Visible Transmittance: Visible Transmittance (VT) is a measure of how much visible light gets through. Lower VT means less glare, but also less nighttime visibility from indoors to out.

NFRC
National Fenestration Rating Council®
CERTIFIED

World's Best Window Co.
Millennium 2000⁺
Vinyl-Clad Wood Frame
Double Glazing • Argon Fill • Low E
Product Type: **Vertical Slider**

ENERGY PERFORMANCE RATINGS

U-Factor (U.S./I-P)	Solar Heat Gain Coefficient
0.35	**0.32**

ADDITIONAL PERFORMANCE RATINGS

Visible Transmittance	Air Leakage (U.S./I-P)
0.51	**0.2**

Manufacturer stipulates that these ratings conform to applicable NFRC procedures for determining whole product performance. NFRC ratings are determined for a fixed set of environmental conditions and a specific product size. NFRC does not recommend any product and does not warrant the suitability of any product for any specific use. Consult manufacturer's literature for other product performance information.
www.nfrc.org

KELLY'S EXPERIENCE *Sometimes window dealers don't understand passive-solar heating; if a window has a low-E coating and a low U-factor, they think it's a great window. Some friends of mine discovered how serious this misunderstanding can be. They had long dreamed of living in a self-sufficient, passive-solar home. When they finally built their dream home, they oriented it to the sun; carefully calculated the areas of south-facing windows and thermal mass; designed for summer shading; constructed a tight, superinsulated envelope; and outfitted the house with sensors to measure the thermal performance. They installed the best windows they could afford, with low-E glass and a U-factor of 0.25. They were assured by the dealer that these were the finest windows available.*

During the first winter, they could tell something was wrong. Despite weeks of mostly sunny days, the furnace ran most of the time. They looked back through their calculations but couldn't find their mistake. Finally, someone asked, "Could it be the glass? They checked the SHGC, and—sure enough—it was very low: 0.25. Only 25 per cent of the sun's radiant warmth was making it through their windows. They returned to the dealer, worked out a compromise, and replaced the glass in their south-facing windows with a high-SHGC, low-E type. I'm happy to report that their house now functions perfectly.

These days, it's increasingly difficult to find residential window manufacturers who offer low-E, high-SHGC glazing. If you are designing passive-solar heat gain as your primary heating strategy, shop around; several Canadian manufacturers offer these options.

WHAT IS LOW-E COATING AND WHAT DOES IT DO?

Low-E (low-emittance) coatings are microscopically thin, virtually invisible metal or metallic oxide layers deposited on glass. They allow visible light to pass through but reflect long-wavelength radiant energy. There are two main types of low-E glass, determined by the type and location of the coating:

• Low-E, high SHGC for climates with high heating needs and for south windows in passive-solar-heated spaces

• Low-E, low SHGC for climates with high cooling needs and for most north, east, and west windows

CHAPTER 8

Energy: Use It Well

*People and nations behave wisely—once they
have exhausted all other alternatives.*
—Winston Churchill

ALL LIVING SYSTEMS USE ENERGY to meet their needs. Every time you breathe, walk in the park, fire up your computer, sip your coffee, or even think, you're using energy. Energy is defined as "usable power," or the capacity of a physical system to "do work."

Letting sun shine in brings free light and heat, reduces fossil fuel use, and helps you tune into natural cycles.

Solar energy powers all life on earth. The sun's heat drives our winds and the movement of water through the hydrologic cycle. Plants and some bacteria use sunlight via photosynthesis to create simple sugars that power their internal systems. We use the sun's energy both directly (for example, to see and to stay warm) and indirectly (as when we consume plants and animals to fuel our bodies). We can also use various technologies to convert sunlight, plants, and the movement of wind and water into storable energy, in the form of electricity, biofuels, and hydrogen.

These homeowners reduced their energy costs by overinsulating and employing natural strategies for cooling and lighting.

Fossil Fuels: Ancient Sunlight

Fossil fuels come from the sun, too—at least originally. Coal, oil, and natural gas are the transformed remains of ancient plants and animals. Fossil fuels could be likened to giant batteries that store millions of years' worth of sunlight. But, as you probably know, there are a few problems with fossil fuel use:

- Fossil fuels are *nonrenewable*. When they're gone, they're gone. We are fast approaching (if not already at) the point where the demand for fossil fuels exceeds the supply, and the shortage is going to affect us all.

- Our current technologies for converting fossil fuels to do the work we need are *inefficient*, with losses in extraction, transportation, generation, and transmission.

- Converting fossil fuels to electricity produces a huge array of *toxic byproducts*. In the United States, coal-burning power plants generate 52 percent of our electricity and are the single biggest air polluter in the country[1].

- The *rising cost* of fossil fuels means that our utility bills are rising and will continue to do so. The cost of staying comfortable is likely to place an increasing burden on household finances.

Living on Current Sunlight

One way or another, fossil fuels are on their way out. Sustainability means meeting our needs with the energy that comes from the sun—directly every day in the form of solar radiation, and also indirectly as it moves air and water and is stored by plants. We are a long way from balancing our energy expenditures with solar income (only 7 percent of United States energy use comes from renewable sources), but the shift is inevitable.

You can do a lot to balance your personal energy budget. Using whole-system design and off-the-shelf technologies, you can reduce your household's need for outside energy (electricity generated off site, natural gas, or oil) by 50 to 80 percent[2]—without sitting in the dark, shivering, or sweating.

Before you even consider the energy efficiency of your appliances or mechanical systems (furnace, air conditioning, fans), base your approach on the following ideas:

The best way to cut your energy use is to minimize your need for it in the first place. Reduce your home's energy appetite with a tight, well-insulated envelope (see chapter 7, page 108). Whether you heat your home with the sun or a furnace, your smartest move is to keep the warmth in the house, rather than heating up the great outdoors.

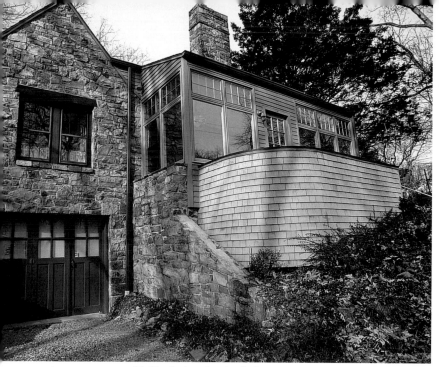

A sunroom can provide "free" winter heating for homes not originally designed to take advantage of the sun.

Use the most direct energy sources. Natural (passive) strategies for heating your water, and for heating, cooling, and lighting your house (as described in chapters 3 and 4), are the most energy-efficient.

Support renewable energy generation. Consider producing your own electricity with photovoltaic panels, a small-scale wind turbine, or even a micro-hydropower installation. If this isn't feasible, ask your local utility about renewable options or purchase renewable-energy certificates called "green tags," or visit www.greentagsusa.org.

"Sustainable. Unsustainable. What do these words really mean? Perhaps peak oil at last provides the word sustainability with teeth. People now speak of 'sustainable development,' 'sustainable growth,' and 'sustainable returns on investment.' That, my friends, is sustainability lite. The word has been diluted and denatured almost beyond recognition. But if you can't do it without fossil fuels, by definition, it ain't sustainable."

—Richard Heinberg, author of *The Party's Over* and *Power Down*, in a 2004 address to the First U.S. Conference on Peak Oil and Community Solutions.

Photovoltaic panels can be integrated into the roof of even historic buildings.

How Do You Use Energy at Home?

Once you have a plan to maximize your use of renewable sources, it's time to focus on using outside power efficiently. In the United States, the average household uses about 10,000 kilowatt-hours (kwh) of electricity[3] and 81,200 cubic feet of natural gas per year[4]. Your own household energy usage may differ significantly from these averages, especially as you remodel to align your home with natural systems.

You can identify the greatest opportunities for saving energy by breaking down how you use it (see figure 1). Start with the biggest energy consumers; improvements here will give you the best returns on your investments.

AVERAGE HOUSEHOLD ENERGY USE

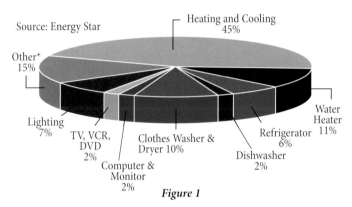

Source: Energy Star

Heating and Cooling 45%
Other* 15%
Lighting 7%
TV, VCR, DVD 2%
Computer & Monitor 2%
Clothes Washer & Dryer 10%
Dishwasher 2%
Refrigerator 6%
Water Heater 11%

Figure 1

Tools for Finding the Best of the Best

Before you shop for appliances, home electronics, or heating and cooling systems, do a little research to avoid confusion and overwhelm. The American Council for an Energy Efficient Economy (ACEEE) publishes lists of the "best of the best" energy-efficient appliances (see Resources, page 267). *Energy Star* is a government-backed program that certifies products based on strict energy-efficiency guidelines set by the EPA and the U.S. Department of Energy (DOE). Look for the Energy Star label when shopping for appliances and lighting products, and consider it to be a minimum standard; you can often find products that exceed these standards. Contact your local utility company for information about special programs and rebates in your region.

Mechanical Heating and Cooling

Heating and cooling represent about 45 percent of the average household's annual energy bill. In hot climates, air conditioning can even account for a whopping 60 to 70 percent of a home's summer electricity consumption. The good news is that you can lower these numbers significantly by using natural heating and cooling strategies (see chapters 3 and 4) and tightening your home's envelope (see chapter 7), especially in milder climates. That way, you may need your mechanical heating/cooling system only during the coldest or hottest times of year. In more extreme climates, using natural comfort strategies will allow you to use a much smaller heating/cooling system (with a much lower price tag) and to run the system less frequently.

Lighting through high windows connects you with sunlight throughout the day and keeps lighting bills low.

Time for Replacement?

Replacing older gas- or oil-burning furnaces and air conditioners with high-efficiency models is almost always cost-effective; they typically pay for themselves in savings within three to five years. The more extreme your climate and the greater your home's current heating and cooling fuel use, the more you will save.

There are several indicators that your heating/cooling system may need to be replaced:

- The furnace, boiler, air conditioner, or heat pump is more than 15 years old.
- The equipment needs frequent repairs.
- Your energy bills are increasing.
- Some rooms in your home are too hot or too cold.
- The system is noisy.
- You've improved your home's energy performance so that you no longer need a large system.
- You've added space to your home.

The efficiency of new boilers and furnaces is measured in terms of their Annual Fuel Utilization Efficiency (AFUE). The AFUE accounts for the efficiency of the furnace or boiler, not the entire system; leaky, un-insulated ducts outside of the envelope will lower system efficiency (see Seal Leaky Ducts, page 119). If you have an older boiler or furnace, its AFUE is probably 70 or less, compared with a possible 90+ for a new, high-efficiency model.

However, if your heating/ventilating/air-conditioning (HVAC) system is less than 10 years old, it may not make sense to replace it. You have to weigh the cost of new equipment, the cost of fuel, and the need to dispose of existing equipment against the fuel savings of a new system. If your existing HVAC system is relatively new and efficient, and you plan to add conditioned space to your home, air sealing and insulating may allow you to use your existing unit, eliminating the need for new equipment.

Super insulating your roof and walls and including a solar hot-air collector may provide all the heating you need.

This straw-bale "wrap" around a concrete block home allows for a small heating or cooling system.

Selecting a New Heating/Cooling System

There are many factors to consider when deciding on the right heating and cooling system for your home:

- Whether you have an existing duct system

- The types of fuel available (natural gas, electricity, or propane)

- The cost of available fuel (keeping in mind that the cost of fossil fuels will continue to climb)

- Your climate

- Your home's design and orientation

- The materials your home is made of

- Your personal preferences

Your first decision is how to distribute the warmth or coolness: Do you want to use ducts, tubing (for a fluid-based, or *hydronic*, radiant heating system, see page 134), or more direct sources such as a wood stove? In most cases, your house will probably determine your distribution method; if your house has a ductwork system, you may want to stick with forced air. But if you don't already have a duct system, you may want to consider some type of radiant heating system for increased comfort and to avoid the health hazards associated with ducts (dry air, fried dust, and microbes).

Tubing for hydronic heating systems can be mounted between existing floor joists or laid down before pouring a new concrete slab.

Low-Hanging Fruit *things you can do today*

- **Install a programmable thermostat.** It's a common misconception that a system runs more efficiently if it is on all the time. You can set the timer/programmer to determine when and at what temperatures your heating/cooling system will operate. According to Energy Star, using a programmable thermostat can save you about $100 per year.

- **Maintain your existing system.** If you have a relatively new system, regular maintenance will keep it running efficiently.

More Advanced Steps *things you can do tomorrow*

- Seal your duct system if it is outside your envelope (see chapter 7, page 119).

- Replace your heating/cooling system with a new energy-efficient unit.

Stained with ferrous sulfate, this concrete floor is smooth and durable. The space is heated via hydronic tubing in the floor.

Second, you need to pick your energy source: electricity or combustion fuel (natural gas, propane, fuel oil, or wood). Your decision will probably be based on availability, what you currently use, and local fuel costs; there are efficient options no matter what the energy source. If your house isn't currently plumbed for natural gas or propane, it may make sense to stick with electricity. Keep in mind that costs of nonrenewable fuels will continue to go up as they become more difficult to find and extract.

KELLY'S EXPERIENCE *If you're replacing a heating/cooling system, don't let the contractor sell you more than the house needs. Oversized systems waste money twice: once when you pay for the excess capacity, and later when you pay your fuel bill (they operate less efficiently by cycling off and on frequently). Worse, in humid climates, oversized air conditioners can cause humidity problems; they cool the air quickly, then cycle off before the air is dehumidified, leaving you feeling sticky.*

Don't settle for old-school, rule-of-thumb calculations such as "one ton of air conditioning per 500 square feet." Insist that your contractor base the size of your new equipment on a detailed, written heating and cooling analysis of your home that takes your energy improvements into account (insulation, air sealing, new thermal mass, new windows, south-facing glass, shading, etc.). The calculations should follow the standards of the Air Conditioning Contractors of America (ACCA) Manual J, American Society of Heating, Refrigerating, and Air Conditioning Engineers (ASHRAE).

Here are some guidelines for choosing heating and cooling equipment from the non-profit American Council for an Energy Efficient Economy:

- **Fuel-fired furnaces** heat air directly and distribute it via ducts. A gas-fired furnace with an AFUE of 90+ and electronic ignition is the most energy-efficient, and therefore has the shortest payback period. Specify a sealed-combustion unit or install the unit in an air-sealed closet to keep air-fouling combustion by-products out of your house.

- **Fuel-fired boilers** use a fan-coil unit (similar to a car radiator) to directly heat water (for hydronic radiant heating systems) or indirectly heat air (for forced-air systems). Select a sealed-combustion boiler with an electric ignition and AFUE of 90+. Combination boilers can provide hot water for both domestic use (at faucets and showerheads) and space heating.

- **Air-source heat pumps** use a refrigerant and the evaporation/condensation cycle to extract heat from outdoor air in winter and transfer it to indoor air. In the summer, the cycle is reversed and the unit functions as an air conditioner. Until recently, the effectiveness of air-source heat pumps was

An efficient wood stove can supplement the heat provided by a furnace.

limited in climates with winter temperatures mostly above 35°F, but newer models can operate efficiently down to -30°F. The heating efficiency of heat pumps is described as the Heating Seasonal Performance Factor (HSPF), and their cooling efficiency is measured with a Seasonal Energy-Efficiency Ratio (SEER). In warmer climates, SEER is more important than HSPF; in colder climates, focus on getting the highest HSPF feasible. Look for equipment with a SEER of at least 14.5 and an HSPF around 9.0.

- **Ground-source (or Geothermal) and water-to-air heat pumps** work like air-source heat pumps, but they extract heat from loops of pipe buried in the ground or immersed in a water well. Since belowground temperatures are relatively stable year-round, these systems can be practical regardless of the outdoor air temperature. However, the extensive system of buried pipes can be quite expensive unless you need to install a well for other reasons. An upside is that they don't involve an outdoor air-conditioning unit that takes up space.

- **Air conditioners** use a refrigerant and the evaporation/condensation cycle to extract heat from indoor air and transfer it to outdoor air (the opposite of a heat pump in heating mode). Central units are the most efficient if you need to cool your whole house, but the system loses efficiency quickly if

Place your wood stove next to a thermal mass wall. It will store heat and continue to radiate it even after the fire is out.

uninsulated ducts run through hot areas (such as uninsulated attics) or if the ducts are leaky. A window unit is a less efficient piece of equipment in itself, but it can be more efficient for cooling a limited area (e.g., a bedroom for comfortable sleep in muggy climates) because it doesn't entail duct losses. Select whole-house air conditioners with a SEER of at least 14.5. Window air conditioners are rated with an Energy-Efficiency Ratio (EER); choose a unit with an EER of at least 10.

- **Evaporative coolers (swamp coolers)** cool air by blowing it through a wetted mesh pad. They are about 75 percent more energy-efficient than air conditioners, but they are effective only in climates with hot dry summers. As with air conditioners, both centralized ducted systems and wall or window units are available.

- **Electric radiant mats** installed under tile aren't particularly efficient, but they can be a good choice for heating a small area (such as a bathroom) for a short time. Always couple electric radiant mats with a timer switch or a programmable thermostat to avoid using excessive amounts of electricity.

- **Electric baseboard convectors** are the least efficient of all heating choices and should not be used except in supertight, superinsulated houses where no other options are practical.

- **Wood stoves** can be a good source of heat in areas with a sustainable supply of wood. Select a clean-burning EPA-certified stove that is sized properly for your home. When a wood stove is too big, residents tend to burn fires at a low smolder to avoid overheating, which wastes fuel and is a significant cause of air pollution.

In a climate with hot, dry summers, a swamp cooler (far right) can replace an air conditioner, at a lower operating cost.

High-mass masonry stoves burn a fast, hot fire to heat the thermal mass, then radiate heat for many hours.

- **High-mass masonry stoves** are much more efficient and clean-burning than conventional wood-burning fireplaces. Also known as *Kachelofen*, or as Russian, Siberian, or Finnish fireplaces, they burn a quick, intense fire to heat thermal mass, which then slowly radiates and conducts heat to the living space.

Equipment Location and Sizing

When possible, heating equipment (except for heat pumps) should be located inside the thermal envelope. If your system is currently in unconditioned space (e.g., an attic or basement) and you plan to replace it, consider relocating it to conditioned space or insulating the area where it will be located. If you plan to have fuel-fired equipment in a conditioned area, be sure to get a sealed-combustion unit; these high-efficiency gas furnaces bring in combustion air from outside the building envelope and exhaust combustion products to the outdoors.

HEATING WATER WITH THE SUN

Whether or not your home is well oriented for passive-solar heating, you can use the sun's energy to heat water for bathing and cooking. All you need is an unobstructed patch of roof or yard that is sunny most of the day. Using the sun's radiant energy to heat water for your home is one of the most cost-effective and energy-efficient uses of solar energy, reducing water heating costs by 50 to 80 percent.

All solar water-heating systems have at least two components:

- A *collector* that collects and concentrates energy from the sun, and
- A *storage tank* for the heated water.

Integral Storage Collectors (ISC) and batch heaters (see figure 3), combine the collector and storage tank in one unit. These passive systems are simple and direct, without pumps or controllers, but they can be used only in areas with minimal freezing. They should be equipped with isolation valves that allow the system to be drained and bypassed in case of freezing.

In colder climates, hot water is typically stored in a tank at some distance from the collector—often in a garage, basement, or utility room. Such systems are called *active* systems (see figure 4); they require a fluid (water or antifreeze) to transfer heat from the collector to the storage tank and a pump to circulate the fluid. *Direct active* systems circulate and heat the potable water that you will be using in your home. *Indirect active* systems, most common in colder climates that experience winter freezing, use a solution of distilled water and antifreeze that circulates in a closed loop, with a heater exchanger to transfer heat from the collector to water in the storage tank. Both direct and indirect systems can use a photovoltaic panel to power a pump. *Drain-down systems* offer the best freeze protection in very cold climates because the water or fluid drains out of the collector into a tank whenever the pump shuts off.

SOLAR WATER HEATING SYSTEMS

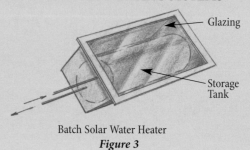

Glazing

Storage Tank

Batch Solar Water Heater
Figure 3

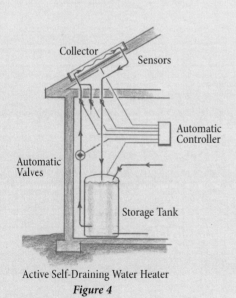

Thermosiphoning Water Heater

Active Self-Draining Water Heater

Figure 4

Electricity Use

Electricity is primarily generated by burning fossil fuels, with water pressure, wind turbines, and photovoltaic cells contributing to the mix. By the time electricity gets to your house, a lot of energy has been consumed to generate and transport it—not to mention the toxic pollution created by most power plants. So use electricity wisely. For example, using electricity to heat a space is highly inefficient. When electricity use is appropriate, use the most energy-efficient appliances, lights, and heating and cooling systems that will do the job.

Appliances

Washer, clothes dryer, refrigerator, freezer, and dishwasher—we love the convenience of modern appliances. Because they last a long time (10 to 20 years), it's important to buy them wisely. Each appliance has three price tags: the purchase price, the cost of repairs and maintenance, and the cost to operate it over its lifetime—which will show up on utility bills every month. The cheapest appliance, or even the one with the best repair record, won't necessarily cost the least to operate. Always compare Energy Guide labels when shopping, and look for Energy Star appliances.

ENERGY GUIDE LABELS

Energy Guide labels tell you the estimated energy consumption of a given piece of equipment compared to other models. They also provide an estimated annual cost of operation. Compare models and look for models with the lowest energy consumption.

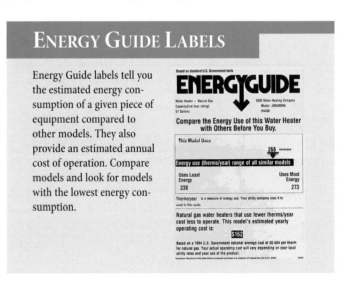

Low-Hanging Fruit *things you can do today*

- **Reduce your use of hot water.** Fix leaky fixtures, install low-flow showerheads and faucets, and use efficient washing machines and dishwashers.

- **Lower your water heater's thermostat setting.** This can save as much as $45 per year and reduce the risk of being scalded by tap water.

- **Minimize waste while you're away.** If you have a gas water heater, lower the temperature setting before you leave. If you have an electric water heater, turn it off at the electrical panel if you will be gone more than two days (and your house will remain above freezing).

- **Insulate your hot water tank.** To reduce heat loss, wrap your water heater with specially designed water heater jacket insulation (some newer energy-efficient models should not be insulated; check the manual). Gas water heaters should not be insulated on top. Set an electric water heater on a piece of rigid foam insulation, especially if it's on a concrete slab.

- **Insulate all exposed hot water pipes.** Use minimum 5/8-inch foam pipe insulation or 3-inch fiberglass wrap.

- **Stop convective losses.** Install a heat trap nipple that minimizes circulation of hot water from the tank into the outlet pipe. A 6-inch pipe loop will also control convective losses.

More Advanced Steps *things you can do tomorrow*

- **Replace your old water heater with a new energy-efficient unit.** Look for models with an Energy Star label or an Energy Factor (EF) of at least .62. Size your water heater to meet your needs; two adults may never use more than 30 gallons of hot water in an hour, but a family of six may use as much as 70 gallons in an hour. The "first hour rating" of a tank should match, but not exceed, your estimated hot water needs.

- **Install an instantaneous (tankless) water heater.** Tankless water heaters only heat water when you turn on a hot-water faucet. They generate plenty of hot water, but they must be sized for the maximum number of fixtures that might be in simultaneous use, or there may not be enough hot water to go around. Look for a model with electronic ignition to avoid having a continuously burning pilot.

- **Install a solar water heating system (see sidebar page 136).**

- **Install a heat-recovery system.** If you have a basement below your main shower, you may be able to use heat from waste water to pre-heat incoming water.

Tankless water heaters are small. In climates where temperatures don't go below 5°F, they can be mounted outside.

Refrigerators

Refrigerators use more energy than any other household appliance, so buying an energy-efficient fridge can make a big difference. And don't just move your old refrigerator to the garage and keep using it! Many utility companies will buy your old refrigerator and recycle it, safely disposing of ozone-depleting refrigerants.

Stoves and Ovens

If you are replacing your stove, consider getting a self-cleaning oven; its higher insulation levels mean lower energy use. If you're buying a gas range, an electronic ignition will save the energy of a constantly burning pilot.

Clothes Dryers

Electric clothes dryers are second only to refrigerators in energy consumption, costing $1,100 to $1,500 to operate over their lifetime. New dryers aren't required to display Energy Guide labels, but you can look for energy-saving features such as a high energy factor (EF), a moisture or temperature sensor that shuts the machine off when clothes are dry, and a cool-down cycle, sometimes known as a "perma-press" cycle. Of course, a clothesline in your sunny backyard is the most efficient dryer of all.

Fresh air and sunshine make laundry dried on a clothesline smell good.

Refrigerators are among the most energy-consuming home appliances. Purchase the most energy-efficient model that meets your needs.

Washing Machines

A washing machine's efficiency is measured by its Modified Energy Factor (MEF), which considers both tub capacity and energy use. Look for models with an MEF of 1.9 and above. And wash with cold water when appropriate!

Home Electronics

Turn out your lights some evening and walk around your home; you'll probably see glowing dots and digital clocks everywhere. In the last ten years, there's been a proliferation of appliances that consume electricity even when turned off. These passive power drains are known as "standby losses" or "phantom loads." A 2001 study performed at Lawrence Berkeley National Laboratory and the University of California at Berkeley found that standby electricity usage accounts for 6 to 25 percent of average household electricity use. Computers, laser printers, TVs, VCRs, cell phone chargers, and set-top cable boxes are the worst offenders, consuming 75 percent of their total energy usage *while turned off.* Energy Star home electronic products reduce standby losses by 50 percent.

To avoid standby losses, unplug appliances when not in use. Better yet, group appliances (for example, a computer,

Two lights mounted directly above the main work surface provide great lighting without shadows.

printer, and other peripherals, or a TV, DVD, VCR, and stereo) on one surge protector that can be turned off when the appliances are not in use.

Lighting

Though lighting isn't the largest consumer of electricity in the average home (only 7 percent), it is one of the easiest arenas for reducing energy use. For starters, maximize your use of sunlight (see chapter 3). Also, don't try to achieve uniformly high levels of light throughout your house. Task lighting, such as desk lamps and fixtures that shine directly on kitchen work surfaces, puts the light where you need it most.

Where electric lighting is needed, consider making the switch to Compact Fluorescent Lamps (CFLs). They are three to four times more efficient than incandescent bulbs, and they last 8 to 10 times longer. Replacing incandescent bulbs with CFLs may appear expensive, but it can actually reduce your lighting energy costs by 50 to 80 percent without any loss in lighting quality.

While conserving electricity is important, the quality of light in your home is equally critical to your health and comfort. Early fluorescent lighting got a bad reputation because of flicker, buzzing, and poor color rendition. Newer CFLs feature electronic ballasts, warmer color temperatures, color rendition similar to incandescent lighting, and even dimming capabilities. To get the best lighting from CFLs, choose high-quality Energy Star–rated units that clearly indicate the color temperature and Color Rendering Index (CRI) (see sidebar, page 141).

CAROL'S EXPERIENCE *People often focus on the rate at which a light bulb—or anything else—consumes energy, overlooking the fact that total energy use is what really matters. Let's imagine that one household replaces all their incandescent light bulbs with compact fluorescents while another one uses only incandescent lamps. Which one uses more energy for lighting? We have no idea.*

Now what if I tell you that people in the first household light every room brightly, leave lights on when they're out of a room, and stay up late at night? Meanwhile, the incandescent family gets up at sunrise, goes to bed early, turns on lights only when they need them, and turns them off as soon as they're through. There's a good chance that the second household uses less energy for lighting.

Fluorescent lights aren't an excuse for wasting energy. Choose light sources that are appropriate for their intended uses, use them with respect, and keep the big picture in sight.

Respect Your Fuel

It's easy to feel paranoid, guilty, or frustrated about energy use. Whatever happened to the good old days, when people could just enjoy their toys without having to deny themselves?

But let's look at this differently. While utility-grid-based comfort systems and appliances can be convenient, their unconscious use can cut you off from the rest of the living world. Consider the possibility that you might enjoy living with more natural light, using hand tools, and choosing forms of recreation that use your physical energy, not electricity or combustion engines. We aren't advocating a life of discomfort and self-denial. But we are advocating a life of caring awareness, accompanied by greater health and fitness.

Fluorescent lights come in a variety of sizes and colors that can be adapted to almost any fixture.

Understanding where your energy comes from and its real costs—not just monetary, but environmental, physical, political, and, social—can enrich your life. In fact, you can graduate from being a consumer to being an empowered participant in natural systems.

CHOOSING COMPACT FLUORESCENTS FOR YOUR HOME

To maintain your current lighting levels, replace incandescent bulbs with CFLs rated at one-third the wattage of the incandescent bulb. For example, a 20-watt CFL produces the same amount of light as a 60-watt incandescent bulb. You will also need to look for CFLs that fit the shape, size, and configuration of your current fixtures. Fortunately, a wide variety is available today.

"Color temperature" allows us to choose the best bulb for a particular use. It describes the color of light produced by a bulb, from "warm" (pink or orange in color) to "cool" (blue in color). For example, early fluorescent lights were known for their harsh blue light, which made people look pale and sickly. Color temperature is rated using the Kelvin scale, which ranges from 1,700° for a match flame to 10,000° for a partly cloudy sky. For general residential use, 2,700 K is about the same color as an incandescent bulb; it provides a bit of color warmth, which makes people look attractive and healthy. However, for task lighting, such as home-office or kitchen surfaces, you might like a higher color temperature, such as 3,000–4,100K; this cooler range allows the eye to see with more precision. Another way to evaluate the color performance of a given bulb is the Color Rendering Index (CRI), which uses a scale of 1–100 to indicate how well a light source renders colors. Bulbs with a CRI of 80 or above reproduce colors accurately.

Cenac Residence
Lake Martin, Louisiana

Typically, natural remodeling strives to *naturalize* a house that ignores its surroundings. But the house that Madeleine Cenac found was built long before the era of mechanical heating and air conditioning. In fact, it hadn't been modified since its creation in the mid-1800s. It was a classic example of vernacular building, designed to keep its occupants naturally cool in the hot, humid climate of southern Louisiana. "These houses were built for that climate, so it's not like you're starting from scratch and trying to figure out what's appropriate," says Madeleine's architect, Eddie Cazayoux, AIA. "It was appropriate, sustainable architecture to begin with." The challenge here was to maintain the house's historic charm and energy efficiency while updating it for 21st-century living.

Madeleine owned a piece of property near Lake Martin and was looking for an old house to move onto the land and restore. A friend told her of a house he'd known about for years. It was being used as a hay barn and was in pretty poor condition. He knew the owners of the old house, and he introduced Madeleine to them.

When Madeleine first saw the house, the front porch had deteriorated, some windows were covered with tin, and most of the shutters were gone. The piers that the house originally rested on had collapsed, and the wooden floor was sitting on the ground. "The house was virginal," says Madeleine. "It had never had electricity; we were the first to turn on a light bulb in the house. It never had indoor plumbing. It had only been painted twice. The house was in a deteriorated state because it hadn't been inhabited since the 20s, but it was easy to see the bones; there weren't layers of other people's remuddling."

The original house's heavy timber structure was preserved, as well as the brick infill at the interior walls.

The house's construction was a classic example of Acadian building techniques, which blended native American and French colonial practices. The structure was a heavy timber frame called *colombage*, with mortise-and-tenon joints. The exterior walls were filled in with *bousillage*, a type of wattle-and-daub made with local mud and cured Spanish moss. Interior walls were filled in with brick. The inside of the house was plastered, and lap siding protected the outside. There was a brick fireplace in the middle of the house, in the French style.

Before the house could be moved, the new site was prepared and footings were poured. In keeping with the historical style, pier footings would raise the house above the ground to escape seasonal flooding. Eddie cleverly tied together the historically accurate piers with a below-grade perimeter footing.

The house also had to be readied for the move; the fireplace was dismantled, rotting wood was shored up, plywood was screwed to the walls to hold the bousillage in place, and the steep roof was taken off so that the house could pass under the utility wires en route to its new home. Before removal, all the parts were numbered for reassembly.

Once the house was in place, the first job was to restore the porch, fireplace, and roof. Then the interior and exterior were renovated,

including repairing the shutters and windows and replacing some of the bousillage and plaster.

The home's new site is near a shallow lake, where a rookery attracts thousands of birds in springtime. Huge cypress trees are hung with Spanish moss, and near

Maison Madeleine has been lovingly revived and now sits near Lake Martin, surrounded by old cypress and live oak trees.

the house is a live oak tree. Madeleine oriented the old house's front porch to the west—not always practical in a hot climate, but the density of the bottomland hardwood forest provides ample shading for this western exposure. Guests park away from the house and walk through a wild area before arriving at the front yard, where a traditional split-board fence defines the formal garden. "The idea is to create thresholds to separate the home from automobiles and the real world," says Eddie.

Old Style, New Strategies

In rebuilding the roof, Eddie combined the old appearance with a contemporary understanding of comfort and energy efficiency. Near the steep gable roof's peak, there was enough height for upstairs bedrooms, but atticlike spaces are notoriously hot. "I needed to insulate the roof, but I didn't want to change the existing fascia and wood gutter," says Eddie. "So I took 2x12s and ripped them diagonally, which gave me zero at one end, and 11¼ inches at the upper end. And we put that on top of the existing framing with the largest end at the peak, so by the time you get to the highest part of the house, where the two upstairs bedrooms are, there was enough room to add insulation, a ventilated air space, and a radiant barrier. That's how heat is transferred: by conduction, convection, and radiation

ROOF SECTION DETAIL

Air Baffle

⅝ Drywall

1-inch Rigid Insulation with Foil Face to Attic

Wood Shingle Ridge Cap

Ridge Vent

1x Cypress

Existing Rafters

Tapered New Rafters

2 x 8 Blocking

2 x 6 Blocking

Attic

Attic

The house's natural ventilation was increased without altering its historic appearance by introducing small screened gaps between horizontal siding boards.

So if you use a radiant barrier, insulation, and ventilation, you're combating that heat gain all three ways in which it can be transferred. That technique also left the rafters and the decking exposed to the inside. And it's very comfortable up there."

The attic is further cooled by a trick Eddie did with the siding. At the gable ends of the house, he inserted a small wooden shim at each stud to open a barely noticeable space between the boards of the lap siding. He then screened the back of the openings to keep bugs out. Air flows in between the boards, up through the little corners of the attic outside the knee wall, through the new tapered rafters, and out the roof through a ridge vent at the top.

The floor plan of the original house was kept intact, and the only concession to modern living was to turn one of the little rooms in back into a bathroom (the house had no indoor plumbing). While the house was upgraded with plumbing and electricity, it's far from obvious. The restorers took great pains to hide switches, electrical outlets, faucets, and other evidence of modern life.

Meanwhile, it was clear that the little cabin wasn't large enough for Madeleine and her children. Eddie designed a second structure to look like a cabin from the 1700s, in an older style of French colonial architecture. This addition houses the kitchen and dining area. Eddie placed the addition behind the renovated old house, with a narrow breeze-

The original house had no indoor plumbing, so the house's functions were "modernized" while retaining the feeling of living in another era.

The kitchen/dining addition adjacent to the original cabin appears to be older than the main house, thanks to exquisite care in design and detailing.

144

way connecting the two. The addition is oriented to the road, with its porch facing south. This allows for better shading in a more open area of the site, a good connection to the old house, and a secondary entrance from the parking area for Madeleine—especially handy when carrying groceries. The location also creates a good relationship between the kitchen and the fruit trees and vegetable and herb garden around the addition.

When it was all done, you'd never know that the extended house hadn't been there for centuries. "It looks like two old houses that are attached by a little enclosed bridge," observes Eddie.

While the house was adapted for life with electricity, evidence of modern conveniences was downplayed.

FLOOR PLANS

Den

Dining

To Loft

Addition

Office

Living Room

Master Bedroom

Historic House

Bedroom

Bedroom

2nd Floor
Historic House

Catching a breeze while sitting on a shaded porch is a time-honored feature of southern living.

Thermal Comfort

The porches are a central feature in the home's natural cooling scheme. Open to the breeze, they provide shade for people sitting on the porch, as well as for the house itself. French doors, operable windows, and high ceilings support natural cooling by ventilating the interior spaces.

The bousillage in the exterior walls is also a natural comfort feature. "A lot of people here refer to the bousillage as insulation," says Eddie. "But it really functions as thermal mass. When massive walls are shaded by large overhangs and porches, they can stay pretty cool in spring and fall. That's when the days are warm enough to get uncomfortable, but the nights are cool enough to cool off that mass. When you walk from outdoors to indoors in a house like this, people are amazed at how cool it is inside." While most experts advise building a light, airy structure in a hot, humid climate, Eddie sees a role for massive walls here. "You can build with mass here *if* you can control its temperature. When you keep the mass cool in summer and warm in the winter, it feels wonderful."

The deep porches made it difficult to bring in winter sun for passive solar heating. But winters are mild enough here that Eddie isn't worried. When heat is needed, there's the fireplace; while reconstructing it to look like the original, he added outside combustion air to improve its efficiency. A damper on the side of the fireplace brings in air from outdoors, rather than drawing on house air and inducing cold drafts. When extra heat is needed—or on those hot, muggy, breezeless days when natural cooling isn't enough—an air-source heat pump located under the house makes up the difference.

Materials

Almost all of the materials used in this project were salvaged, and most of the rest were locally harvested. The heavy timbers for the new cabin came from old barns nearby. The blocks that the new cabin rests on were made from thousand-year-old cypress trees recovered from a local river, where they'd sunk on their way to the mill during the Depression. "The French called cypress 'wood eternal' because termites don't eat it and it weathers beautifully," says Eddie. "But only the old-growth cypress is like that."

The new bousillage, used to repair the old house and fill the walls of the new wing, was made of clay from the yard and Spanish moss from the trees on site. They replaced the original soft fireplace bricks with old reclaimed solid brick. Madeleine tracked down authentic old materials to complete the house, including hand-forged metal hinges, old-style faucets, wavy old glass for the windows, and cypress wood for the structure and the finishes. "There's a circle of old-house lovers online," offers Madeleine. "That saved me a lot of time."

In keeping with tradition, the cabin addition rests on decay-resistant cedar, in this case salvaged from a local river.

Home at Last

The bulk of the project took about five years to complete, with many small tasks remaining. As the French say, "some things can't be rushed." Today, Maison Madeleine looks as if it's always been there. "I'm really happy with the way it fits into the natural environment," says Eddie. "It's a good fit, and it was very satisfying to save a historic building."

Madeleine agrees: "I love beauty and tranquility, and that's what this house gives me—and a sense of place. I lived in a subdivision, and I found it draining. It's as if I'm a battery, and I have to come home to get recharged. The solid walls give this house a really different feeling. Friends try to get me to go out on the weekends, but they know I'll refuse; this is a much better place to be than most places they want me to go."

Madeleine and a friend relax on the front porch of the main house.

Eddie Cazayoux's Top Five Criteria for Hot Humid Climates

1. Shading

2. Ventilation

3. Insulation

4. Attention to moisture: thoughtful site use, especially drainage, and protection from rain (this area gets 57 inches a year)

5. A radiant barrier in the roof (and any walls that are in direct sun)

"I look at structure and drainage first," says Eddie. "If you're going to restore an old house, make sure the structure is sufficient (or can be corrected) and that the site can drain well. That's a problem here; the land is very flat, we have a high water table, and we get lots of rain. If water stays around the footings, you'll have problems."

The south-facing porch helps shade the house while linking the kitchen addition with the food gardens.

Devise a Strategy

What's the use of running if you are not on the right road?

—German proverb

One strategy for this home was to use the addition to create multiple indoor and outdoor spaces on the east side.

UP TO THIS POINT, you've been like a hawk, soaring above the fields, scouting the territory. You've gathered information about the ecosystems in and around your home. You've thought about your needs and desires, and now you're ready to start making decisions. Your next step is to formulate a personalized strategy for your remodeling project.

A strategy is a description of where you want to go with your house and how you plan to get there. It sums up the basic systems and relationships that will fit your home seamlessly into its surroundings while creating a nurturing environment for you.

Defining your strategy is a crucial step; it will give you a touchstone for making good decisions as you design, select systems, and choose materials. It increases the likelihood that the parts of your home will function harmoniously. Not having a strategy is risky; you could overlook opportunities or end up with different aspects of your project at odds with each other.

Set Your Course

This is where things get really fun. You're going to devise a strategy that will help you make the best use of nature's gifts in your unique location and in support of your personal goals.

Your first step is to establish your broad goals for your remodeling project. Natural remodeling projects generally have four core goals:

• Make the most of nature's renewable resources

• Use nonrenewable resources with great care

• Restore your personal relationship with the living world

• Increase vitality—the planet's and your own

Refer to these for guidance as you develop specific goals based on your circumstances.

A dormer admits sunlight from above in this renovation of an old barn in Germany.

Here, goals included integrating an access ramp with a covered sitting porch.

Now, it's up to you to interpret these core goals as they apply to your home:

• Get out your Project Notebook and look over everything you've recorded there: your personal survey, site plan, climate information, house plan, list of what does and doesn't work in your home, desired budget for the project, other resources, and so on.

• Jot down your ideas for:

    Using nature's gifts

    Remedying your top problems

    Building on what's working well already

To help structure your thoughts, here are some basic areas to consider:

Natural thermal comfort: How will you stay warm in winter and cool in summer with maximal use of renewable resources and minimal use of nonrenewable ones?

Lighting: How will you maximize your use of daylighting where needed and provide appropriate lighting for various functions (tasks, entertainment)?

Sparkling light through colored and clear glass blocks brings beauty and delight to this interior stairwell.

Indoor-outdoor connections: How will you develop outdoor areas to draw you out of the house, provide habitat for others, and improve energy efficiency?

Other energy use: How will you minimize energy waste?

Write or sketch your responses to these questions in your Project Notebook. Feel free to add other items that are basic to your needs: beauty, functionality, durability, clean water and air, mitigating hazards—whatever feels central to you and your family. Take as much time as you need; you are laying the groundwork for all the decisions that follow.

A simple table and chairs under a sheltering apple tree supports the homeowner's goal of spending more time outside.

Define Your Basic Strategy

Now sum up your basic strategy in a sentence or a short paragraph. For example, if you live in a mixed climate with good solar access, your basic strategy might be this:

Improve passive solar heating by adding thermal mass and increasing the area of south-facing glass; improve summer cooling with deeper overhangs and good night ventilation; create outdoor rooms on all sides of the house.

By contrast, if you live in a cold climate and your house is on a north-facing slope in acres of dense forest, your basic strategy might be this:

Air-seal and superinsulate the house; add an efficient nonpolluting wood-burning stove; augment daylighting with tubular skylights.

The Core of the Matter: Natural Heating and Cooling

Most contemporary homes were not built to take the best advantage of sun, shade, and breezes. So it makes sense that the heart of your remodeling strategy should be a plan for achieving thermal comfort in a way that delights you and your family while being kind to the earth. Because of its importance, we want to outline some techniques you can use to help you better understand your situation and make appropriate changes.

When you identified your climate zone in chapter 1, you took the first step in the right direction. Now it's time to consider the best natural heating and cooling approaches for your house in that context. The table on page 152 provides an overview of which strategies generally work best in each climate zone, along with some vernacular examples that may be familiar. As you'll see, there are many overlapping approaches, especially in the mixed climates. Your house, your site, the surrounding microclimate, and your budget will give you clues about which will be best for your project.

Reducing your need for heating and cooling through superinsulation is a highly effective remodeling strategy in most climates.

Keep in mind that this table provides general guidelines; always let your own circumstances guide you. You might live in a mixed dry climate, but if the sun doesn't shine on your house and you can't change that fact, there's no point in basing your heating strategy on passive-solar heating.

NATURAL THERMAL COMFORT STRATEGIES

CLIMATE ZONE	Passive-Heating Opportunities	Passive-Cooling Opportunities	Building Form and Materials	Vernacular Examples
Very Cold Very Cold Winter Mild Summer	Windbreaks, earth sheltering, passive-solar tempering	Very little cooling required. Shading (shade south-facing windows as needed during hottest month), natural ventilation	Compact form most efficient to insulate and heat. Thermal mass and south glass required for passive-solar tempering.	Igloo, saltbox, Scandinavian farm courtyards, Finnish masonry heaters, Swiss chalets with shallow roofs to retain snow, Asian and European roofs insulated and weather-proofed with thatch
Cold Dry Cold Winter Warm Dry Summer	Windbreaks, earth sheltering, passive-solar heating	Shading (shade south-facing windows as needed during hottest month), natural ventilation, evaporative cooling, night ventilation of thermal mass	Compact form most efficient to insulate and heat, but narrow forms good for ventilation. Thermal mass and south glass required for passive-solar heating; thermal mass also effective for passive cooling	Igloo, saltbox, Scandinavian farm courtyards, Finnish masonry heaters, Swiss chalets with shallow roofs to retain snow, Asian and European roofs insulated and weather-proofed with thatch
Cold Humid Cold Winter Warm Humid Summer	Windbreaks, earth sheltering, passive-solar heating	Shading (shade south-facing windows as needed during hottest months), natural ventilation, night ventilation of thermal mass	Compact form most efficient to insulate and heat, but narrow forms good for ventilation. Thermal mass and south glass required for passive-solar heating; thermal mass also effective for passive cooling	Igloo, saltbox, Scandinavian farm courtyards, Finnish masonry heaters, Swiss chalets with shallow roofs to retain snow, Asian and European roofs insulated and weather-proofed with thatch
Mixed Humid Cold Winter Hot Humid Summer	Passive-solar heating, earth sheltering	Shading (east, west, and south sides in summer), natural ventilation, thermal mass	Narrow form with openings on opposite sides most efficient for ventilation. Promote good ventilation for drying materials in summer.	Shaded open porches, summer kitchens, Asian and European roofs insulated and weatherproofed with thatch
Hot Humid Mild Winter Very Hot Humid Summer	Passive-solar heating during 1-2 coldest months	Shading, natural ventilation, decoupling heat-producing functions (e.g., cooking). Use high-mass materials only when well shaded.	Narrow form with openings on opposite sides allow for ventilation. Light colors reflect strong sunlight.	Elevated pole houses, shaded open porches, summer kitchens
Marine Mediterranean Mild, Wet Winter Mild Dry Summer	Passive-solar heating, wind-breaks, earth sheltering.	Shading, natural ventilation, thermal mass, night ventilation. The ocean's breezes provide cooling.	Narrow forms with openings on opposite sides most efficient for ventilation. Light colors reflect strong sunlight.	Italian hill towns, summer kitchens, outdoor living
Mixed Dry Cold, Dry Winter Hot Dry Summer	Passive-solar heating, wind-breaks, earth sheltering	Natural ventilation, shading, interior mass, night ventilation, evaporative cooling, earth sheltering, decoupling heat-producing functions (e.g., cooking)	Narrow wings with openings on opposite sides allow for ventilation. Courtyards and loggias provide shading.	Courtyard houses, earth-sheltered houses, high-thermal-mass adobe houses, summer kitchens
Hot Dry Mild, Dry Winter Hot Dry Summer	Passive-solar heating during 1-2 coldest months	Natural ventilation, shading, interior mass, night ventilation, evaporative cooling, earth sheltering, decoupling heat-producing functions (e.g., cooking)	Narrow wings with openings on opposite sides allow for ventilation. Courtyards and loggias provide shading.	Courtyard houses, earth-sheltered houses, high-thermal-mass adobe houses, summer kitchens

Refine Your Strategy

The next step is to flesh out your strategy by looking at your situation in more detail.

- For each of the basics (thermal comfort, lighting, indoor-outdoor connections, energy use, and anything else you add to that list), write a simple statement of what you can do in response to your context—your house, yourself, and your climate.

  For example, the best thermal strategies in a hot, humid climate for a city townhouse that faces east and west might be these: good roof insulation, ceiling fans, and movable west shading. For a home exposed to the sun in a mixed-dry climate, passive-solar heating will work well for winter warmth, but you'll want to develop summer shading with plants or built structures.

- For each statement, list the steps you can take to make your goal a reality. If there are several steps, you might want to list them in order of your priority or cost.

You might also want to include a diagram or some photos. A simple diagram can visually clarify how you want, for example, your solar access, landscaping, and water collection/distribution systems to interact. Evocative pictures from magazines, or sketches that embody the overall feelings and functions you're seeking, can inspire you and keep you on track.

The goals: bring more daylight, eating space, and an expansive feeling into this kitchen; the solution was enclosing an unused porch as a dining area and opening up the ceiling.

High operable windows meet two goals: natural lighting and stack ventilation (aided by a ceiling fan).

153

- Look for dependencies, overlaps, and synergies. Try to make each proposed change meet several needs.

  For example, opening up a wall between the kitchen and dining room could improve functionality, daylighting, and indoor/outdoor relationships (see the Sanders Residence Case Study, page 222). If you replace the whole wall with chest-height bookshelves, you'll be creating storage and display space as well (see the Lerner Residence Case Study, page 85). You may want to include some diagrams or photos to visually clarify; for instance, a diagram might better illustrate than words how your solar access, landscaping, and water collection systems will interact.

- Finally, prioritize your options and plan your phases. Remember that a home is always a work in progress. You'll probably have more ideas for your home than money or time will let you accomplish immediately. You can phase your remodeling project over several months, years, or even decades. For smooth phasing, group together similar projects. You might group projects by location, type of work, related functions, level of urgency, or a combination of such factors.

Starting a remodeling project by developing a porch and exterior gardens provides a place to relax and restore yourself during the rest of the project.

Half-height bookcases imply a boundary between the entry and living room, while providing valuable storage space.

For example, you might start with the backyard because the work can be completed without changing the shell of the house, then move on to the adjacent kitchen and half-bath because they're adjacent to the backyard and they both require a plumber.

As you work through the specific changes you want to make in your home, you will find that this is a continuous process of making choices. Keep referring to the four core goals of natural remodeling (at the beginning of this chapter) to help you make those choices. Use the notes and sketches you've made in your Project Notebook to help you think of ways to address more than one goal with a single change. Let the specific strategies that you've defined guide you in making choices that are suited to you and your circumstances.

SPELL OUT THE DETAILS

Here's an example of a well-thought-out remodeling strategy. Use it as a guide as you organize your thoughts on the specifics of your project.

BASIC STRATEGY

We are remodeling our house to have passive cooling via natural ventilation, good air quality, lots of indoor/outdoor living spaces, and lush habitat gardens.

DETAILED STRATEGY

Keep our second story from overheating in summer so we can sleep well and reduce air conditioner use.
- Plant trees to shade the west side of the house.
- Build a trellis over the south windows and moveable shutters on the west second-story windows.
- Add screens so we can leave windows open at night without being eaten by mosquitoes.
- Add attic insulation.
- Air-seal the house envelope.
- Within the next 10 years, replace the roofing with light-colored shingles.
- Install a whole-house fan when we replace the roof.

Improve access to the garden and make it more inviting, more like a living space.
- Shade the doors with a trellised pergola covered with grape vines.
- Pave the area under the pergola with flagstone and arrange the columns to accommodate a dining table for six, or two hammocks.
- Install new French doors on the west side of the dining room.

Relieve our daughter's allergies and asthma.
- Remove all solvents from the basement.
- Seal the air ducts.
- Create a good air barrier between the house and the garage.
- Remove wall-to-wall carpets throughout the house and refinish the wood floors with a water-based sealer.
- Investigate options for installing additional filters and a return-air makeup system on the existing furnace.

Wake up with the sun on our faces and see the stars at night.
- Move the bed closer to the windows and leave the curtains open at night.
- Plant a screen that blocks the neighbor's view into our bedroom.
- Add an east-facing window to the bedroom.
- Shade the window with a new redbud tree to the southeast of the window.

Bring Your Strategy to Life

How will you translate your strategies into nuts and bolts? Let's say you want to pick flooring materials. Using the examples we gave earlier—a house with good solar access or a house in dense forest—the thermal mass of thick Mexican tiles could be a perfect flooring for the first case, and uncomfortably cold and hard in the second case. And the warm area rug that might be just the solution in the forest house could frustrate efforts at storing solar heat in the sunny house.

Laying your strategy out on paper will also help you identify ways to integrate your design ideas for maximum benefit. For example, you may note that the porch on the west side of your house allows too much sunlight to enter the living room on a summer afternoon. You could consider hanging bamboo blinds; that would solve the problem, but it would achieve only one objective. Or you might consider adding a well-placed trellis with a fruiting vine. The vine could provide summer shading, attract butterflies, block a view of the neighbor's house, and delight you with fruit and flowers. The trellis could help define an outdoor room, calm the breeze, and even support a hammock. Of the two choices, the second satisfies many more needs and wants, all with one gesture.

If you are looking to buy a home to remodel, your strategy might also include what kind of neighborhood you want to be in, how to shorten your commute, and other sustainable lifestyle considerations.

Thick Mexican floor tiles help keep this sunny Southern California bedroom cool in summer and warm in winter.

RETHINKING OUR GREEN HOME
by Beth Meredith and Eric Storm

We thought we were doing fairly well at living green, having reduced our "ecological footprint" to about half the U.S. average of 24 acres (www.myfootprint.org). However, even after designing and building a very green 1,400-square-foot home, we realized that there were limitations to how sustainably we could live in a car-dependent, single-family house on a large rural lot. Not surprisingly, driving comprised a large part of our energy use, and this meant that we were still consuming and producing waste at four times what the earth can support.

We decided to challenge ourselves to find a way to live yet more sustainably, with one important additional requirement: *every change had to improve our quality of life.*

In the end, we found it easiest to reduce our impacts most by reconsidering the location and type of house we lived in. By living in a multi-family home in an urban area with good public transportation, our energy use would be equal to that of living in a green home. By then greening our home in this greener context, we could further reduce our footprint to about 8 acres.

The key was to find a neighborhood close to the things we love (we work at home, so we were somewhat free in terms of location). Eventually we settled on northwest Portland, Oregon because of its easy walking distance to shops, cafés, and downtown, as well as great outdoor spaces like the Japanese Garden and Forest Park.

For homeowners, this downtown neighborhood provides lots of amenities and a sense of community within easy walking distance.

Shared spaces and resources make it "greener" to live in a multi-unit building than in an isolated house.

Eric and Beth take time to relax on their porch and chat with neighbors. Their space-efficient condo doesn't take much time to clean and maintain.

The next goal was to find an affordable place in a building that worked for us. While we didn't find a green condo building per se, we did choose a building and a community where there was a relatively high degree of shared common spaces (porches, garden, work areas, etc.), resources (tools, laundry, etc.), and responsibilities (maintenance, gardening, etc.). In this way, we were able to enjoy some of the benefits of a cohousing situation without having to find or create one in our neighborhood.

We chose a relatively small place (769 square feet), with a good floor plan and light. We were attracted to a smaller home in order to simplify our material lives and reduce the time and effort spent on maintenance. Choosing a smaller place also meant that it was more affordable and allowed us to consider a wider range of locations. The one major improvement we made to our new home was to open up the kitchen to the dining room and hall, creating a bright, multifunctional space where we dine and work. We updated the kitchen, saving what elements we could and using green materials such as wheatboard and salvaged wood for the new cabinetry and flooring. We improved energy efficiency by installing a smaller refrigerator, lighting with fluorescents, insulating the attic, and changing to double-glazed windows. We used no-VOC paints and finishes and nontoxic materials throughout. To see more, you can take a virtual tour of our home at www.livingspacesdesign.biz. Including remodeling, our new place cost us just over $200,000, a reasonable price in Portland for a green home, and less of a financial burden than where we were living before.

While we aren't yet living at the global fair-share level of 3 acres per person, we have moved closer to this goal and, in the process, improved our quality of life. We now have an affordable and easily maintained home with better access to a broad range of great services, cultural events, and beautiful natural places to walk.

We offer our experience as one model for putting the idea of "green home" in the larger context of the "green lifestyle." It's an accessible approach that many people may find appealing.

Beth Meredith and Eric Storm of Living Spaces provide design and coaching services for green home remodeling.

Beth and Eric revamped their kitchen, improved energy efficiency, and made minor floor plan changes—and still paid less for their attached home than the price of an average new home in Portland, Oregon.

REGENERATION-BASED CHECKLIST FOR DESIGN AND CONSTRUCTION

Carefully thought-out checklists can be used to help you distinguish positive ecological choices from negative ones. The following example is based on a checklist developed by members of the Society of Building Science Educators, based on Malcolm Well's original *Wilderness-Based Checklist for Design and Construction*.

The Site

1. **Pollutes Air—Cleans Air.** Combustion (furnace, automobile, lawn mower), ventilation, and off-gassing pollute the air. Native vegetation creates oxygen, absorbs CO_2, and removes pollutants.

2. **Pollutes Water—Cleans Water.** On-site toxic wastes, pesticides, insecticides, fertilizers, and petroleum products pollute water. Retaining water that falls on or flows through the site and allowing it to percolate to the water table cleans water (see chapter 5).

3. **Wastes Rainwater—Stores Rainwater.** Consider rainwater harvesting, water recycling, and water conservation (see chapter 5).

4. **Consumes Food—Produces Food.** Consider food produced for humans and other species (see chapter 6).

5. **Destroys Rich Soil—Creates Rich Soil.** Construction, paving, pollution, erosion, pesticides, and herbicides destroy soil. Soil-building ground covers, earthworms, composted organic wastes, and mulch will restore ailing land to healthful life (see chapter 6).

6. **Dumps Wastes Unused—Consumes Wastes.** Consider the fate of all wastes created on site (waste water, trash, pollutants) while the building was being constructed and during its lifetime. Organic wastes can be composted; waste water can be a nutrient for other life forms; construction wastes, consumer goods, and packaging can be recycled.

7. **Destroys Wildlife Habitat—Provides Wildlife Habitat.** Consider the impact of the building, its site development, and its occupants on wildlife habitat (see chapter 6).

8. **Imports Energy—Exports Energy.** Consider the energy required to heat and cool the home, maintain the site, and provide electricity for lights and equipment. Meet or exceed these needs with solar energy, wind power, and hydropower.

9. **Requires Fuel-Powered Transportation—Requires Human-Powered Transportation.** Consider getting to and from your home by automobile, mass transit, bicycle, and foot.

10. **Intensifies Local Weather—Moderates Local Weather.** Consider the microclimatic effects caused by the building and site development. Pavement, masonry walls, and waste heat intensify the city effect while green space and water retention moderate the effect.

The Building

11. **Excludes Daylight—Uses Daylight.** Consider the use of daylight indoors, augmented by electricity only as needed (see chapter 3).

12. **Uses Mechanical Heating—Uses Passive Heating.** Minimize the need for heating with a good building envelope (see chapters 7 and 8), and look to the sun for the heat you need (see chapter 3).

13. **Uses Mechanical Cooling—Uses Passive Cooling.** Provide shade with landscaping, exterior shading devices, and interior shades (see chapters 3 and 6). Look to natural ventilation for more cooling (see chapter 4).

14. **Needs Cleaning and Repair—Maintains Itself.** Emphasize durability in design and material choices (see chapter 12), and favor passive heating and cooling systems that require little maintenance.

15. **Produces Human Discomfort—Provides Human Comfort.** Consider thermal, luminous, and psychological comfort (see chapters 3, 4, and 6).

16. **Pollutes Indoor Air—Creates Pure Indoor Air.** Consider the building materials, furnishings, and maintenance requirements as sources of indoor air pollution (see chapter 12 and Resources, page 268).

17. **Built of Virgin Materials—Built of Recycled Materials.** Consider materials used for paving, structure, finish, and furnishing (see chapter 12).

18. **Cannot Be Recycled—Can Be Recycled.** Consider building materials and construction techniques (see chapter 12), as well as suitability of the structure for new uses in the future.

19. **Serves as an Icon for the Apocalypse—Serves as an Icon for Regeneration.** A building with high visibility and appropriate responses to ecological issues can serve as a role model and inspire regenerative design.

20. **Is a Bad Neighbor—Is a Good Neighbor.** A bad neighbor hogs the sun in winter, sends water off site, intensifies neighbors' climates, and causes glare, air pollution, and noise pollution.

21. **Is Ugly—Is Beautiful.** Make an aesthetic judgment. When architecture draws its lessons from the wild, beauty will no longer have to be a consideration. Organic rightness and appropriateness will repair the broken connection between architecture and its roots.

Project:

	degeneration				sustainability				regeneration
	- 100 always	- 75 usually	- 50 sometimes	- 25 a bit	0 balances	+ 25 seldom	+ 50 sometimes	+ 75 usually	+ 100 always	

the site

	- 100 always	- 75 usually	- 50 sometimes	- 25 a bit	0 balances	+ 25 seldom	+ 50 sometimes	+ 75 usually	+ 100 always	
pollutes air										cleans air
pollutes water										cleans water
wastes rainwater										stores rainwater
consumes food										produces food
destroys rich soil										creates rich soil
dumps wastes unused										consumes wastes
destroys wildlife habitat										provides wildlife habitat
imports energy										exports energy
requires fuel-powered transportation										requires human-powered transportation
intensifies local weather										moderates local weather

the building

	- 100 always	- 75 usually	- 50 sometimes	- 25 a bit	0 balances	+ 25 seldom	+ 50 sometimes	+ 75 usually	+ 100 always	
excludes daylight										uses daylight
uses mechanical heating										uses passive heating
uses mechanical cooling										uses passive cooling
needs cleaning and repair										maintains itself
produces human discomfort										provides human comfort
uses fuel-powered circulation										uses human-powered circulation
pollutes indoor air										creates pure indoor air
is built of virgin materials										is built of recycled materials
cannot be recycled										can be recycled
serves as an icon for the apocalypse										serves as an icon for regeneration
is a bad neighbor										is a good neighbor
is ugly										is beautiful

negative score
possible 2,200

positive score
possible 2,200

final score:

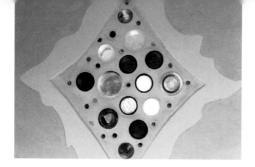

You're on Your Way

When you've developed your strategy, place the strategy outline and images at the front of your Project Notebook so that you can refer to them easily. Like anything natural, your strategy may continue to evolve as you reflect, cogitate, and see more options. Don't be afraid to revise it as you move through the design process.

Now it's time to give yourself a pat on the back! Clear thinking at the beginning is the basis of a successful project. You've created a roadmap that will guide you through the rest of your remodeling project. Refer to your strategy often as you design your spaces, choose materials, and begin construction.

Determining your strategy at the beginning allows your creativity to blossom.

KELLY'S EXPERIENCE *Once I was asked to design an addition to a home in California's Central Valley. My clients had a typical suburban ranch house with an open great room along the south side. They wanted to add an informal dining room for entertaining guests, away from the sound of kids playing in the great room. They also wanted to lower their energy use, but they were feeling a little flummoxed on that front. On the advice of a weatherization contractor, they had installed low-E replacement windows and added aluminum siding with ⅜-inch rigid-insulation backer board. Although the house felt slightly cooler in summer, their air conditioner still ran nonstop—and the great room was actually colder in winter. They were concerned that adding a new dining room would require an even larger air-conditioning unit.*

I explained to my clients that they had been the victims of "weatherization marketing," aimed more at putting money in the contractor's pocket than improving their energy efficiency. The thin insulating backer board on the siding was for the installer's convenience and added little to their wall insulation. The low-E windows had a low solar heat gain coefficient (SHGC) that kept the sun's warmth from entering the house—helpful in summer, but counterproductive in

winter. Because they hadn't looked at their goals in the context of how their home functioned and what nature had to offer, they had missed some obvious, cost-effective opportunities.

I suggested that we step back and look at their goals—a functional dining area, thermal comfort, and efficient energy use—and some possible holistic solutions. With a little redesign of their floor plan, we solved their thermal and space problems for far less money than an addition would have cost.

We began by shading their east and west windows with carefully placed bushes and trees. This cut their summer cooling bills in half and kept them from having to replace their formerly overloaded air-conditioning system. On the south side of the house, we created a new patio with an open, wisteria-covered trellis. This shaded their south-facing windows in summer and served as a relaxing outdoor dining room separated from the great room. We rounded

This patio has enough sunshine and thermal mass (in the pavers) to be warm in cool weather, and enough shade to stay cool in summer.

out those design changes with some basic energy-efficiency measures: insulating the roof, sealing the air ducts, and caulking air leaks throughout the house made every room in the house more comfortable. Finally, when we replaced the glass in the south-facing replacement windows with high-SHGC glass, the winter sun warmed their home once more.

CHAPTER 10
Making Space for Your Life

A house is a home when it shelters the body and comforts the soul.

—Phillip Moffit

Upper bookcases and built-in benches with under-seat storage create a cozy dining nook.

FOR MOST PEOPLE, REMODELING MEANS building an addition; they feel they need more space. When clients come to us for remodeling, they often say things like, "Our family is growing and there's no place for the kids to play," "This kitchen is too small; we don't have room to store food," "I don't have a quiet place to pay bills or work on the computer," or "We like to entertain and we just don't have enough room for guests." They automatically think that more space is the answer. But by reorganizing and rearranging the space they already have—or simply changing the way they use that space—they can often solve their problems with less expense, fewer headaches, and less consumption of natural resources.

Although this is a book about remodeling, we actually want you to *build* as little as possible. Why? Construction uses resources, so staying within your home's existing footprint makes both financial and ecological sense. It almost always costs more to add on to a house because you'll have to deal with structure and weatherproofing and integrating the new section with the old. Adding on also creates more space to heat, cool, light, clean, and maintain. Staying within your house's existing walls means less expense for structure and maintenance. This may free up money to pay for the signature details and quality materials that personalize a house and give it soul. If, by redesigning the house you've got, you can avoid or minimize the need for an addition, you'll have done one of the greenest things you can do.

WHY SMALLER IS BETTER
by Ann Edminster

When remodeling your home, think small. It's tempting to adopt an "in for a penny, in for a pound" approach to additions, but bigger is not necessarily better. In fact, precisely the opposite is often the case.

A modest home has many virtues. It uses less of your time and money. It encourages you to get along with your housemates. And perhaps most compelling of all, a smaller home represents less global environmental burden.

In 1963, the median new U.S. single-family home was 1,365 square feet and housed 3.2 people. According to the U.S. government, by 1999, the median new U.S. home had grown nearly 50 percent—to 2,030 square feet—while average household size had decreased to 2.4 people. The net effect? Nearly twice as much home area *per person*: an increase from 427 to 839 square feet.

A bigger home—no matter how energy-efficient—uses more energy than its smaller counterpart, contributing proportionately more to air pollution, global warming, and ozone-layer destruction. It also consumes more land and building materials, chiefly wood. Most Americans dearly love our forests, yet few make the connection between the roof over their heads and the threat to natural forest ecosystems.

Older homes, like these brick bungalows in Chicago, usually had a floor area of under 1,500 square feet.

Home construction is among the top consumers of wood in North America and a primary driver of natural forest devastation. In British Columbia, forests are being clearcut at the rate of about one acre every minute (Rainforest Action Network). Plantation tree farming, while it may be able to produce much of the wood fiber that our society demands, cannot replace the richness and complexity of these forest ecosystems.

Residents of the United States consume 1.83 cubic meters of wood per person every year—more than any other country, and well above the worldwide average of .32 cubic meters per person. And much of that wood is wasted; wood is typically the largest constituent of the residential construction and demolition waste stream.

The United States, once a timber-rich country, now imports much of its construction lumber from Canada and Siberia; we are already unable to meet our own demands. With residential building (and consumption) outside North America increasingly modeled after ours, the world's forests—and with them, thousands of dependent plant and animal species—are in great danger.

In order to reduce our demands and begin to restore the earth's bounty, we must begin to live more modestly. Remodeling an existing home rather than buying a new one is a conservation measure. It keeps you in your community, enriches that community through economic activity, and offsets demand for new homes in what are often sterile, unsustainable new tracts. Keeping your remodel as modest as possible maximizes the value of your conservation effort.

Ann V. Edminster *is an environmental design consultant and educator. She is cochair of the U.S. Green Building Council's Leadership in Energy and Environmental Design (LEED) Homes Committee and coauthor of* Efficient Wood Use in Residential Construction.

Do You Need More Space or Better Space?

Size alone is a poor measure of how well a house works. Many houses have plenty of floor area, but because the rooms don't relate to each other well or match the family's activities, much of the space may be wasted. Making space is about designing rooms for the way you really live—designing around the particular activities that you and your family enjoy. You may not need more square footage, but rather a redesign of your existing space to make it more functional and comfortable. After all, what is comfort but the ability to move through your day with ease, able to wake in pleasant surroundings, bathe with bliss, find your keys and sort the mail, cook meals with pans and food within reach, gaze out into the garden, chat with friends, relax in a cozy space at the end of the day, and sleep in a quiet, secure area. Making space is about evaluating your home, your climate and site, what you love, and what you need, then massaging the space you have so that it works for you. Consider building an addition only after you've been creative with what's already there.

But how can you make your existing house function better without adding more floor area? Start by evaluating how you use your house now: Where are the problem areas? What works well? What rooms are seldom used and why? Ask yourself, "What would it take for me to use all of these rooms (indoors and outdoors) every day?" Bear in mind that if a public room can't be seen from the main gathering area, you probably won't use it much. Often all it takes to remedy such a problem is moving a doorway, opening up a wall between a kitchen and living room, or installing French doors to a garden patio. Seldom-used rooms can do double duty, increasing their usefulness. For example, with a little good storage, such as built-in bookcases and drawers, a formal dining room can host guests at holidays and also serve for daily after-school study or weekly bill paying. A dark dungeon can become a welcoming project room if you install a new skylight or glazed door and paint the room a light color.

A wide hallway can become a working office space with the addition of storage shelves.

CAROL'S EXPERIENCE *A woman came to me recently for a consultation. She wanted to move out of her rented apartment into an eco-friendly home, but she had a limited budget. She wondered if she should buy an existing home or build a new one. One thing she was sure of: she needed at least 1,200 square feet for herself and her home office. The problem was, her budget wouldn't allow her to buy or build that much space—to say nothing of the resource waste involved.*

Having lived and worked successfully in spaces half that size for many years, I questioned her requirement. "Well, I lived in a house once that had 1,000 square feet, and it wasn't big enough. And another time, I had a 1,200-square-foot house, and it was fine."

I asked her to sketch the floor plans of her past homes for me, and the problem was immediately apparent. As I'd suspected, the 1,000-square-foot home was chopped up into hallways and small, awkward rooms; anyone would have a hard time making the most of the space. Then I made my own sketch, showing her how she could meet all of her needs in 900 square feet. She could hardly believe it. I think she suspected me of sleight of hand.

The moral of the story is this: unless you think like a designer, you're likely to know only what you've experienced. And you've probably experienced a goodly share of poorly designed spaces. Don't fall into the square-footage trap. Learn to think about function, flow, and feeling. Satisfy your actual needs without waste.

Some rooms become more inviting at particular times of day, especially as sunlight falls across the floor.

Evaluate Your Current Living Patterns

A graphic analysis of how you use your current house can be enlightening. Pull out the floor and site plans that you drew in chapter 2 and make copies to draw on. With colored pencils, locate the activities in your home during different times of day (see figure 1):

- Morning in yellow
- Midday in red
- Afternoon in green
- Evening in orange
- Night in dark blue

Do these patterns change seasonally with longer hours of sunlight or different thermal conditions?

Now rank the rooms according to how much time you spend in each (including outdoor rooms and the garden). You might be surprised by the patterns that emerge. Your family may be migrating to follow the light, warmth, or coolness. Some large rooms, such as formal dining and living rooms, may not see much use. The point is to identify which parts of your home

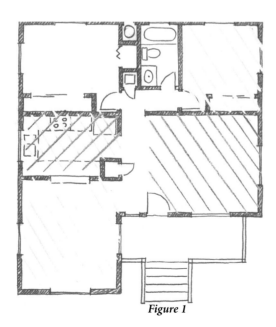
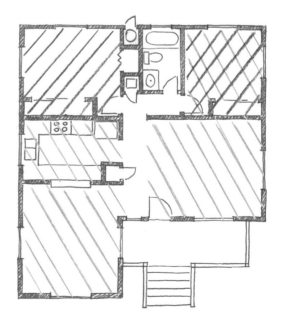

Figure 1

Lowered beams, archways, and a varied color palette can differentiate adjacent spaces.

Heavy wood trusses reflect the rugged beauty of the northern Idaho forest just outside this lakeside home.

aren't being well used. Why aren't they used more? Consider whether the problem might be the following:

- **Space:** Is the room too big or too small for the activities? Is there a lack of storage space?

- **Function:** Does the room lack light or have too much light and heat? Does it not suit its function well (often a problem in kitchens and offices)?

- **Circulation Patterns:** Is there a lack of connection with other rooms, or do too many people pass through or near the room?

- **Appearance:** Does the room lack character? Does it feel too dark and heavy or out of proportion?

After you identify the least used rooms and their problems, consider how you might reconfigure the spaces to better fit your activities: moving doorways, adding a closet, adding beams, taking down or building walls, installing new windows or bookcases.

Remodel Your Home to Fit You

Eco-remodeling doesn't mean spartan, frugal, or minimal design—quite the opposite. "Doing more with less" really does mean *more*: more ease, more comfort, more vitality, more joy, more of your authentic self. Close your eyes and imagine the most beautiful place you've ever been in. What elements made

you feel most comfortable? Was it the color of the walls, the warmth of sun on your cheeks, the dappled light, the soft cushion, the spectacular view? How can you translate and replicate those elements in your home?

For example, perhaps you feel most "at home" hiking in the mountains—the feel of organic duff below your feet, dappled sunlight through the trees, framed "zen" views of distant peaks, textures of rough basalt or granite, the trees just budding out. Distill this experience into elements in your home: wood-chip paths through your garden, light filtering into the living space through a vine-covered trellis, a small window to a stunning view, a bathtub surrounded by rough-hewn stone, a special tree just outside the kitchen window. With this attention to detail, your home can become the place that grounds you, the place where you nourish your physical and spiritual health by reconnecting with the primal cycles of the natural world that you hold dear.

Expressing your personal style doesn't preclude functionality. In fact, uniqueness and functionality support each other. Spaces designed to fit your everyday life—how you sleep, play, cook, eat, bathe, pay bills, and socialize—allow you to surround yourself with the things you love while eliminating the unnecessary. A family room that fits your family's activities can be both smaller and more enjoyable. A kitchen with storage well matched to the way you shop and cook is more comfortable and works better. The best personal solutions are universal.

A PLACE OF YOUR OWN

by Sarah Susanka

A simple altar in a private corner allows for a moment's peace in the midst of a hectic day.

An important space that is missing in most homes today is a small "place of one's own" for each adult. Children typically have their own rooms, but, once coupled, adults share their private space, leaving no place for what I like to term "inner listening" and self-discovery. By making such places, and giving them importance in our lives, we can, on an individual level, give ourselves the gift of connection to the greater mystical universe, and we can learn to hear the voice of the true Self.

Joseph Campbell wrote of the need for such a place. He said, "You must have a room or a certain hour of the day or so where you do not know what is in the morning paper. A place where you can simply experience and bring forth what you are and what you might be. At first you may think nothing's happening. But if you have a sacred space and take advantage of it and use it every day, something will happen."

Whether it's a place to engage in a hobby, to listen to music, or simply to be quiet and away from the hubbub of family life for a while, such a spot can offer the opportunity to nurture individual delights and passions. Such a place does not need to be large. It can be an alcove off a bedroom, an unused corner of the basement, or an attic, as in my own home. Take time to make it beautiful, make it an expression of who you are, whether simple and unadorned or filled with treasures collected over a lifetime. And make it a pattern of your daily routine to spend time there each day, in meditation, in contemplation, or in creative exploration. We are amazing creatures, every one of us, but we forget so easily, when we don't take the time to listen to our inner beings.

Over the years, I've designed "places of one's own" for all kinds of longings, from a location to practice calligraphy, to a writer's attic retreat, to an alcove for a friend to indulge her love of collage making. None of these places required a lot of space. In almost every case, if you are creative, you can find a small area that's rarely used in the house to make the place, without incurring the expense of adding on. Although these gestures seem small and perhaps insignificant, the effect such a space can have on your life is enormous.

I believe that the rebalancing of our lives, and of our planet, is not something that can be done by massive planning. But through actions like the making of such sacred spaces, it will happen of its own accord. All that is required of us is to tune in and listen to Earth's requests of each of us, and to act accordingly. It sounds like such a simple thing, but it requires clarity, compassion, and collaboration from all those who can already hear her voice.

Sarah Susanka is an award-winning residential architect and the author of the best-selling books The Not So Big House *and* Home by Design.

A quiet, enclosed, private garden right outside French doors invites relaxation.

Use the Space You Have

There are many ways to revamp the feel and function of your home without moving the exterior walls. They range from simple steps that don't cost a thing (cleaning, organizing, or moving furniture), to low-investment projects (painting, tiling, or adding built-in furniture), to more serious changes (moving or adding walls and doorways). It's a good idea to make the small changes first; not only are they less expensive, but also undertaking them will allow you to better understand what you actually need and want, then decide whether larger changes are warranted.

Declutter and Rearrange

"A place for everything and everything in its place" is an ideal that few of us live up to, but it can make a huge difference in how well a home functions. Rooms that are cluttered, dark, or too full of furniture feel cramped and often collect unhealthy dust. Casting off your excess stuff lets you use your existing space better and it often leaves you with more energy.

When a house goes up for sale, the realtor often recommends cleaning thoroughly, repainting, and removing half the furniture so that the house feels more spacious. Why not take the same approach to creating more space for yourself right now? Commit 15 minutes a day to organization and you'll be surprised how much gets done.

Here are some thoughts to guide your clearing-out process:

- Pass along things you don't need or use. Ask yourself, "Does this have sentimental value? Have I used it in the past year? Do I expect to use it in the coming year?" Less stuff in your life means less to take care of and a more sustainable lifestyle.

- Contain and organize collections and similar items so they're easy to access. Labeled boxes, photo albums, magazine files, and drawers (designated by type of item) can help you stay sane.

- Install simple storage units. Recycling bins, a compost bucket, bookshelves, hanging racks for pans and kitchen tools, baskets, file boxes, magazine racks, and shelves all provide neat and attractive storage.

- Create places for organizing things that enter and leave your home: coat racks and hooks, shoe storage, recycling bins.

- Reorganize your existing storage: kitchen cabinets, closets, understair areas, and so on.

This cabinet has shelves of many sizes to snugly accommodate a range of possessions. Covering the television keeps it from being intrusive when not in use.

A simple coat rack and bureau for hats, gloves, and keys make even a small entry functional.

KELLY'S EXPERIENCE *When I remodeled my California home in 2001, I grappled with how to make the most of a small 1940s tract house on a limited budget. One of the central problems in the house was the lack of a dining room. The kitchen was a tiny, dark "L," so we ate at a table in the living room. But no matter where we placed the table, it never worked well. As I drew and redrew plans, I was tempted to add a dining room, but with remodeling costs in the Bay Area then close to $200 per square foot, I knew that a large addition would mean giving up other custom design features I wanted, such as a vaulted ceiling in the kitchen, beautiful kitchen cabinets, saltillo tile on the lower floor, or a second-story deck. Adding a dining room adjacent to the kitchen (on the southeast corner) would also have shaded the living room, master bedroom, and part of the patio.*

In the end, I added just five feet to the kitchen to accommodate a built-in corner bench and dining table (see figure 2). To keep the new eat-in kitchen from feeling cramped, I brought in sunlight via new windows and replaced the wall between the kitchen and the living room with half-height bookshelves. To define the rooms, I raised the ceiling in the kitchen and added a lowered beam between the kitchen and living room. I expanded the kitchen further with an exterior door to a deck for alfresco dining and grilling. In the end, the eat-in kitchen with deck access became the most used space in our house—and I got my beautiful kitchen cabinets (see the Lerner Case Study, page 85)!

FLOOR PLAN—BEFORE AND AFTER

Main Floor Before

Main Floor After

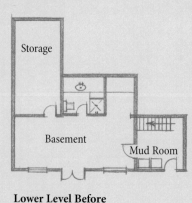

Lower Level Before

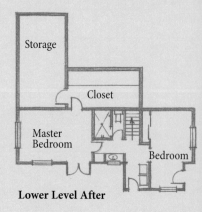

Lower Level After

Figure 2

Bring in More Light

Humans are phototropic by nature. We move toward light. We seat ourselves facing the light. Rooms with poor natural lighting often aren't well used because they feel small, confining, and uninviting. Adding light to a dark room or hall makes it feel large, inviting, and thus more useful. Rather than adding floor space, consider adding sunlight to your existing rooms to make them better fit your needs. There are many ways to bring light to dark space (for more, see chapter 3):

- First, see if you can reflect light from an existing opening farther into the space by painting the opposite and/or adjacent wall and ceiling a light, reflective color. Extending the jambs of a window with built-in bookcases will also reflect light into the room and give you extra storage (see figure 3).

- Borrow light from another room. Opening rooms to each other by removing or punching through a wall provides both light and an extended visual range. Well-sealed interior windows or glass blocks can allow two spaces to share light without compromising acoustic privacy.

- Add a window or glazed door. Windows placed high in a wall will throw light deeper into the room. A window or glazed door adds more than just light; views to the outside can expand a room by drawing the eye outside. Don't for-

A large window next to the tub expands the bathroom and gives the illusion of bathing in a garden.

get to shade your windows with overhangs (on the south) or vegetation (on the east and west).

- Add a skylight. Use skylights in rooms where wall space is at a premium or in attics where windows aren't an option. (See chapter 3 for more on skylights.)

BOUNCING LIGHT FROM EXISTING WINDOWS

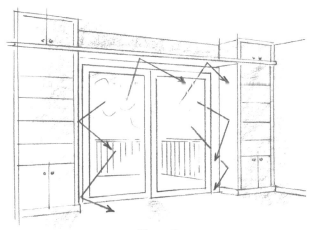

Figure 3

Daylight can be at a premium in townhouses, but the problem is solved here by a translucent panel in the upper bathroom floor, which lets light pass through to the living space below.

Add Built-In Furniture

Built-ins are a great way to make your existing spaces go farther. Though they take up floor space, built-ins simplify rooms and increase their usability by eliminating the need for additional furniture. Built-ins can also divide rooms and provide storage at the same time. Here are some good ways to use built-ins to make your space live larger:

- Bookcases are great for adding thickness and display space to existing walls. Half-height bookshelves can replace interior walls, providing both functional separation and visual connection between rooms.

- Built-in seating eliminates the need for a sofa and chairs, and can even function as a sleeping place for guests. Flip-top storage extends its functionality. With a flat place to lean back against, a window seat is often the most sought-after place in the house, whether for reading or napping in the sun.

A built-in bench allows a dining area to fit into a small space.

- Dining nooks with built-in tables and seating allow the table to be closer to the wall, saving valuable floor space.

- Built-in work surfaces and bookshelves are often the only furniture needed in a home office.

- Lofts in rooms with high ceilings can double the available square footage and provide good spaces for working, meditation, or sleeping.

- Built-in cabinets used as room dividers take up a little more space than a stud wall, but they give back a lot more in functionality, while stud walls give little.

Half-height bookcases and an archway separate the entry from the living room.

A built-in cabinet provides storage while separating the family room from the kitchen beyond.

170

Add Flexibility

You can extend the usefulness of your present spaces by designing them to adjust for different functions at different times of day. Creating convenient or movable storage for different activities is often the key to multiuse rooms.

• Movable cabinets or bookcases can act as room dividers for some activities, then be rolled against the wall to accommodate functions that require more space.

• A kitchen island on wheels can roll away for flexible floor space, or roll on out to the garden for outdoor cooking.

• An interior or exterior wall can slide into place to hide a home office or a kitchen for more formal meals.

• A Murphy bed quickly changes a den, an office, or a family room into a guest room.

THINKING IN PATTERNS

Cooking, eating, sleeping, resting, bathing, socializing—your home contains the same activities as homes all over the world throughout time, and you face the same design challenges in housing those activities. Fortunately, you can learn from what has worked for others.

A "pattern" is a description of a common design challenge and the core of its solution, based on how people have addressed the same issues over time. *A Pattern Language* (APL), assembled by architects and students at the Center for Environmental Structure, has inspired countless designers and homeowners with its commonsense approach based on human and natural considerations. Though APL covers everything from the design of cities to the size of trim, many of the patterns, such as "Front Door Bench," "Sunny Place," and "Garden Growing Wild," describe the interactions of buildings with natural cycles in ways that resonate on a visceral level. Such patterns remind us of guiding principles that we can use in redesigning our homes. For example, here's an excerpt from Pattern 161, "Sunny Place":

> "…the most important sunny places occur up against the exterior walls of buildings, where people can see into them from inside and step directly out into the light, leaning in the doorway of the building…"

Two other books, *Home by Design*, by Sarah Susanka, and *Patterns of Home*, by Max Jacobson, Murray Silverstein, and Barbara Winslow, focus on the patterns that make a house a home without excess square footage. Susanka's pattern "Shelter around Activity" lays out how to get the most from a modest space:

> "Creating a sense of shelter around each activity area can make a space seem much larger than it actually is, because our eyes and senses perceive multiple defined spaces and we assume there must be more floor area there as a result. This principle is one of the keys to doing more with less."

Full of photographs, floor plans, and diagrams, these books will inspire you to change the way you think about your home.

With sheltering walls on two sides, this dining room is open to the kitchen through a wide archway and a patio through French doors.

CRAFTING A SUCCESSFUL KITCHEN-FAMILY ROOM RELATIONSHIP

Many older homes were designed for the lifestyles of a previous era, when wives stayed home all day doing housework and preparing food. Kitchens in these homes are often isolated from the main living spaces; they accommodate only one cook, and they lack space for the appliances we've come to expect. But many contemporary families—in which parents and children are away from the house all day—crave the comfort of preparing food together at the end of the day. In more modern houses, the kitchen has expanded into one big "great room" to accommodate dining, socializing, and food preparation. Unfortunately, the competing needs of the various spaces often make such great rooms chaotic.

While neither isolated kitchens nor open great rooms work very well, partial openness can be the key. Raised countertops screen the kitchen mess from view and provide an informal eating bar. Regular-height counters and islands define spaces and double the workspace because helpers can work from both sides. Upper cabinets add an extra layer of separation—but remember to hang them high enough to see underneath. Built-in eating spaces between the kitchen and family room strengthen both rooms by preserving each one's independence while linking it with an eating space. For more on the special role of kitchens, see chapter 11.

Change Interior Walls and Traffic Patterns for Shelter and Openness

A closed room can feel oppressive and cut off from social contact, but a room that is too open can feel uncomfortable if people, noise, and clutter from other rooms intrude. To be most comfortable, social spaces need a balance between the openness that facilitates interpersonal contact and the separation that allows conversations and activities to flow uninterrupted.

As you consider how you might change your interior walls, remember that rooms and activity centers need spatial differentiation. Changes in ceiling height, lowered beams, columns, built-in furniture, or even changes in flooring can signal the end of one room and the beginning of the next. Rooms that are sheltered on three sides, with circulation or openness on the fourth side, provide both the sense of refuge and the outward view that we all crave. At a minimum, each activity center should be protected by walls, built-ins, or furniture on two sides.

Bits of recycled glass, abalone shell, pottery, stones, and jewelry, pressed into the grout, add a playful element to a pantry floor.

Up into the Attic

In homes and garages without roof trusses, an attic may be the perfect place for more private uses, such as an office, a guest bedroom, a master suite, or a meditation room. The sloped ceilings can provide a sheltered, comforting feeling—as long as they are well lighted and well insulated. Dormers can enlarge your attic further by extending the area that has standing room. If you're finishing out your attic, you'll face these common design challenges:

- **Access.** Do you have an existing stair, or is there room for a stair or ladder? A full stairway may be legally required for a bedroom; check with your local building department. Stairs gobble up space but can often be accommodated by giving up a closet or one side of a larger room.

- **Insulation and moisture control.** Expanding into your attic will change the boundary of your thermal envelope (see chapter 7, page 108). Insulate knee walls (the short walls at the outer edge of an attic) to the same level as your exterior walls. You'll want to insulate the roof, too, but rafters are usually too shallow for adequate roof insulation (see figure 4). If so, you might want to extend the rafters and install rigid insulation, or use a blown-in foam insulation to eliminate the need for roof ventilation. If you are creating a living space in your garage attic, protect your indoor air quality by air-sealing completely between the new space and the garage.

A change in flooring and an archway accentuate the transition between rooms.

- **Structure.** Ceiling joists with long spans may need to be reinforced to support the added floor loads of people and furniture. Roof framing may need to be reinforced to support dormers. Consult with an architect or a structural engineer to evaluate your current structure.

This attic has been transformed into a cozy, private master suite.

RIGID INSULATION BELOW RAFTERS

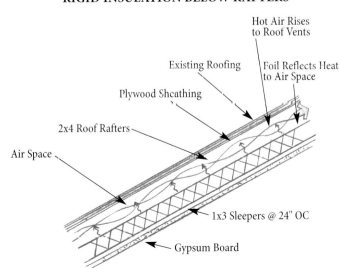

Hot Air Rises to Roof Vents

Existing Roofing

Foil Reflects Heat to Air Space

Plywood Sheathing

2x4 Roof Rafters

Air Space

1x3 Sleepers @ 24" OC

Gypsum Board

Figure 4

Skylights bring light into a dark attic.

- **Light.** Lighting your attic may be as simple as adding windows at gable ends or building dormers. Skylights may be appropriate.

Down into the Basement

Turning a basement into living space presents special challenges because its masonry or concrete walls and slabs are in direct contact with soil. The ceiling may also be too low; most building codes require at least 7 feet for legal habitable space. Before you expand into your basement, you will also want to check for radon gas in the soil and take mitigation measures if it is present.

- **Insulation and moisture control.** It's always better to block groundwater before it gets to the basement walls. Nevertheless, you should select basement interior finishes with moisture in mind. Even with the best efforts, some moisture may migrate into the basement through the footing, walls, and slab, and water is likely to condense on the cool wall and floor surfaces—especially in climates with humid summers. Unless your basement walls are insulated on the exterior, you'll need interior insulation to minimize condensation and heat loss. See chapter 7 for tips on insulating your basement.

- **Indoor air quality.** Basements often house combustion appliances, such as furnaces, water heaters, or clothes dryers. If you are extending your living space into your basement, make sure these appliances have sufficient combustion air and are properly vented to the exterior. Basements often have limited ventilation from windows and are cut off from the house's heating and cooling systems, so extend your ventilation and heating system into your basement.

Entering through a gate into a fenced yard heightens the sense of arrival.

Outdoor Rooms: Porches, Patios, and Gardens

Outdoor rooms are the best way to add seasonal living space without the high cost of weatherproof, insulated construction. They can also be coupled with new windows and doors to add visual space to existing interior rooms. A gated entry courtyard, trellis, or porch can add gracious, welcoming charm to a plain house by making an arrival feel like a journey through many well-crafted spaces.

In mild climates, such as in northern California, decks and patios are usable spaces most of the year.

Additions: Out and Up

You've analyzed how you use your home, cleaned up and organized, considered how your existing rooms could be reconfigured, and looked to your attic, basement, and the outdoors. But what if you still need a little more space? Before you add a whole new room, consider what adding just a few feet to an existing room could do for you. If your upper story is nestled under the roof, dormers can add ceiling height for expanded living space as well as light and ventilation from new windows. A cantilevered pop-out bay with built-in seating can expand a dining, living, or

A good addition doesn't keep sunlight from reaching existing windows, and it can help define new outdoor spaces.

family room by eliminating the need for a sofa or chairs without the cost of foundation work (see figure 5).

If you decide to add more space, don't forget to improve the comfort, functionality, and energy efficiency of your whole house at the same time. For example, consider reinsulating your existing house when the new addition is being finished and insulated.

Going Out

If you are extending your house outward, be careful that your addition doesn't shade other rooms or block their sunlight. Additions that are narrower than the existing house are generally better because they don't cover all the existing windows (leaving interior rooms dark), and their narrower roofs integrate more easily into the main roof. They also help define "positive" outdoor space that creates a welcoming microclimate (see chapter 6).

Sunrooms are a special type of addition that can improve your passive-solar heating while adding floor space. In cold climates, design the sunroom to be sealed off from the house at night to minimize heat loss through all that glass. Avoid overheating by including adequate thermal mass and summer shading (see chapter 3).

POPPING OUT A BAY

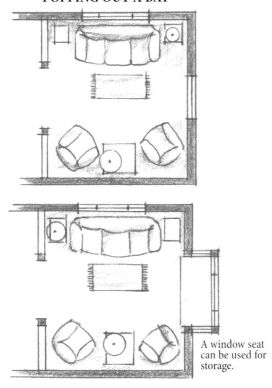

A window seat can be used for storage.

Figure 5

Going Up

Adding another story is usually more expensive than building out because old foundations are rarely adequate for the additional loads. If you build up, you may want to build during the driest time of the year and plan for weatherproofing during construction. As with attic remodeling, adding an upper story requires finding a good location for a stairway and changing your thermal boundary. Insulate carefully at the floor rim joist, and plan for both good insulation and good ventilation in your new roof.

Looking Good

Driving through old neighborhoods, you've probably noticed homes that have been "remuddled" with additions that don't match the original house, often destroying its charm. If you add to your house, carefully integrate new rooflines into the existing roof and match details such as overhangs, roof pitches, window patterns, and trim. The best additions look like they've been there all along. If your house is plain, an addition can give it interest and detail, but be sure to carry those new details into the existing house for an integrated appearance.

After: Cream-colored paint keeps the brick cool by reflecting the sun's rays while visually tying the original first floor to the second-story addition above.

During construction: A lot can be done to transform a brick house, but it's important that the redesign incorporate the look of the original materials.

176

Less Is More

In this era of rampant consumption, it's easy to think that a big house is synonymous with the good life. Even many new "green" homes are oversized for the families and activities they contain. The real measure of a home is how well it shelters and sustains you, connecting you with the larger web of life. Remodeling needn't be about more square footage, but it can be about creating a paradise for yourself and your loved ones. Value quality over quantity, comfort over volume, elegant functionality over impersonal square footage, and a relationship with the sun, wind, and web of life over isolation. When you pause to tune in to your body, your soul, and your true sources of sustenance, it's much easier to know the difference between too much and just right.

Heating and Cooling

If you've air-sealed and insulated your existing home, it's likely that you've reduced the heating and cooling loads enough that your existing HVAC system can serve your well-insulated new space. Before deciding to replace any equipment, get a "load calculation" that takes into account your air sealing and insulation upgrades. If you do need additional heating or cooling, it may be less expensive to install a separate system in the addition, such as a direct-vent gas or electric wall heater (with a programmable thermostat, of course). You can also consider heating the addition with a hydronic system that runs off your existing water heater (see figure 6).

USING A WATER HEATER FOR SPACE AND WATER HEATING

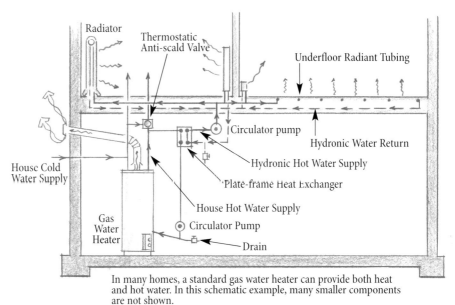

In many homes, a standard gas water heater can provide both heat and hot water. In this schematic example, many smaller components are not shown.

Figure 6

177

Decisions that you make in planning your addition can have a huge impact on construction waste. In residential construction, 6 to 8 percent of the total weight of building materials delivered to the site typically ends up as waste[1]. About 12 percent of the drywall used in new construction ends up as scrap[2]. When construction waste leaves your building site, you've paid for the material three times: once at purchase (material cost), once when it's moved around (labor cost), and once when it's disposed of (dumpster, hauling, and dump fees). You can avoid creating much of this construction waste with good design. A few simple guidelines can reduce waste and save money on labor.

Two Feet

Most building materials come in 2-foot modules: a 4-foot by 8-foot piece of wheatboard, plywood, or sheetrock; dimensional lumber in 2-foot increments; tile sized to fit a 2-foot module. Every time you can avoid sawing, trimming, or shaping a building material, you'll reduce waste.

Fabulous Framing

Back in the day of never-ending forests and inexpensive lumber, three-stud corners, solid 4x12 headers, and double top plates were just dandy. But now, with shrinking mature forests and sky-high lumber prices, *optimum value-engineered framing* methods can help you use less wood and save money on labor. These techniques include the following (see figure 7):

• Spacing wall studs on 2-foot centers

• Aligning rafters with wall studs

• Building two-stud corners (which also allow for more insulation in exterior walls)

• Sizing headers for actual conditions (a 3-foot opening might only need a 4x4 header)—or better yet, using insulated headers

If you're adding to your home, consider using a slab-on-grade floor; it eliminates the need for wood floor framing, and it provides thermal mass (see page 54). Prefabricated roof trusses are another way to use less wood; now available in a wide range of designs, they can eliminate up to 26 per cent of the wood typically used in roof framing, and they usually provide more space for insulation in cathedral ceilings, boosting your energy efficiency (see figure 8).

FRAMING TECHNIQUES

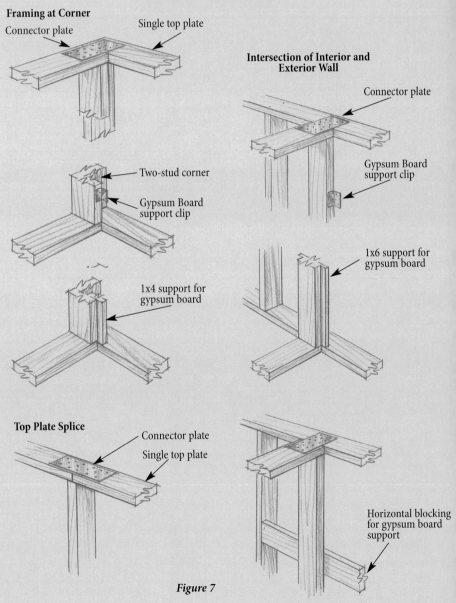

Framing at Corner
Connector plate
Single top plate

Intersection of Interior and Exterior Wall
Connector plate
Gypsum Board support clip

Two-stud corner
Gypsum Board support clip

1x6 support for gypsum board

1x4 support for gypsum board

Top Plate Splice
Connector plate
Single top plate

Horizontal blocking for gypsum board support

Figure 7

Stick Framing

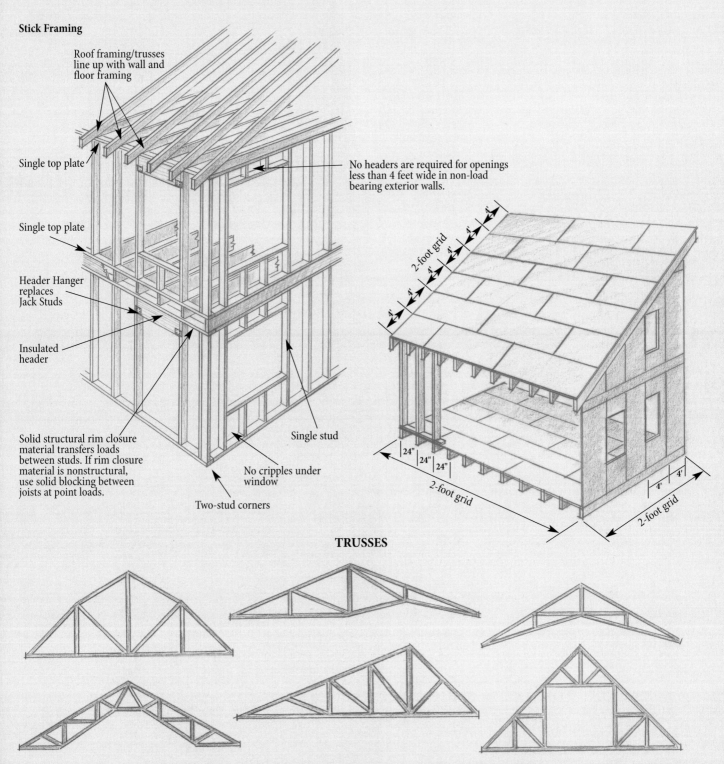

Roof framing/trusses line up with wall and floor framing

Single top plate

Single top plate

Header Hanger replaces Jack Studs

Insulated header

Solid structural rim closure material transfers loads between studs. If rim closure material is nonstructural, use solid blocking between joists at point loads.

Two-stud corners

No cripples under window

Single stud

No headers are required for openings less than 4 feet wide in non-load bearing exterior walls.

2-foot grid

4' 4' 4'

4'

24" 24" 24"

2-foot grid

4' 4'

2-foot grid

TRUSSES

Trusses are economical to build and install, and can accommodate almost any roof form.

Figure 8

179

Katzmann Residence
Ithaca, New York

Brent and Diana's remodeled home has become a life-size portfolio of natural design options.

Brent and Diana Katzmann's conversion to green living started with family camping trips. "We suddenly became more aware of nature and of how little we really need," says Diana. "We began to learn about the impact of household cleansers and stains and finishes on the environment—and on our kids!"

Numerous challenges awaited the Katzmanns: weathered siding, an uninviting entry, an awkward floor plan, a mildewed basement, and noise pollution.

Around the same time, decades in corporate careers had them feeling out of touch with their core values and motivations. They decided to make several changes at once. They quit their jobs, moved from Chicago, Illinois, to Ithaca, New York, to be near family, and wrote a business plan that drew on their beliefs and earlier training: a home design and consulting firm, specializing in green building. And what better way to launch their business than by remodeling their new home, essentially creating a life-size portfolio?

The Katzmanns found a plain ranch house on 10 acres, built in the late 1970s. It was in pretty good condition and had some auspicious features: a wonderful open plan, lots of natural light, hydronic baseboard heating, good insulation, east and south exposures, a beautiful pond for swimming and fishing, a two-car garage to the north (protecting the house from cold north winds and snow), and Ithaca's Eco-Village next door.

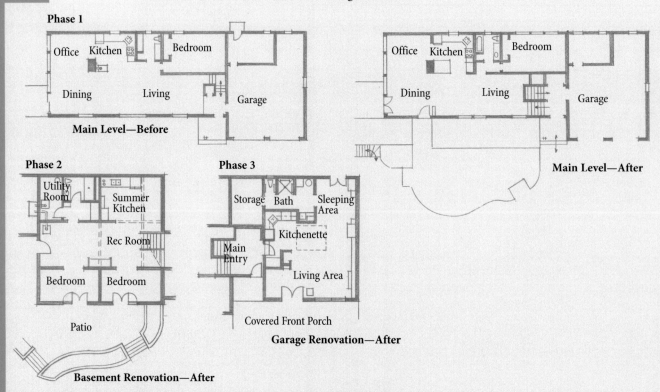

Phase 1

Office | Kitchen | Bedroom
Dining | Living | Garage

Main Level—Before

Office | Kitchen | Bedroom
Dining | Living | Garage

Main Level—After

Phase 2

Utility Room | Summer Kitchen
Rec Room
Bedroom | Bedroom
Patio

Basement Renovation—After

Phase 3

Storage | Bath | Sleeping Area
Kitchenette
Main Entry
Living Area
Covered Front Porch

Garage Renovation—After

The addition of an interior stairway made the newly expanded and refurbished basement rooms part of the main house for the first time.

Nevertheless, the house needed their help. The downstairs was a dark, mildewed rental apartment. The entry was uninviting. The layout of the main level was awkward, with only one bedroom. And there was a major state highway with noisy traffic about 50 feet away.

The Katzmanns wasted no time. They moved into the house in July 2001 and began reconstruction two months later. Acting as owner-contractors, they brought in local craftspeople as needed and helped with the physical labor when they could.

Going Below

The greatest challenge was the downstairs apartment, so Brent and Diana attacked it first. A suspended ceiling had become home to an array of critters. It was a haven for moisture and mold, with its uninsulated concrete slab and subterranean cinderblock walls. To make a bad situation worse, there was little daylight down there, and the interior finish materials were either impervious (a plastic vapor barrier, rigid foam insulation, and fake wood paneling on the inside of the block walls, keeping moisture from escaping) or moisture loving (wood furring strips on the walls, gypsum board, and pressboard that held moisture and encouraged mold growth).

They began by gutting the apartment, removing all the finish materials and kitchen cabinets, and cleaning up the mold. To avoid future moisture problems, they installed gutters on the roof above, caulked every place where the slab and wall intersected, and added window wells to the west side of the basement, enabling them to improve drainage by sloping the ground surface away from the house.

Then they extended the lower level to accommodate two new bedrooms and reconfigured the existing space into a family room, craft kitchen, bathroom, and laundry area. Next, they opened a stairwell between the upper and lower level, uniting them as one house for the first time.

Brent and Diana also brought sunlight and ventilation to the bedroom addition via French doors that open onto a new stone patio and gardens overlooking the pond. The walls of the downstairs addition are poured-in-place concrete for thermal mass, the new slab floor incorporates hydronic radiant heating, and it's topped with a living roof.

Because Brent, Diana, their son, and Brent's parents were all camping out upstairs, the next priority was to finish the downstairs rooms. They moved a wood stove from the kitchen, where it had felt in the way, down to the new family room. Now it augments the radiant heat downstairs, and its warmed air rises through the new stairwell and a floor grate to heat the upstairs.

The new downstairs bathroom was designed to control mold growth via natural light, ventilation, and clever material choices.

They avoided choosing new materials that would trap moisture, preferring to allow transpiration. In the bathroom, they used unglazed clay tile, which they treated with linseed oil and beeswax. The shower wall is glass block to admit light and avoid the need for a moisture-trapping shower curtain; the ceiling is T&G cedar, which is mildew-resistant and "adds a nice aroma." They left the new concrete walls unfinished, enjoying the wood-grain pattern from the form boards. Other walls received clay paint to help modulate moisture and zero-VOC paint, using sponging and glazing techniques.

The French doors admit sunlight, while the concrete walls and earth berm block highway noise.

"We sleep really peacefully there," says Diana. "The concrete walls and the garden roof block the highway noise. It's like a sanctuary."

Tweaking an Open Plan

Once they could sleep downstairs, the family began to improve the main floor. "While we liked the airiness, the disadvantage of an open plan is that it's more difficult to define space," observes Brent. "I think some of the greatest work we've done here is to make this entry and the main living space function well; we added visual cues about where one area begins and another ends."

They started with the entry. "The whole entry was really distressing before we worked on it," Brent says. "From outside, it was out of scale and uninviting. Inside, it was a strange, small, confining entry into a chaotic space. You entered halfway between the two floor levels, but all you could do was go up." Brent and Diana reconfigured the entryway, adding a coat closet, a flight of stairs to the lower level, and an entry to the adjacent garage (soon to become an apartment for Brent's parents).

Brent and Diana removed cabinets from the basement apartment, then reused them upstairs to create a kitchen peninsula.

The countertop is FSC-certified birch plywood, finished with casein paint and waxed; the playful "river of stones" delights guests and continues to grow via stone gifts.

Sliding windows now open to allow the Katzmanns to pick herbs and strawberries from the "green roof" of the downstairs addition.

Upstairs, they added "small suggestions of walls" to better define the space, painting them in contrasting tones to create visual boundaries without interrupting the open plan. Where the bathroom opened directly onto the living room, they lengthened a wall and created a short hallway. They'd found the kitchen layout awkward, too, so they expanded the kitchen and created a peninsula, using cabinets taken out of the former downstairs kitchen.

To improve energy efficiency, they replaced the floor-to-ceiling windows with new double-pane sliding windows. These now open onto the garden roof below, allowing them to easily pick the herbs and strawberries growing there.

The original garage became a wheelchair-accessible in-law apartment, complete with a trellised front porch and a well-integrated ramp.

Extended Family

Brent and Diana spent ten months working on the main house, then turned their attention to converting the garage into an ADA-compliant, 720-square-foot in-law suite for Brent's parents. Because the existing roof trusses spanned the whole space, they were able to develop an open plan, minimizing partition walls. At the center of the space, they created a cupola with clerestory windows to bring in light and aid natural ventilation. To allow for superinsulation, they added a second stud wall inside the existing 2x4s and packed the spaces with cotton batt insulation. The R-35 walls now aid thermal comfort and minimize noise from the highway. The roof was insulated with blown-in cellulose.

The cupola not only adds visual charm, but also provides natural light and ventilation.

In hot weather, a ceiling fan helps pull warm air up and out through the cupola.

To upgrade the garage floor, they laid a layer of blueboard (rigid foam insulation) on the existing slab, then a layer of sand, radiant heating tubes, and finally a soil-cement layer using clay-rich soil that had been excavated for the bedroom addition (cutting cement use by over two-thirds, compared with a standard slab). The slab was colored with powdered earth pigments and finished with linseed oil, tung oil, carnauba wax, and larch resin. Expansion joints are freehand-cut reused studs.

Finishing Touches

With all the spaces livable, the Katzmanns focused on the exterior finishes. They removed and recycled the uninteresting aluminum siding, replacing it with local white pine Adirondack-style siding with mitered joints. A stain of sunflower and thistle oils (from OSMO in Germany) adds the final natural touch.

The asphalt shingle roof was covered with galvalume-finished steel roofing to allow future rainwater collection. A new entry porch roof is held up with local, hand-peeled, oiled red pine posts. Above the in-law apartment's porch, a trellis made from local hemlock will soon sport grapevines.

Outside the new French doors on the lower level, Brent and Diana laid a flagstone patio and stone garden retaining walls. They took a weekend course at Cornell on dry-stacked stone building, so they were able to help a hired local mason by doing much of the physical labor themselves.

The final major project was back indoors: they built a small kitchen on the lower level, which came in handy for mixing natural paints and experimental finishes. In the future, it will serve as a canning and crafts kitchen. They found a reclaimed restaurant sink and a small cooktop where they can make their morning tea, to be enjoyed on the flagstone patio just outside.

The new entry is much more welcoming; its boldness comes from posts of local red pine, hand-peeled and oiled to carry through the Adirondack look of the siding.

Local white pine with the bark attached adds an organic touch to the lap siding.

Red pine posts support the trellis at the front of the converted-garage apartment.

Together with a local mason, Brent and Diana were able to do much of the labor involved in laying their dry-stacked stone walls.

A Work in Progress

The Katzmanns still have a few projects to complete. For one, the new concrete walls downstairs aren't insulated; the original design was for interior insulation, but they found that they liked the wood grain left behind on the inside surface—and they now better understand the utility of interior thermal mass—so they're considering which type of exterior rigid insulation and plaster to add.

They also plan to tweak the natural heating and cooling upstairs. Off the kitchen is a sunspace that was added by previous owners, which now serves as Brent and Diana's office. Lacking thermal mass and adequate shading, it tends to overheat. They've planted trees on the west side and have added solar shades to the windows for summer. They plan to introduce thermal mass in the form of thick wall plaster and perhaps some mass in the floor, and install an insulated whole-house fan to pull up cooler replacement air from the lower level.

A small kitchen downstairs employs a reclaimed restaurant sink and a small cooktop for canning projects and morning tea.

Dry-stacked retaining walls are durable and yet allow moisture to pass through.

185

The trim is made from locally harvested hardwoods, much of it from trees that fell naturally.

Delightful details like this cedar tree (found standing dead, and wirebrushed prior to installation) make the in-law suite come alive.

Looking Back

Reflecting on their remodeling project, Diana says, "We had a vision of what this home could become, and it's really rewarding to see it actually done—to see spaces work better. And the house smells clean now. It feels good to have cleaned up that mold problem and to be surrounded by healthy materials."

Brent found it very satisfying to work with natural finish materials. "The process of mixing and applying plasters and soil-cement and natural paints and stains is a tactile, sensual experience. It's a great olfactory experience, too, which isn't true of conventional materials with all their VOCs. And it's been really encouraging that others have reacted so positively to our handiwork."

Diana also enjoyed working with salvaged materials. "Allowing the materials to be what they are is an important aspect of using reclaimed materials," she says. "If there's a little ding in the sink, it's okay; it's *wabi-sabi* (see page 212). The same goes for reused woods; weathered barn siding can look gorgeous as trim."

Would they do anything differently if they could? "This house, candidly, is probably too big," offers Brent. "The main house has about 2,200 square feet of living space for three of us, which we've begun to recognize as grotesquely more than anybody should really need. Our next house is going to be much smaller."

A wall sconce fashioned from an old air register.

Moving Ahead

And how are the Katzmanns doing with their new business? Balance Studio is off and running, specializing in "design, collaboration, and sustainability." Potential clients come to the house to see their natural finishes and be inspired about the possibilities for their own home. "Our house has become a three-dimensional portfolio," says Diana.

Through this project, they've also come to know several like-minded tradespeople, with whom they've founded the Ithaca Green Building Alliance. The group's mission is to educate people about sustainable ways to build and remodel. Recently, the Alliance held a local Green Building Fair, and they've offered a seminar series on environmentally responsible design and construction.

Balance Studio is now involved with several sustainable building projects, including interior design for a straw bale house, design and construction management for an earth-sheltered timber-frame home, and restoration of a barn that will be a natural candle shop.

And at the end of the day, "I love coming home to this house," glows Brent. "It's very inviting now; I feel fortunate to live here."

Small flagstones and pebbles mimic the flow of water in a stream.

The Katzmanns' Top Five Suggestions For Remodeling in a Cold, Wet Climate

1. Insulate—"above and beyond what's required."

2. Manage moisture. "Handle all the water and moisture issues from the get-go."

3. Bring in natural light and ventilation. "They're underutilized in this climate by most builders."

4. Use local materials. "The northeast is rich in natural materials—clay, stone, and wood. The forests here have regenerated, so there's quite a bit of second-growth plantation pine and black locust, which is a great rot-resistant wood. So there's no need to buy foreign or even nonnortheastern wood."

5. Be aware of the toxicity of all the materials that come into the house. "You'll be sealed up indoors with them all winter. We don't usually use wallpaper, carpeting, or conventional paints and cabinets. We prefer to incorporate many reclaimed materials—tested and treated for lead, of course."

Integrated Design of Special Rooms

A tiny change today brings us a dramatically different tomorrow.

—Richard Bach

THE KITCHEN, THE BATH-
ROOM, and the bedroom all
provide rich opportunities to
deepen your relationship with
nature. How you design these
areas can play a big role in your
health and in your attitude
toward yourself, others, and life in
general. In the kitchen and the
bathroom, you can indulge your
senses while using the resources
of water and energy appropriately.
And what better place than the
bedroom to restore your own personal energy resources? Let's take
a closer look at how you can
transform each of these areas of
your home.

The Global Kitchen

The kitchen is widely regarded as the heart of the home, and its nurturing qualities can emanate throughout the house. But this is also where many households consume the most energy, release the most airborne toxins, and produce the most noise via kitchen appliances. Furthermore, your choices here affect everything from your family's health to global warming. Nowhere does "think globally, act locally" apply more.

It's About the Food

The defining characteristic of an ecological kitchen isn't energy-efficient appliances or recycled-content countertops (though those are good, too). Kitchens are about food. And food is about many things we sometimes forget: plants, soil, rain, pollinators, farmers, weather, and seasons. Unfortunately, in this era of industrialized agriculture, it's also about genetic engineering, monocrops, pesticides, soil destruction, lowered water tables, nutrient loss, and the combustion of vast quantities of fossil fuels to chill, process, package, and ship food around the globe.

So the most important, far-reaching thing you can do to "remodel" your kitchen ecologically is *pay attention to the source of your food*. Look for local, organically grown food. With that simple act, you can support family farms, reduce the pesticide load, decrease fuel use (and thereby global warming), minimize packaging waste, and improve your health. Better yet, grow your own food. When you experience the connection between

Kitchens are all about food. Let all of your choices support the enjoyment of fresh, local fare.

Warm colors, plenty of sunlight, good storage and work surfaces, and a door to the garden make for a happy, healthy kitchen.

healthy soil and thriving plants, the relationship between freshness and flavor, the oneness of healthy food and happy people, and the satisfaction of nourishing your garden with composted food scraps, you will have learned some of the most important lessons about ecology.

If you plan to redesign your kitchen, think of ways to enhance its connection with the act of growing food. If your kitchen lacks a door that opens onto your garden, consider adding that

Hanging herbs and flowers to dry in the kitchen keeps us beautifully aware of food cycles.

In this house, the kitchen window opens directly out onto the green roof planted with herbs and strawberries.

important link. If you have no yard, or none that will support food growing, you can grow herbs on a windowsill. Cutting fresh herbs and dropping them into the pot brings a joy and vitality that can't be matched by opening a spice jar. If you don't have a window in your kitchen, consider adding one—or plant those herbs nearby and hang them to dry in the kitchen. At the very least, you can hang pictures of gardens and vegetables on your kitchen walls to keep alive a mental connection with your food sources.

Such a wholesome relationship with food has other design implications. For example, if you have even a tiny garden, you'll want a place to save food scraps for composting. A pullout bin below the main cutting surface is useful.

Another great idea is to create a space that acts as a natural cooler for grains and produce. This space should be kept cool,

but not as cold as a refrigerator. Such a cooler can be as small as a cupboard or as large as a small room. The essential features are screened vents (operable, if necessary) high and low on a shaded outside wall, slatted shelves for air circulation, and insulation on any sides exposed to sunlight or heat. Having a natural cooler may mean that you will need only a small refrigerator, which saves both space and energy.

Who's in the Kitchen?

Let's not forget the other living element in the kitchen: the cook. In many traditions, it is believed that the cook's mood profoundly affects the food; meals prepared with love will be nurturing and healthful, while food cooked with tension can leave people unsatisfied and out of sorts. With this in mind, let the kitchen be a place of peace, happiness, and love. A convenient layout helps—neither cramped nor inconveniently large.

Consider kitchen ergonomics: appropriate counter heights and resilient flooring help keep the cook physically flexible.

A pleasant, functional kitchen helps make a happy cook, so pay attention to both layout and delight.

Before remodeling, this kitchen had one small window over the sink, flanked by upper cabinets; now it feels like cooking in the garden.

Fluorescent task lighting directly on the work surface helps improve a kitchen's energy efficiency.

Store tools where they are needed and minimize annoying clutter. Appliance noise can fray the cook's nerves, so ask yourself whether you really need all those electrical tools; many cooks find more pleasure in using a cleaver than a food processor. Finally, a resilient floor surface and counters set at different heights for different tasks will keep the cook's limbs and spine supple.

Supporting Players

With the heart of the kitchen in place, the physical components should further enhance global and personal health. Here are some things to keep in mind:

Energy

- Let the sun light your kitchen, but avoid glare and overheating from south or west sun (see chapter 3).

- Choose pleasant, energy-efficient electrical lighting (warm-colored electronic-ballast fluorescents, halogen lights, or incandescent fixtures with dimmers); place fixtures directly above the main food-preparation areas; provide separate switches so that you don't have to turn on all the kitchen lights at once.

- Use energy-efficient appliances (and only the ones you really need); clean and service them regularly.

- Don't overcook food; when possible, bake several dishes in the oven at once to conserve energy.

- Cook outdoors in summer to lessen the cooling load on the house.

- Use a solar cooker; it keeps your house cooler in summer and it's perfect for slow-cooked dishes.

Energy-efficient appliances will pay you back for years to come.

Water

- Filter tap water if necessary.

- Conserve water, use a low-flow faucet, and don't heat more water than needed.

- Reuse water—install a greywater system (see chapter 5).

- Use copper or PEX pipes; avoid PVC pipes and lead-containing solder.

- Use an energy-efficient, water-efficient dishwasher, or hand-wash dishes with modest amounts of water.

- If it takes a long time for hot water to reach your kitchen tap, consider installing a hot water circulation system.

Materials

- Cabinets: instead of replacing, consider reusing old ones, resurfacing or replacing doors, or using new ones of solid sustainable wood, metal, or least-toxic board products; seal existing toxic cabinets with a water-based sealer; avoid vinyl doors.

- Countertops: consider salvaged or recycled-content materials.

- Floors: use natural linoleum, tile (with resilient mats where the cook stands), wood, or sealed cork; avoid vinyl.

Wood cabinets sealed with natural oils or water-based sealers bring a warm glow to a kitchen.

Cork flooring is a good choice for kitchens; it's warm and resilient, and it comes from a sustainable biosource.

Air Quality

- Provide good ventilation, especially over gas stoves (a range fan vented to the outdoors, operable windows).

- Use low-toxic cleaning supplies.

Waste

- Have composting and recycling centers in or near the kitchen.

- Buy good-quality appliances that last longer; repair rather than discard.

Keep in mind that the most important aspect of the ecological kitchen is life itself. If your kitchen increases vitality, supports the natural world, and promotes awareness of the web of life, it is a natural kitchen.

A couple once approached me for help in remodeling the dark, cramped kitchen of their charming 1920s bungalow. The appliances, cabinets, and finishes were all dilapidated, and the areas near the kitchen were chopped up into a hall-way, a mudroom, and an undefined wood stove-and-storage area. What they want-ed was a place of sensuous eco-healthy delights.

At one end of the kitchen, we created a plastered inglenook.

The working end of the kitchen is now warm and bright, while the cabinet fronts reflect the owners' whimsical penchant for soft angles.

We began by opening up the space, turning it into one big live-in kitchen. We added larger, double-pane wood windows, a skylight, and a pair of French doors that opened onto a new deck and the kitchen garden beyond. While all this glass might have led to overheating in other locations, the tall surround-ing trees filter the sunlight and keep the space comfortable. We also insulated the roof, walls, and floor to increase comfort and lower heating bills, using four spaced layers of foil-faced bubble-pack insulation, chosen for its low tox-icity and ease of application.

We transformed the no-man's-land at one end of the kitchen into a cozy Southwest-style inglenook with a built-in fireplace and plastered benches. Because the house is small, this area has become a place to rest, to read, to play the guitar, to socialize, or to warm up on a cold day.

The owners wanted the walls to look like the inside of a seashell, so we used three coats of gyp-sum plaster with a mineral pigment in the finish coat. It has since become one of their favorite features of the kitchen. When the sun shines in, the walls have a warm, sensuous glow.

Wanting to avoid rectilinear kitchen cabinet fronts, one of the owners found a cabinetmaker through a local Waldorf school who was happy to help. The cabinets' unique, sculptural look—and the fact that they're made of solid, sal-vaged wood—draws rave reviews from visitors.

To store grains and fresh produce, we carved a "cool room" out of the north corner of the kitchen. With insulation all around, screened vents high and low on a shady outside wall, and slatted shelves for airflow, it stays cooler than the rest of the house without using fuel energy.

A look at the kitchen before remodeling.

We brought in extra sunlight, and used natural plaster, solid wood cabinetry, and arches to create a sensuous place to cook.

193

A bathroom needn't be cramped and cold; let your body temple be as sensuous as you want.

The Bathroom as Body Temple

The bathroom is just as important to creating a harmonious home. It involves major water use, energy use (heating, lighting, and ventilation), and disposal of bodily wastes. It also reflects and influences how we feel about our bodies. Yet bathrooms tend to be tucked out of sight and are often cramped and utilitarian.

If the goal of ecological building is to increase our active respect for all of life, and because our own bodies are our nearest and dearest portals to understanding the nature of life, shouldn't the bathroom—where our bodies commune with the elements—be one of the most important rooms in a natural home?

In the bathroom you have an unparalleled opportunity to grasp the dance of life, in your mind and in every cell of your body. What a great place to practice weaving together the sensual and the sensible! Your sensory experience there is just as important as the mechanics of a healthful, resource-conserving bathroom.

When your bathroom experience is nurturing and comforting, you feel good about life from the inside out. When your bath water nourishes your garden, you feel more involved with the cycles of life. And when your use of water, heat, light, and materials is respectful of natural systems, you can relax deeply, knowing that your pleasure is not gained at the expense of the biosphere.

In the Flow

Bathrooms are all about water—water to wash your face, brush your teeth, bathe your body; water to drink, and then to pass into the toilet where more water flushes it away; water condensing on walls and tiles; and water running down the drain.

When we bathe, we relax, we touch ourselves, we cleanse our bodies, and we wash away our cares. In the shower, the pressure of the spray invigorates us. In the tub, the womblike water relaxes taut muscles and calms the mind. We are reborn from the waters of life.

You will feel especially good if you also know that the water you're using isn't depleting precious reserves. You can reduce your water usage by installing flow restrictors or low-flow faucets. You can also reuse your bathing water by piping it to the toilet tank for flushing, to the washing machine for its first cycle, or into the garden. And for truly wonderful bathing, collect rainwater, filter it, and siphon it into your bathtub or run it into a holding tank for your shower. While you're at it, don't squander fossil fuels to warm your bathing water; use an energy-efficient water heater—even the sun, wherever possible.

There's an unseen health issue in the bathing area, too: you can absorb radon, chlorine, or volatile organic compounds (VOCs) from the water through your skin and lungs. Have your water tested; you may want to filter it at the faucet or showerhead, or even for the whole house.

Finally, don't let all that moisture hang around. Minimize mold growth via sunlight, ventilation, and moderate air temperatures. An operable window is the best way to let in sunlight and fresh air, but every bathroom should also have a quiet, energy-efficient extraction fan controlled by a timer or humidistat.

Sunlight and fresh air in bathrooms are a natural way to discourage mold growth.

You can really enjoy your bath if you know that you've collected your bathwater as rainfall, or if it will later water your fruit trees.

The Throne of Presence

There is a story about a man who made a special trip to a Zen monastery to see a famous painting. Upon his arrival, however, he was told the painting was not available for viewing. While he was there, he needed to visit the toilet room. As he squatted over the pit toilet, he looked up to find himself gazing at the very painting he had traveled to see. It had been thoughtfully placed in the one spot in the monastery where a person would be fully present to appreciate it.

People have some of their most profound insights while seated on the toilet. This is one of the few times when we are absolutely "in the moment"—not distracted by the outside world and completely aware of our thoughts and our own physical presence. In fact, it was while sitting on the privy that Martin Luther developed the ideas that led to the Protestant Reformation.

Artwork, sunlight, a pleasing view, appealing textures, and restful colors can all enhance the toilet visit. Anthony Lawlor, author of *A Home for the Soul*, suggests, "Make a little shelf near the toilet where you can place a picture of a beautiful view, an interesting object, or a poem to contemplate. Change the object you put on this shelf occasionally to reflect the season or your mood."

Meanwhile, back up your sojourn with sound resource use. Minimize the volume of fresh water used for flushing: install a low-volume flush toilet; use rainwater or greywater for flushing; install a tank-lid sink that lets you wash your hands with water before it flushes the toilet; or, best of all, install a composting toilet.

When remodeling or doing new construction, consider separating the toilet from the bathing area. A separate toilet

Having your water tested for radon, chlorine, and VOCs can make your bathing experience healthier.

compartment isolates odors and allows multiple people to use the bathroom with privacy. This, in turn, reduces the number of bathrooms needed, which saves money and resources.

Radiance

The best source of warmth and light is the sun. Bathroom windows needn't mean a loss of privacy; a shoulder-height sill preserves both views and modesty, or big windows can look out onto a protected garden. A wide windowsill allows you to put toothbrushes, sponges, and razor in the sun for natural disinfection by the ultraviolet rays, unimpeded by glass.

For additional warmth, hydronic radiant heat is the most comfortable and energy-efficient type. In new construction, you can install heating tubes in the floor, the wall, or a heated towel rack, and for retrofits there are self-contained units. Hold on to that heat by insulating the bathroom well.

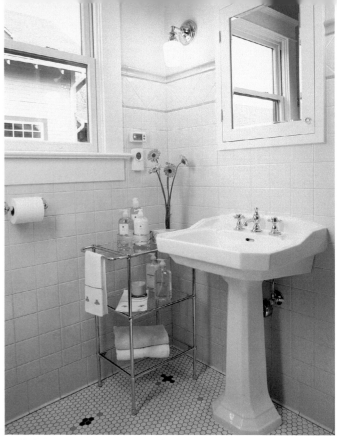

Sunlight brings natural disinfection into a bathroom—and a view of the garden is nice, too.

With good design, bathroom privacy and sunshine needn't be mutually exclusive.

Decor that suggests flowing water or natural scenery can enhance the primal bathroom experience.

Knowing Nature

Lawlor goes on to suggest evoking natural bodies of water by using smooth river stones and seashells at the sink and tub to hold soap, sponges, and grooming tools. "On the walls, hang pictures that honor the grace and beauty of the body. Use photographs and paintings of waterfalls, rivers, and lakes, and water creatures such as fish, dolphins, mermaids, sea horses, and starfish." Consider installing a door from your bathroom into a private garden; there's little as primal as outdoor bathing. You can also water the garden by draining your outdoor tub or shower directly toward thirsty plants.

Creating a bathroom that marries the sensuous and the sensible is a radical act. Whether you add a bathroom or transform an existing one, dedicate it to the truth that caring for ourselves is harmonious with caring for the earth.

A Place to Sleep

Dr. William Dement of the Stanford University Sleep Research Center, and author of *The Promise of Sleep*, says that average Americans now sleep an hour-and-a-half less each night than they did a century ago, at great cost to health and safety.

In the name of productivity, people now treat sleep as a disposable commodity; fewer than 35 percent of American adults regularly get the seven to eight hours of nightly sleep that researchers consider necessary for most people. But rather than increasing productivity, sleep loss lowers it by causing memory loss, increased error rates, slower reflexes, lower motivation, and shorter tempers. Driver fatigue contributes to more than half the vehicle collisions in this country. And Dement points out that sleep deprivation played a role in the grounding of the Exxon Valdez, the 1986 Space Shuttle explosion, and the nuclear incidents at Chernobyl and Three Mile Island.

Chronic sleep loss also affects our health, causing lowered immune function, elevated stress hormone levels, slowed metabolism, and increased risk of high blood pressure, heart disease, certain malignancies, and diabetes. Is all this enough to

The characteristics of the bedroom are a major factor in the quality of our sleep.

convince us that that there's something to the notion of living in harmony with nature?

When we sleep, our brains consolidate the day's experiences into memory while our bodies reenergize our muscles and organs and replace old cells with new ones. Researchers have identified several phases of brain-wave activity during sleep, and we need to experience all of them each night in order to get the full benefits of sleep.

A Sleep Oasis

Our surroundings play a crucial role in the quality of our sleep. We need to create havens that will help us relax and sleep well. Even if you spend enough hours sleeping, a poor environment can contribute to sleep deprivation. In other words, the place where you sleep is a vital element of your health, happiness, and success in your life.

Unfortunately, the bedroom is often the last place we pay attention to when spiffing up our homes. Guests rarely see it and we're unconscious most of the time when we're there, so why should it matter? As a result, the bedroom is often a catchall, serving as TV-viewing room, office, personal library, storage area, dressing room, laundry-staging area, and sickroom. All of these are stimulating distractions that can keep our minds and bodies alert when we need to be letting go of the day's cares.

You can make your bedroom a haven of tranquility.

Fresh air and warm covers on a cool night are a healthy combination for good sleep.

Researchers say we should pay attention to four primary factors in the sleeping environment:

Light

If you can see your hand after the lights are turned out, your bedroom is too light. Streetlights, nightlights, hall lights, clocks, phone dials, baby monitors, and electric blanket controls can produce enough light to disrupt the production of melatonin, the hormone that helps regulate the sleep cycle, causing a state similar to jet lag. Most of these can be moved or covered; if streetlights invade your bedroom, you may need to install light-blocking drapes. Equally important is your light exposure before bedtime; being surrounded by electric light in the evening—even checking e-mail before bed—provides enough light to reset your biological clock and make falling asleep difficult.

Noise

Sudden loud noises can awaken us, and even passing traffic can cause fragmented sleep. Sleeping as far as possible from the street and from noisy equipment and appliances is a good start. While some researchers suggest masking other sounds with a "white noise" generator or a fan, you might prefer something more natural, such as a recirculating fountain with a quiet motor. Insulating your bedroom and replacing single-pane windows with double-pane ones can quiet a room significantly—but only if you keep the windows closed. If you like sleeping with a window open for fresh air, you'll need to address nighttime noise in other ways.

Temperature

Overheating the bedroom in cold weather isn't just a waste of energy; it makes sleep difficult. Air temperature of 65°F has been found ideal for sleep. Keep your body warm with a comforter or blankets that retain your body heat, but not so warm as to induce sweat.

The Bed

Not only should your bed be comfortable, relaxing, and good for your back, it shouldn't expose you to toxic fumes, dust mites, or mold. Such things can wreak havoc with your nights and, consequently, your days. Look for natural bedding—organic cotton, wool, or natural latex—and keep it clean and well-aired.

Completing Your Sleep Experience

Other factors can also support your sleep haven. Soothing colors may relax your body and mind, putting you in the right mood for sleep; many people find lavenders, blues, or light greens appropriate. Minimizing electromagnetic fields near the bed is a good idea, too. Finally, consider removing clutter, visual distractions, stimulating colors, bright lights, and the television from your bedroom; their effects can remain in your mind and body even after the lights are turned out. Above all, pay attention to what works for you; everyone is different.

On the morning side of the equation, being awakened gradually by sunlight is the healthiest way to go. Whether you wake up at dawn or later, the increasing light levels synchronize your circadian rhythms for the day and allow your body to make a

Seeing beautiful things and feeling soothing textures when you awaken can start your day off right.

smooth transition into activity. However, given set work and school schedules, that's not always easy to do—especially in the northern latitudes during the darkness of winter. Even if you can't awaken with morning light year-round, let yourself linger in bed for a moment to ease the transition. Also, pay attention to what surrounds you when you first awaken; feeling sensuous textures and seeing pleasing colors and objects when you open your eyes can go a long way toward starting your day on a good note.

The Soul of Sleep

Amid the technicalities, let's not forget the magical side of sleep. Sleep is our daily portal to the mysteries of dreaming. It's the realm in which we must relinquish our striving, logical minds and surrender our tense, hardworking bodies to an archetypal journey. In our fast-paced culture, we haven't just lost sleep; we've paved over its power to renew our imaginations as well as our bodies.

Creating a haven for sleeping and dreaming honors the mysteries of life. It restores our oneness with our source. It unites us with dreamers throughout time and space in the land of the moon and stars. It brings us home to the deepest levels of our soul. What better place from which to be reborn each day?

The Big and Little Picture

As you can see, each room in your house provides an opportunity to integrate a range of features into a healthy, nurturing experience. While we may split up the topics for the sake of discussion—treating, for example, solar heating, water use, and building materials separately—the real fun of ecological remodeling is weaving them together in one special place. In fact, nature never separates these subjects; it's profoundly good for us to experience their oneness, too.

And don't stop with your kitchen, bathrooms, and sleeping areas. Explore every area of your home in a similarly holistic way. Think about how you want to use each area, considering how you will use it at different times of day and in different seasons. Think about your needs for warmth, coolness, sunlight, fresh air, water, and outdoor connections. Diagram the resources and functions that flow through each space. Think about what your body needs and how it wants to feel there. Ask your soul what it wants. Look for ways to meet multiple needs with simple gestures. Bring your rooms to life.

Natural, nontoxic bedding and finish materials go a long way to support restful sleep.

CHAPTER 12

Choosing Materials Wisely

Not everything that can be counted counts,
and not everything that counts can be counted.
—Albert Einstein

YOUR DREAMS BEGIN TO take physical form when you choose materials for your home. But natural remodeling involves much more than using sustainably produced or recycled materials. You will also want to choose materials that delight your senses, support your thermal comfort strategy, reflect your locale, fit your budget, and do no harm. How do you know which materials will best suit your specific needs and strategies? The information in this chapter will help you decide.

The Role of Materials in Natural Remodeling

The materials you choose are the physical tools for creating a healthy, comfortable home in harmony with the rest of the planet. The right materials can make a home sing, while poor material choices can ruin a design, both functionally and aesthetically.

Our bodies respond to materials directly through our senses:

- **Touch:** texture, softness, hardness, conductivity, warmth

- **Sight:** color, reflectivity, smoothness, irregularity

- **Sound:** reflection or absorption of sound waves

- **Smell:** aroma, toxicity

Warm wood floors balance the cool-colored, light-reflecting plaster of the ceiling and walls.

Bringing life to the floor of a short hallway, this classic design is rendered in bamboo flooring and reclaimed marble.

For example, a room with too many hard, reflective surfaces, such as tile floors and hard plaster walls and ceilings, may be too acoustically "live." It may also feel too cool if these thermally massive materials aren't warmed by the sun or another source (e.g., a wood stove, a radiant heating system).

Our bodies also sense subtler material characteristics. Wood feels more alive than plastic, even if the plastic is stamped with a wood grain; wool and cotton feel more alive than nylon, even when it's spun into fiber; clay plaster feels more alive than gypsum plaster, even with similar textures. Synthetic materials often lack the irregularity and moisture transmission of materials that began their life as plants or earth. Natural materials, such as rock, clay, wood, and fibers, express the vitality, beauty, and uniqueness of living systems. By surrounding ourselves with natural materials, we are reminded of our place in the living world.

The Myth of the Perfect "Green" Material

Choosing good green materials is not, in itself, the primary goal of natural remodeling; it's a means of helping you achieve the goals you laid out in your strategy. Your overall design strategy comes first; it's the foundation for your choices. Our clients often ask us, "What are the best green materials?" "It all depends on the context," we answer. What may be a good "green" material in one context could turn out to be disastrous in another. For example, using a natural, nontoxic water-absorbent flooring next to a shower could create a mold problem, especially in a humid climate. Even materials with stellar "green" reputations can be used inappropriately, such as putting cork tile (an insulator) over a radiantly heated floor. No single factor or attribute determines the impact of a given material, and no material is perfect from an environmental perspective—just better or worse depending on your goals, the nature of your project, and how the material is installed.

Also keep in mind that choosing between two materials may involve considering their impacts on other parts of a system or assembly. For example, a heavy roofing material may increase the load on your walls and foundation, requiring additional structural material.

The fact that there is no easy way to evaluate materials may sound like bad news to some, but it also gives you great freedom. Barring toxicity, most materials are never completely good or completely bad. A local material may not have recycled content, but it doesn't require much energy for transportation, and buying locally supports your community. Rigid polystyrene insulation is produced with nonrenewable fossil fuels, but when used correctly it will save countless barrels of oil over its useful life. The challenge is to match materials to your context in a way that brings life to your home. So relax, do your best, and enjoy the process; there's no such thing as a perfect ecological choice, just a choice that's right for your home as a total system.

This whimsical earth-plastered addition helps enclose a protected garden.

A Process for Choosing Materials

A seemingly simple remodeling project can require hundreds of decisions that leave your head spinning. While there's no perfect "green" material, there *are* real differences in performance, toxicity, durability, life-cycle costs, and *embodied energy* (the total of all the energy that went into its acquisition,

processing, and transportation). And some characteristics of materials are more important than others. For example, particle board with recycled content may keep material out of a landfill, but it can still endanger your family's health if it off-gasses toxic chemicals.[1] Then there are other tough questions: Is recycled content more important than local sourcing? Is a highly insulative material produced with fossil fuels better than a natural product with a lower R-value?

To help you sort through materials for your remodeling project, we've devised a step-by-step process that puts the most important issues first. Using such a process saves time, makes the job of choosing materials easier, and helps you get the results you want. The process involves a series of questions that guide you to first match materials to your climate and your thermal comfort strategy, then weed out materials that are harmful, and finally sort through a list of additional attributes.

LOOKING FOR BALANCE

- Renewable Source
- Local Material

- Recycled Content
- Durable

Figure 1

This formerly dark, plain living room has been transformed by the addition of daylighting, clay plaster, and a sculpted cob wood stove surround.

While you consider all these issues, don't forget beauty. Natural systems are beautiful because of their vitality, complexity, functionality, resilience, and imperfections. Buildings that are modeled on living systems, with their integration and symbiotic relationships, take on a similar beauty. Maybe that's why people feel healthier and happier living and working in beautiful buildings. Furthermore, people care for beautiful things—which makes them more durable, and thereby sustainable. In the words of Christopher Alexander, "Those buildings which work are the ones which create relatedness between a person and the universe."[2] Beautiful buildings inspire replication. How will you know beauty when you see it? Forget fashion and style. Observe living systems, then go with your gut feelings.

FINISHING YOUR WALLS WITH THE GROUND WE WALK ON
by Janine Björnson

Earthen plasters, also called clay plasters, are nontoxic, easy and fun to apply, and beautiful to look at. Whether or not your eye detects earth on the walls, your body is immediately at ease around earthen plasters. This is what happens when you are surrounded by a material that you have coevolved with for thousands of years. Your body registers the material; it is your friend.

Earthen plasters are made from simple ingredients, most commonly clay, sand, pigment, fiber, and water. There are many combinations of these basic materials as well as many possible additives, depending on your needs and desires.

You can make clay plasters yourself, or you can purchase them premixed. If you want to make your own earthen plaster, you can harvest the clay from the earth, or you can purchase dry powdered bag clays from ceramic stores. If you go with a premixed clay plaster, the price may seem high, but the manufacturer has taken all the guesswork out of the system for you; you can look at a color chart, purchase clay plaster by the bag or the bucket, and apply it yourself *after acquiring some basic plastering skills*. Most clay plasters can be applied to either conventional or natural wall systems, with the appropriate substrate.

Earthen plasters can give you years of long lasting enjoyment. Your walls will be a reflection of nature; calming, inspiring, and beautiful. If you care for them gently, they will care for you in return.

Janine Björnson is a natural building educator, practitioner, and consultant, with a focus on natural plasters (e-mail: claybonesandstones@yahoo.ca).

Is This Material Green for My Home?

There are four topics essential to selecting materials for natural remodeling. We call them the Core Characteristics: climate suitability, toxicity, durability, and functionality. Additional Characteristics, such as recycled content, local sourcing, and embodied energy, are also important, but usually not as crucial (see figure 2).

Many of these characteristics are interrelated. For example, if a material comes from a sustainable source or if it is salvaged, chances are it will have low embodied energy. If a material is suitable for your climate and is installed properly, it may well also be durable.

When selecting materials, also keep an eye to getting the most bang for your buck. The cost of a material should be in line with your values and with its importance in the building. It's worth paying more for materials that directly affect your health and your home's energy usage. Durable materials may cost a little more up front, but they save you money and time in the long run. They can also give you a lifetime of satisfaction, which has no price tag.

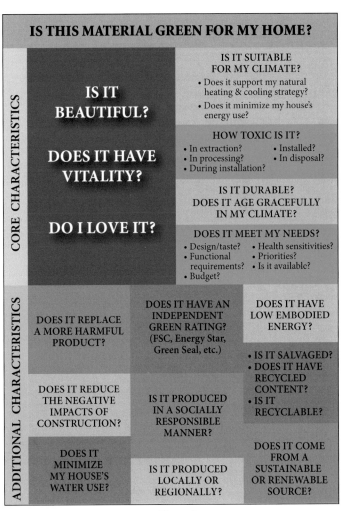

Figure 2

IS THIS MATERIAL GREEN FOR MY HOME?

CORE CHARACTERISTICS

IS IT BEAUTIFUL?

DOES IT HAVE VITALITY?

DO I LOVE IT?

IS IT SUITABLE FOR MY CLIMATE?
- Does it support my natural heating & cooling strategy?
- Does it minimize my house's energy use?

HOW TOXIC IS IT?
- In extraction?
- In processing?
- During installation?
- Installed?
- In disposal?

IS IT DURABLE? DOES IT AGE GRACEFULLY IN MY CLIMATE?

DOES IT MEET MY NEEDS?
- Design/taste?
- Functional requirements?
- Budget?
- Health sensitivities?
- Priorities?
- Is it available?

ADDITIONAL CHARACTERISTICS

DOES IT REPLACE A MORE HARMFUL PRODUCT?

DOES IT HAVE AN INDEPENDENT GREEN RATING? (FSC, Energy Star, Green Seal, etc.)

DOES IT HAVE LOW EMBODIED ENERGY?

- IS IT SALVAGED?
- DOES IT HAVE RECYCLED CONTENT?
- IS IT RECYCLABLE?

DOES IT REDUCE THE NEGATIVE IMPACTS OF CONSTRUCTION?

IS IT PRODUCED IN A SOCIALLY RESPONSIBLE MANNER?

DOES IT MINIMIZE MY HOUSE'S WATER USE?

IS IT PRODUCED LOCALLY OR REGIONALLY?

DOES IT COME FROM A SUSTAINABLE OR RENEWABLE SOURCE?

205

COLOR YOUR HOUSE, COLOR YOUR LIFE

by Virginia Young and Janie Lowe

Color can be one of the most exciting aspects of the remodeling process. It has the power to change the feeling of a space quickly at a relatively low cost. It can create flow, bring out character, or highlight architectural details. It can draw people to gathering spots or add a sense of tranquility to spaces.

Selecting your paint colors should be fun; it's just paint, and it can be easily adjusted if you change your mind. There is never only one perfect color for a space; many hues can work beautifully.

When thinking about color for your project, first consider the physical space:

- Is it open, with high ceilings?

- Is it small and cozy?

- Does one room flow openly to the next?

- How much natural light does the space get?

- What is the color of the reflected light from outdoors? (Is it green due to foliage? Does a blue house next door cast a cool light?)

If the space has high ceilings, light colors may float away and get lost. If the room is small, walls will reflect each other, making the hue stronger than intended. When one room flows to the next, you could use similar families of color to unite the spaces or different colors to distinguish the rooms from each other.

No-VOC paints, like those of YOLO Colorhouse, are becoming more readily available.

In many areas of the country, green light is reflected off plants at least half the year. In summer, light, golden colors tend to absorb the green cast, changing sunny colors to greenish yellows. In this situation, choose stronger hues that aren't as affected by the reflected green light.

Next, think about how you want the room to feel and how it will be used. Certain hues evoke feelings that can guide your use of color.

Rich reds and terra-cotta hues exude an earthy warmth and energy—perfect for social gathering spaces. These strong colors will draw the eye. Think of a rich red clay rock set against a soft green landscape; your eye is drawn to the red clay.

Soft greens are tranquil, restful, and calming. They work well in bedrooms, bathrooms, living rooms, dens—places where you want to kick back and relax, much like you would in a meadow of soft, green grass.

Neutral hues let objects and art come forward. If you have a lot of color in rugs, furniture, or art, the stone hues make an elegant backdrop for them. These are the colors of river rock; any leaf or flower that falls on the rock will pop out from this neutral backdrop.

Soft blues are soothing, calm, and warm. Blue is a cool color, but when used with rich woods, it can create a beautiful, calming space, emphasizing the warmth of the wood.

Golden tones make a room feel like it's bathed in light from the setting sun. They are warm, neutral, and versatile. Their rich colors invite people into gathering spots such as dining rooms and family rooms.

Don't forget strong accents or color spots, like wildflowers in a field. Bright colors are exciting; they draw the eye immediately, like a cobalt-blue front door, a magenta pinstripe, or a lime-green porch chair.

Light, space, and other nearby colors constantly alter how each color is viewed. The process of choosing color to live with is an exciting endeavor, from your first inspirations to actually putting the paint on the wall.

Virginia Young and Janie Lowe are the cocreators of YOLO Colorhouse, a system that provides a palette of 40 interior colors, suspended in no-VOC paint.

The galvanized corrugated metal ceiling in this cupola reflects light into the apartment below.

This bedroom addition was designed to increase passive-solar heating for the whole house.

Core Characteristics
Is this material suitable for my climate?

A common mistake is to overlook the critical role that materials play in long-term heating and cooling strategies. Many people agonize about the embodied energy in their building materials, but ongoing energy use has a much greater impact in nearly all homes. A Michigan study found that, of all the energy used to build and operate a particular house over a 50-year period, 94 percent was related to operating the house, while only 6 percent was used for construction[3].

Your choice of insulation, flooring material, or windows will affect energy consumption and durability for your home's entire lifetime. Matching your materials to your thermal strategy will keep you more comfortable, too. This is doubly true in extremely hot or cold climates.

Use the Natural Thermal Comfort Strategies table (see chapter 9, page 152) to harmonize your materials with your thermal comfort strategy. Regarding their thermal characteristics, most materials can be viewed in terms of a few broad categories:

- **Insulators**, such as cork, resist heat conduction. As finish materials, they feel neither hot nor cold to the touch.

- **Conductors**, such as metal, transfer heat easily. As finish materials, they will seem cold to the touch unless heated.

- **Thermally massive materials**, such as stone, tile, brick, plaster, and water, have a high potential for heat storage. They moderate interior temperature swings by storing heat when the air temperature rises and releasing it when the air temperature falls. Thermal mass is most appropriate in climates that experience relatively high temperature swings from day to night.

This interior stone wall stores heat during the day and releases it at night when the temperatures drop.

How toxic is this material?

Dioxins, lead, mercury, and volatile organic compounds (VOCs) in building materials have been linked to health problems such as asthma, learning disabilities, and cancer. Some materials may be benign in their finished form but release toxic chemicals during manufacturing (e.g., dioxin from vinyl and CFCs from some extruded polystyrene). Other materials, such as solvent-based finishes, adhesives, carpeting, and particleboard, release formaldehyde and other VOCs into the air, endangering your family's health and contributing to smog and ground-level ozone pollution. Even some natural materials can create dangerous by-products during construction and must be installed using appropriate safety practices; sawdust from aromatic woods, such as redwood and cedar, can be carcinogenic to woodworkers. And don't overlook what may happen down the road; many synthetic building products are highly toxic in a fire or release toxic substances after disposal.

When it comes to human health and the vitality of the ecosystem, it's always better to err on the side of caution.

How Can You Tell if It's Toxic?

Building material manufacturers aren't usually required to label their products. As a starting point, check the "toxicity" column in the materials tables on page 218. If the material you are considering isn't listed, check product listings in green materials guides (see Resources, page 267), do a quick Web search, question the manufacturer, and ask for a Material Safety Data Sheet (MSDS).

In addition to known toxicity, be aware of your own allergies or sensitivities. You may already know that particular substances irritate your sinuses or give you a headache or rash. Or you may be having "flulike symptoms" that you've chalked up to whatever's going around. In either case, pay attention to what your body is telling you. If you know or suspect that you are sensitive to a substance, take great care in selecting materials. Personally checking out questionable materials ahead of time can save you time, money, frustration, and health challenges in the long run.

Locally grown, rough-sawn white pine siding (with the bark still attached) is sealed with a natural stain of sunflower and thistle oils.

Is it durable?

Replacing a worn-out material costs time and money, sends volumes of "waste" to the landfill, and consumes energy. Manufacturing is usually energy-intensive, so you will save energy by using long-lasting materials that require little maintenance. Even a material high in embodied energy can be appropriate if it has a long useful life. For example, producing the steel for metal roofing uses more nonrenewable energy than manufacturing asphalt shingles, but standing-seam metal roofing can last up to twice as long as asphalt shingles—and it can be recycled when it's removed, instead of becoming a waste product. In addition to the durability of a material itself, consider how the material may contribute to your home's overall longevity. For example, good flashing is critical in preventing water intrusion around windows and doors, as are the materials that go into a drainage system around the outside of your home.

While the production of ceramic tile is energy-intensive, the material can last indefinitely, even in a wet environment such as this kitchen.

Graceful aging is closely related to durability. A material might last a long time, but if it looks terrible you'll wish it didn't. You'll get more value from durable materials that keep looking good through the years. Natural materials often show their years of wear in a more appealing manner than synthetics. A worn butcher-block counter takes on an attractive patina that makes it more valuable with time (as antique shop prices show), while a worn laminate counter just looks scratched, marred, and dated.

Keep in mind that the longevity of a given material may have as much to do with whether it is used appropriately and how well it is installed than with the qualities of the material itself.

Does it meet my functional needs?

You can't truly analyze a material for sustainability without considering your needs. Before you begin to choose materials, generate a list of your functional and aesthetic requirements,

A copper windowsill directs water away from the wall below, protecting it from moisture damage.

TIMELESS OR TRENDY?

It often pays to consider durability at the design stage—long before you choose materials. Ask yourself if a given design concept is timeless or trendy. Timelessness is a potent combination of beauty, functionality, durability, and graceful aging. Timeless design looks good for the whole useful life of a material. Trendy styles, by contrast, look outdated after a few years and lead to frequent-makeover syndrome—discarding materials before the end of their usefulness and consuming limited resources for new installations just for a different look. In other words, if you tear out a kitchen every 10 years to update its look, it doesn't matter how "green" the materials were.

Marble tile flooring and cast-stone details support the passive-solar heating scheme without introducing toxicity. Decorative finishes were created with low-VOC paints.

room by room. For example, the functional requirements for a bathroom flooring in a hot humid climate might be these:

• Mold- and mildew-resistant

• Nonabsorbent

• Slip-resistant

• Easy to clean

• Durable

The functional requirements for a roof in a hot dry climate might be these:

• Reflective

• Light colored

• Good for collecting rainwater

• Able to stand up to bright sun

Your own ecological goals and priorities are also important. Some people feel passionate about preserving old-growth forests, while others are most concerned about creating a safe environment for a child with asthma. Whatever your concerns, listing and prioritizing your goals gives you a touchstone that can help you decide among several options. To help you identify your personal priorities, refer to the self-exploration you did in chapter 2.

Composite countertops made of recycled paper and resin resemble slate or soapstone and resist damage from heat and water.

Natural materials, obtained locally, like this brightly colored earth plaster on a bathroom addition in Germany, naturally have low embodied energy.

Additional Characteristics

The following material attributes have consequences for the environment, but very few materials will score high in all categories. The point here isn't to get a perfect score; it's to use these criteria to help you make appropriate choices for your circumstances.

Embodied Energy

Embodied energy refers to all the energy consumed in producing and delivering a material to its destination in your home. This includes extracting natural resources, manufacturing, transportation, and even administration. Embodied energy is also an indicator of how much a material contributes to global warming. Put simply, natural building materials and products with minimal processing generally have low embodied energy—as long as they're obtained locally.

Don't forget to keep things in perspective. You might use a material that has a high level of embodied energy, but if you use little of it you could be consuming less energy than you would if you used a large quantity of a material with low embodied energy. For example, copper wire has a high level of embodied energy, but you may use relatively little for your wiring.

Recycled Content and "Recyclability"

Recycling diverts material from landfills, but it doesn't address broader environmental issues: energy required for remanufacturing, impacts on global warming, or depletion of the ozone layer. The type and percentage of recycled content in products varies widely. In general, high percentages of postconsumer reclaimed material (recycled after a consumer uses it, such as old newspaper) are better than postindustrial reclaimed material (from materials recycled during the manufacturing process, such as paper trimmings at the pulp mill).

Consider, too, whether a material can be recycled if it is removed from your house in the future. The reusability of a material depends in part on its own nature (metals, for example, are fairly easy to recycle, while composite materials are less so), as well as on how the material is installed—whether it's easy to separate the material from others around it.

Salvaged Material

Salvaged, refurbished, and reused materials are a special subset of recycled materials; these are products that can be reused without being remanufactured. Salvaged building materials can also remind us of our cultural and architectural history. Old clawfoot tubs, sinks, hardware, and doors can often be used directly in a remodeling project. Flooring or structural wood can be remilled from salvaged timbers with relatively little energy input.

This marble countertop was salvaged from the fabricator, and the backsplash is a mosaic of recycled glass.

THE WABI-SABI OF SALVAGE
by Robyn Griggs Lawrence

Pared down to its barest essence, *wabi-sabi* is the Japanese art of finding beauty in imperfection and profundity in nature—of accepting the natural cycle of growth, decay, and death. It's simple, slow, and uncluttered—and it reveres authenticity above all. Wabi-sabi is flea markets, not warehouse stores; aged wood, not Pergo; rice paper, not glass. It celebrates cracks and crevices and all the other marks that time, weather, and loving use leave behind.

Over the past decade, materials salvaged from abandoned or demolished buildings—shutters, windows, columns, bricks, fixtures—have become a design staple. Homeowners and designers with wabi-sabi leanings have snapped up centuries-old iron gates to use as wall hangings, turned mantels into headboards, and divided rooms using old shutters. Solid, handcrafted beams made from woods that are no longer available add permanence and long-lost quality to new homes.

The use of salvaged materials is a positive trend in many ways. Environmentally, it's a boon, keeping debris out of landfills and mitigating the use of new resources. For homeowners, salvaged materials bring charm and interest—and often provide a link to the community. Many people love the fact that their wide-plank heart pine floor came from a schoolhouse just down the road or that the cabinets in the kitchen were once in the local university's chemistry building.

Building materials can be found in salvage yards, at garage sales and flea markets, through classified ads, and increasingly through online resources. While the Internet may be convenient, keep in mind that salvage should be studied and touched to determine whether there's chemistry before you bring it home to live with. Be prepared to dig through piles of musty windows and rusty fixtures before you find what you're looking for. Salvaging is a scavenger's game, and you can expect to get dirty. Be on the lookout for rusty nails and tin, and make sure your tetanus shot is up to date. Be aware that the paint clinging to old wood might contain lead. If that's the case, don't strip it yourself. A better bet would be to seal it with clear polyurethane (to keep the distressed look) or to paint over it. You also want to check all items carefully to make sure they're not too rotten to resurrect. Attempting to salvage the unsalvageable will lead only to frustration and waste your time.

All that said, keep in mind that wabi-sabi is not the same as slobby. A solid yellow line separates tattered and shabby, dust and dirt from something worthy of veneration. Worn things take on their magic only in settings where it's clear they don't harbor bugs or grime. One senses that they've survived to bear the marks of time precisely because they've been so well cared for throughout the years.

Robyn Griggs Lawrence *is the editor in chief of* Natural Home & Garden Magazine *and the author of* The Wabi-Sabi House.

A weathered board fence creates an authentically old enclosure for this historic residence.

A salvaged bridge trestle supports a new second floor, while adding a feeling of visual interest and timeless solidity to this living room.

Sustainable Biosources

Some of the products with the lowest embodied energy come from biosources, also known as "rapidly renewable resources." These are raw materials that grow, such as trees, straw, bamboo, corn, wool, cotton, and soybeans. Agricultural waste products form the basis of many biosourced building products, such as straw bales used to build walls, sunflower-hull board, or sorghum-stalk panels. Others, such as wood, may or may not have been grown in a sustainable manner.

Identifying and obtaining sustainably forested lumber can be particularly challenging. Find out where your wood comes from, and request wood certified in accordance with the rules of the Forest Stewardship Council (FSC). The FSC is the only credible, independent, third-party entity certifying that lumber and wood products have been grown in well-managed forests. Tropical hardwoods, in particular, should be purchased only if FSC-certified. Wood that comes from the salvage of local trees may also be available in some areas; look under "salvaged wood" in your phone book or on the Web.

Odd pieces of wood, reclaimed from a lumber mill, were used to build this fanciful fence and entry gate.

Engineered wood, such as this laminated beam, not only makes efficient use of forest resources but is strong and beautiful as well.

Many species of FSC-certified flooring are available.

Local Products

In our worldwide economy, building products are often shipped from one side of the globe to the other, guzzling fossil fuels and producing clouds of pollution in the process. Furthermore, many products come from countries that lack high environmental standards. For example, China allows high levels of formaldehyde in glues for bamboo flooring, and there are few restrictions on the cutting of tropical hardwoods in Brazil, Mexico, Thailand, and elsewhere.

Don't overlook local materials because they aren't labeled as "green." Buying local materials, such as native hardwoods instead of imported tropical species, reduces energy use and requires less packaging. In addition, native materials add to the regional character of your home. Using a local supplier and a local installer familiar with the material also supports the local economy, builds community, and may give you better results. Local companies are often more responsive to local customers because they depend on your referrals and repeat business.

Replacing a More Harmful Product

Sometimes a product's primary positive attribute is that it replaces a more harmful or toxic product. Low-toxic wood preservatives can substitute for more toxic products; high-density polyethylene (HDPE) pipe can substitute for polyvinyl chloride (PVC) pipe. Engineered wood products (small pieces or fibers of wood, glued together into a product that's stronger than its tree-sawn counterpart) can span long distances and reduce demand for large, solid-wood beams cut from old-growth trees.

Reduction of Construction/Demolition Impact

Minimizing the impacts of demolition and construction is a small but important consideration. This includes erosion-control materials, foundation systems that don't require excavation, and systems for controlling dust during remodeling.

Minimizing Water Use

Low-flow showerheads and plumbing fixtures are obvious features, but this category also includes products like rainwater catchment and greywater irrigation systems.

Socially Responsible Production

Caring about the planet includes caring about all its inhabitants. It's a good idea to investigate whether the production of a material involves unfair wages, inhumane working conditions,

or mistreatment of animals. If a material is mass-produced or comes from far away, it may be difficult to address this criterion. Look for "Fair Trade" labels. Check out the company's mission statement or environmental record on the Web. If a material is produced locally, you can usually get a good idea of the working conditions and the company philosophy.

Independent Green Ratings

Sometimes it's difficult for a novice to weigh all the attributes of a given material or get trustworthy information from manufacturers or retailers. Fortunately, several organizations rate the environmental impact of projects. Before you put your trust in a "green" certification, make sure that the organization is independent and has no financial incentives for recommending a particular material. For example, some certification schemes, such as the Sustainable Forestry Initiative (SFI) and the Canadian Standards Association (CSA), are industry-funded.

Here is a list of some independent rating organizations:

• *GreenSpec* (www.buildinggreen.com) lists materials based on the judgment of a panel of expert evaluators, using objective and qualitative criteria.

• *Green Label Plus* identifies carpets with very low VOC emissions (www.carpet-rug.org).

• *Energy Star* guidelines are set by the U.S. Environmental Protection Agency and the U.S. Department of Energy. They cover many residential building products, including appliances, heating and cooling systems, lighting, fans, roof products, and windows and doors (www.energystar.gov).

• *Forest Stewardship Council* certifies sustainably grown and harvested wood products (www.fscus.org) (see the sidebar in this chapter, page 213).

• The *Greenguard Certification Program* is a third-party testing program for low-emitting products and materials. Greenguard has developed standards for adhesives, appliances, ceiling, flooring, insulation, paint, and wall-covering products (www.greenguard.org).

• *Green Seal* is a nonprofit organization that sets standards for environmentally preferable products, conducts product evaluations, and certifies products that meet their standards (www.greenseal.org).

• *Scientific Certification Systems* identifies Environmentally Preferable Products and Services (EPP), including adhesives and sealants, cabinetry and casework, carpet, doors, flooring, paints, and wallcoverings (www.scscertified.com/manufacturing/manufacture_epp.html).

• *FloorScore™* is the green label of the Resilient Floor Covering Institute for flooring products that meet low indoor emission standards. See www.rfci.com.

Here's an example of one way to analyze material options.

Floor and Wall Materials for the South-Facing Living Room

My Strategy: I am revamping the living room for passive solar heating and good air quality; I need thermal mass, more insulation, and least-toxic materials.

CORE CHARACTERISTICS

Materials Being Considered	Thermal Comfort	Toxicity	Durability	Function
mortar-set tile floor	thermal mass	doesn't off-gas (use no-VOC mortar and sealer)	highly durable; look for a nonslip texture that is easy to clean	seems a little hard, and not sure floor structure could handle the weight
half-wall of rammed earth	thermal mass	doesn't off-gas	durable, but may need to be sealed	
cement-board wainscot with plaster and chair rail	thermal mass, if I apply plaster thick enough	doesn't off-gas	durable, but may need to be sealed	a wainscot would look nice; could add rigid insulation behind cement board, and plaster with clay myself
hardwood floor	thermally neutral	use least-toxic sealer/finish	black locust is dense and rot-resistant and ages well	I love sitting on hardwood floors and have a source for local black locust

Additional Characteristics:

- I can get black locust locally from salvaged urban trees, produced in a socially responsible manner with low embodied energy.

- The production of polyisocyanurate insulation uses energy, but it doesn't cause other pollution and it does have some recycled content.

- Cement board has low embodied energy, and I'm using a limited amount for thermal mass.

- Clay plaster has very low embodied energy, but I do have to ship it from several states away if I can't find a local source of clay to mix my own.

Final Material Choices:

- Black locust floors sealed with water-based sealer

- Wainscot: Rigid polyisocyanurate insulation behind cement backer board with clay plaster finish; black locust chair rail to match floors

- Clay-based paints for walls above the wainscot

Bringing It All Together

Working with materials is especially enjoyable because, unlike drawings, diagrams, or abstract concepts, materials have a real, three-dimensional existence that you can see and touch. As you consider various materials, get samples and play with them—smell them (carefully), stroke them, soak them in water, abuse them, look at them in different kinds of light, put them next to each other and see how they look together. Along with being as analytical as you can, don't forget to trust your gut feelings; if a material has that hard-to-define quality of vitality, it just might help bring your home to life.

The durability and beauty of this bamboo flooring made it perfect for an unusual application: the wall finish of a laundry room.

RESPECTFUL REMODELING
The "Eco-Logical" 1909 House by Arciform LLC Design

The "1909 House" is a recent eco-logical remodeling showcase in the Alameda Ridge-Hollywood district of Portland, Oregon. The "eco" element of this 1909 craftsman bungalow incorporated many sustainable, environmentally friendly materials and design features while increasing the home's energy efficiency and overall health. The "logical" element was the design challenge of retaining and restoring the original charm of this home as much as possible.

The 1909 bungalow had undergone decades of "remuddling" and suffered from structural as well as decorative dismantling. Poor ventilation, an awkward first-floor plan, and poor natural lighting were just a few of the challenges Arciform had to contend with. Incorporating the finer details long lost while making the home structurally sound was the goal set—ensuring that in preserving the past, a sustainable future could be secured. One of the most unique aspects of this project was that every Saturday morning throughout the entire five-month construction process, the public was invited to learn about the restoration/remodeling process onsite. Topics ranged from home/neighborhood history and alternative green/sustainable materials, to energy-efficient systems and native landscape design.

More information on this project can be found on its website: www.1909house.com. For more information on Arciform, please visit their website www.oldhomesnewlife.com.

The 1909 House is an interactive, educational prototype of natural remodeling in Portland, Oregon.

Materials Tables

We've created tables that summarize some non-context-specific attributes of common materials. The tables are divided into four broad material types: structural materials (for an addition or major interior remodeling), exterior finishes (where durability rules), insulation (see chapter 7), and interior finishes (where appearance, maintenance, and low toxicity rate high).

Life isn't really as simple as these tables imply; they're just a snapshot and not meant to be comprehensive. If you are new to green building, you can use them as a guide for further research. If you are familiar with green building, you can use them as a quick reminder of the major issues. For further assistance in choosing green materials, there are several excellent green building material guides available (see Resources, page 267).

STRUCTURE					
	TOXICITY/POLLUTION FROM EXTRACTION, MANUFACTURING, OR DISPOSAL	TOXICITY: IMPACTS ON INDOOR AIR QUALITY	EMBODIED ENERGY	RECYCLED CONTENT AND RECYCLABILITY	RENEWABLE OR PLENTIFUL SOURCE
TRADITIONAL WOOD STUD OR STICK FRAMING					1
WOOD STUD OR STICK FRAMING WITH ENGINEERED WOOD PRODUCTS	2	5	2	2	1
STEEL-STUD FRAMING					4
LOG CONSTRUCTION					1
POST-AND-BEAM OR TIMBER FRAME					1
STRUCTURAL INSULATED PANELS (SIPS)	2	5	2	3	2
STRAW-BALE CONSTRUCTION			2		
INSULATED CONCRETE FORMS (ICFS)		2		3	6
CONCRETE BLOCK					6
EARTH					
POURED-IN-PLACE CONCRETE				2	6

BETTER

SO-SO (see comments)

NOT SO GREEN

1. SEEK SUSTAINABLE SOURCES (certified, renewable, bio-source, etc.)
2. VARIES WITH SPECIFIC PRODUCT OR APPLICATION
3. USE PRODUCT WITH RECYCLED CONTENT
4. RAW MATERIALS PLENTIFUL BUT NOT RENEWABLE
5. MAY OFFGAS TOXIC CHEMICALS; USE LOW-VOC TYPE, SEAL, OR ISOLATE FROM INTERIOR SPACES
6. USE HIGH-FLY-ASH-CONTENT CONCRETE
7. HIGHLY TOXIC IN FIRE

INSULATION AND RADIANT BARRIERS

	R-VALUE/inch (RSI/meter)	TOXICITY/POLLUTION FROM EXTRACTION, MANUFACTURING, OR DISPOSAL	TOXICITY: IMPACTS ON INDOOR AIR QUALITY	EMBODIED ENERGY	RECYCLED CONTENT AND RECYCLABILITY	RENEWABLE OR PLENTIFUL SOURCE
FIBROUS INSULATIONS						
CELLULOSE (LOOSE-FILL, DAMP SPRAY, DENSE-PACK)	3.0-3.7 (21-26)		5			
FIBERGLASS (BATTS, LOOSE-FILL, SEMI-RIGID BOARD)	2.2-4.0 (15-28)		5		3	4
MINERAL WOOL (LOOSE FILL, BATTS, SEMI-RIGID OR RIGID BOARD)	2.8-3.7 (19-26)		5			4
COTTON BATT	3.0-3.7 (21-26)					
SHEEP WOOL	3.7-3.9 (27-28)					
FOAM INSULATIONS						
POLYISO-CYANURATE	6.0-6.5 (17-23)		7		2	
EXTRUDED POLYSTYRENE (XPS)	5.0 (35)					
EXPANDED POLYSTYRENE (EPS)	3.6-4.4 (25-31)	2				
CLOSED-CELL SPRAY POLYURETHANE	5.8-6.8 (40-47)		7			
OPEN-CELL, LOW-DENSITY POLY-URETHANE (SPRAY FOAM)	3.6-3.8 (25-27)		7			1
AIR-KRETE	3.9 (27)				2	4
OTHER INSULATIONS						
PERLITE	2.5-3.3 (17-23)					4
RICE HULLS	high level of settling, not commonly used					
RADIANT BARRIERS						
FOIL-FACED BUBBLE-PACK (INSULATION AND RADIANT BARRIER)	depends on installation	2	2		2	
FOIL-FACED POLYETHYLENE FOAM (INSULATION AND RAD. BARRIER)	depends on installation	2	2		2	
FOIL-FACED PAPERBOARD SHEATHING	depends on installation	2		2	3	1
FOIL-FACED ORIENTED-STRAND BOARD (OSB)	depends on installation					1

BETTER

SO-SO (see comments)

NOT SO GREEN

1. SEEK SUSTAINABLE SOURCES (certified, renewable, bio-source, etc.)
2. VARIES WITH SPECIFIC PRODUCT OR APPLICATION
3. USE PRODUCT WITH RECYCLED CONTENT
4. RAW MATERIALS PLENTIFUL BUT NOT RENEWABLE
5. MAY OFFGAS TOXIC CHEMICALS; USE LOW-VOC TYPE, SEAL, OR ISOLATE FROM INTERIOR SPACES
6. USE HIGH FLY-ASH CONTENT CONCRETE
7. HIGHLY TOXIC IN FIRE

INTERIOR FINISHES

	TOXICITY/POLLUTION FROM EXTRACTION, MANUFACTURING, OR DISPOSAL	TOXICITY: IMPACTS ON INDOOR AIR QUALITY	EMBODIED ENERGY	RECYCLED CONTENT AND RECYCLABILITY	RENEWABLE OR PLENTIFUL SOURCE
FLOORING					
SOLID WOOD (HARDWOOD OR SOFTWOOD)					1
BAMBOO		5		2	1
LAMINATES (PERGO AND OTHERS)	2	2		2	
CORK				2	
NATURAL LINOLEUM				2	
VINYL					
RUBBER	2	2	2	2	1
STONE				2	4
TILE			2	3	4
CONCRETE	2			2	4
CARPET	2	5		3	1
CARPET TILES	2	5		3	1
WALL AND CEILING FINISHES					
GYPSUM WALLBOARD (DRYWALL)	2	2	2		4
FIBER WALLBOARD (PANELING, ETC.)	2	5	2		
PAINT	2	5	2	3	1
VINYL WALLCOVERING					
WALLPAPER		5	2	3	
CORK			2	2	
CABINETS AND FURNISHINGS					
SOLID WOOD				2	1
PLYWOOD	2	5	2	2	1
WOOD PARTICLE BOARD (MDF)	2	5	2		
PARTICLE BOARD WITH NON-WOOD FIBERS (STRAW, ETC.)	2	5	2		
PLASTIC				2	
COUNTERTOPS					
SOLID WOOD					1
NATURAL STONE (e.g. GRANITE, SLATE, MARBLE)				2	4
ENGINEERED STONE			2		4
CONCRETE AND CONCRETE COMPOSITES	2	5	2	2	4
CERAMIC TILE		5	2	3	4
SOLID SURFACE	2		2	2	
LAMINATES			2	2	
METAL					4
TRIM					
SOLID WOOD					1
FINGER-JOINTED WOOD					
MEDIUM-DENSITY FIBERBOARD (MDF)	2		2		
HIGH-DENSITY POLYURETHANE (HDP)	2	2		2	
EXPANDED POLYSTYRENE FOAM (EPS)	2				
POLYVINYL CHLORIDE (PVC)					
POLYVINYL CHLORIDE GLASS-FIBER-RENFORCED COMPOSITES					

EXTERIOR FINISHES				
	TOXICITY/POLLUTION FROM EXTRACTION, MANUFACTURING, OR DISPOSAL	EMBODIED ENERGY	RECYCLED CONTENT AND RECYCLABILITY	RENEWABLE OR PLENTIFUL SOURCE
ROOFING				
ASPHALT SHINGLES				
WOOD SHINGLES OR SHAKES				1
RECYCLED SYNTHETIC SHINGLES	2			
METAL ROOFING				4
SLATE				4
CERAMIC TILE	2			4
FIBER-CEMENT SHINGLES			3	4
BUILT-UP ROOFING (TAR-AND-GRAVEL OR HOT-MOPPED)				
MEMBRANE ROOFING			3	
SIDING				
SOLID WOOD				1
WOOD SHINGLES OR SHAKES				1
PLYWOOD	5	2	2	1
MDF HARDBOARD	5	2		1
VINYL				
FIBER-CEMENT			3	
SHEET METAL				4
ALUMINUM PANELS				4
CEMENT PLASTER (STUCCO)				4
LIME PLASTER	2	2	2	4
EARTH PLASTER				4
BRICK				4
STONE				4
TRIM				
SOLID WOOD				1
FINGER-JOINTED WOOD				
HIGH-DENSITY POLYURETHANE (HDP)	2		3	
EXPANDED POLYSTYRENE FOAM (EPS)	2			
POLYVINYL CHLORIDE (PVC)				
GLASS-FIBER-REINFORCED COMPOSITES (GYPSUM, PLASTIC, OR CONCRETE	2	2		

BETTER

SO-SO (see comments)

NOT SO GREEN

1. SEEK SUSTAINABLE SOURCES (certified, renewable, bio-source, etc.)
2. VARIES WITH SPECIFIC PRODUCT OR APPLICATION
3. USE PRODUCT WITH RECYCLED CONTENT
4. RAW MATERIALS PLENTIFUL BUT NOT RENEWABLE
5. MAY OFFGAS TOXIC CHEMICALS; USE LOW-VOC TYPE, SEAL, OR ISOLATE FROM INTERIOR S
6. USE HIGH-FLY-ASH-CONTENT CONCRETE
7. HIGHLY TOXIC IN FIRE

Sanders Residence
Washington, D.C.

Scott Sanders's remodeling project proves that you don't need a freestanding house, a country property, or even a big yard to get closer to nature. Scott's home is a two-story, hundred-year-old row house in Washington, D.C. On two sides, its walls are shared with the neighboring row houses, and the property provides no room in which to expand. Scott and his architect used sunlight, breezes, plants, and space design to transform a small, dark, cramped house into a light, open, outdoor-oriented home.

Scott, a communications consultant to nonprofits, had lived in his present home as a renter for seven years before buying it. When he was ready to buy, he considered moving farther out from his central downtown neighborhood, but he found that the locale worked for him; he liked walking to work, restaurants, shops, and a large nearby park. He also liked the fact that the row house had a backyard—an important feature for a dog lover.

The house presented several challenges from the start. At 1,100 square feet, it was small by some standards, but there was no room to add on. The only window walls were at the front and back, facing north and south. Even with air conditioning, the second floor (where the bedrooms are located) tended to overheat in summer. The kitchen was small, dark, and "fairly beat up," with one small door out to the backyard.

Formerly a "messy" space several steps down from the kitchen, the backyard is now a delightful area enhanced by "vertical gardens."

The yard wasn't a lot of fun, either. In fact, the little yard was what launched the renovation. "I was thinking of hiring a landscape architect to redo the backyard," says Scott. "You had to walk down some steps to get from the kitchen to the yard, which was just uneven stone pavers on dirt; it was messy. But then I thought it would be nice to do the kitchen at the same time, so I began to look for an architect." Aesthetic taste was on the top of Scott's list of criteria, but he was pleased when he found an architect who was also experienced with green building.

In the evening, candles make the patio a magical space; in cooler seasons, Scott and friends warm themselves around the custom-crafted fireplace.

Phase One: Kitchen and Patio

"We started out looking at the backyard and the kitchen," says Rick Harlan Schneider, AIA, of Inscape Studio. "But when we realized that these two spaces are only separated by a wall, we began to think of them as a whole: How do you flow from the kitchen to the patio, open up the kitchen, and make a patio that feels like an extension of the house?"

The outside kitchen wall had only one window, so the first step was to make it more transparent by putting in double French doors and operable windows. The second step was to raise the patio so that Scott could walk straight from his kitchen to his new outdoor room. With the kitchen and patio redefined as one continuous space, Rick and Scott went to work on improving livability. "We reconfigured the small kitchen to give him more storage and workspace, an eating area, and a cleaner look," says Rick. They used natural linoleum for the floor, a recycled-glass countertop, Energy Star-rated appliances, and elegant fluorescent light fixtures. With light and air coming through the newly opened back wall, the kitchen became a whole new place.

But perhaps the most dramatic transformation was outdoors. "Scott wanted garden space," Rick recalls. "But there really wasn't enough area to plant things horizontally. So we came up with what we call his "vertical gardens." Around the newly raised patio is a fence of sustainably harvested cedar, with a planter box at the top. The fence also supports hanging planters, crafted by local metalsmith Charles Danley. The patio's floor is stone from a local quarry. All of this improves the view from the kitchen, as well.

Opening the back wall with windows and oversized French doors brought light and air into the kitchen.

The patio's utility is extended by a fireplace that functions as a cookstove in summer and a source of heat and social focus in the cooler seasons. Danley also crafted a custom grill for the outdoor fireplace.

"I really like being out there now," grins Scott. "I just open the doors and walk out. It's easier to take food in and out, so I eat out there much more, especially in summer; I used to only eat out there on special occasions. I'm more serious about gardening now, too, because it's so much more pleasant to be there. And the dogs like to lie on the long wooden steps in the sun; even they spend more time out there than they used to!"

A south-facing patio can be a boon in cool weather but a challenge in summer. Fortunately, some tall trees provide some summer shade. In addition, Rick has designed a canvas canopy system for additional shade, soon to be installed.

In this highly paved, built-up city, the patio garden also does its part to manage water wisely. "Instead of paving the whole backyard," says Rick, "we created a strip of pea gravel; any runoff from the patio goes back into the ground to recharge the groundwater. The built-in planters hold some of the rainwater on site, too."

Even the hallway mirror is eco-friendly, framed in reclaimed wood from southern barns.

The upstairs hallway got a new coat of low-VOC paint, and the newel post got a cap of recycled glass.

The kitchen and patio were Scott's original focus, but a holistic process in such a small place rarely leaves other areas untouched. While the team worked on the kitchen, the adjacent powder room was reconfigured and finished out with eco-friendly materials. The upstairs hallway and bathroom got a green facelift in the bargain, with low-VOC paints and sealers and water-efficient fixtures.

Although green building wasn't Scott's top priority in the beginning, once he got into it, he went all out. "It's my nature," says Scott. "If I'm going to do something, I want to do it right. And it felt like the right thing to do. The Web made a huge difference; I did a lot of digging around. I wanted to find as many sustainable products as possible. There's a great website called homeclick.com, which has really affordable products and free shipping. I bought my Toto toilets (normally considered excellent but expensive) and my bathroom sinks from them, delivered right to the door. I bought the lighting fixtures online, too. And I identified other green materials online that we then bought locally."

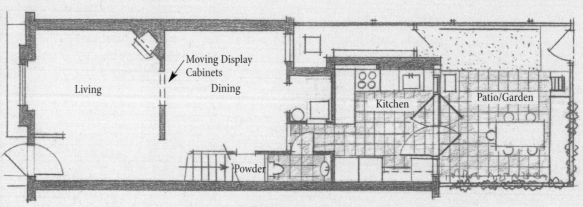

FLOOR PLAN-AFTER

The display cabinets slide into different positions to separate or open up the living room and dining area.

The wall between the dining and living areas was replaced with see-through display cabinets for Scott's pottery.

Phase Two: Living and Dining

After living with these changes for a year, Scott got the urge to update more of his house; once he had a taste of the possibilities, he wanted more light and more storage. Scott and Rick turned their attention to the living area, where a solid wall separated the living and dining rooms. "We could have just done away with the wall to bring in more light and air," observes Rick, "but Scott also wanted display space for the pottery he makes and collects." The solution? An open partition of hanging cabinets slides into different positions for flexibility of use. The cabinets are of veneered formaldehyde-free MDF, with open fronts and backs that admit light to the dining room for the first time.

For even more storage, Rick designed a built-in buffet that runs along the dining room wall. The cabinet is solid maple with perforated metal doors. To carry through the metal theme, Rick also designed a fireplace grill to match the patio's fireplace grill.

Looking back on the renovation, Rick reflects, "If you think about it, the two major walls that we changed were the back wall and the wall between the living and dining room. In both cases, the idea was to take an opaque wall that separated spaces and make it much more flexible and transparent so that spaces could join and flow. In both cases, the idea was to make the wall do more— to make it permeable and flexible, and also to have it serve multiple functions. Scott loves to entertain, too, so once we opened up those two walls, it's suddenly a lot easier to invite people over."

In the living area, a room divider sports a top made from colorful recycled glass, and the carpet squares are made from recycled plastic bottles.

Built-in buffet storage in the refurbished dining room makes it easier to live gracefully in a small space.

225

Comfort Systems

Daylight, fresh air, and outdoor living space are the main natural comfort improvements to Scott's house. The new back wall of the kitchen was designed to maximize natural ventilation, and new ceiling fans in the upstairs bedrooms augment the airflow.

Scott had replaced his old furnace with a new energy-efficient model before remodeling, so there was no need for an upgrade there. But some of the ductwork and grills were old and funky, so Rick suggested having various parts of the system cleaned, repaired, or replaced to improve energy efficiency and indoor air quality.

In the kitchen area, where the bulk of the renovation was done, Rick upgraded wall insulation levels to R-19. The roof insulation was good, but the roofing needed upgrading, so Rick suggested that Scott use a light-colored membrane to cut back on solar heat gain; that step alone can reduce energy bills.

A glass block wall next to the toilet allows light to stream into the bathroom without compromising privacy.

Living There

"I'm delighted with the renovation," says Scott. "It feels like a different house now, more like *my* house—and with a lot more storage space. The main difference is the link between indoors and out, which changed dramatically when we opened up the back of the house. It feels much lighter and more open. And I can eat in my kitchen now; I really like that. The house is better for entertaining, too. When people come in, they really notice the difference; they're moved by the design. The kitchen and backyard are great for dinner parties."

Scott also found it rewarding to work with professionals. "I'm a consultant in a different field, and I've learned the value of bringing in people who are knowledgeable in their own fields. Rick worked collaboratively with me, which was good, but at times he'd push me in directions I wouldn't have thought of. He knows what he's doing, I trusted him, and I've been very happy with the results."

Scott also enjoyed working with the metalsmith and other craftspeople, as well as color consultant Zoe Kyriacos: "She helped me pick out the colors and patterns, which was an incredibly smart investment. She had a good eye, and she gave me the confidence to do things I'd only vaguely thought of. Between Rick and Zoe, this place looks significantly better than it would have if I'd done it by myself. It really made a difference having people who pay attention to the details. It reinforced the value of bringing in people who do this all the time—who have experience and can see things differently."

Rick Harlan Schneider's Tips for Remodeling in a Mixed Humid Climate

1. Get to know the site. "It's really important for any architect in the service of good design to analyze a site and get to know its challenges and opportunities—which sometimes are one and the same."

2. Design with the sun in mind. "In this climate, you have to take into account the fact that we have hot, humid summers and cold winters. It blows me away when people design these beautiful glass boxes that face directly south without any consideration about excessive solar gain. You're either creating a very uncomfortable space or a very high energy bill. It doesn't seem smart at all."

3. Create outdoor living spaces. "Take advantage of three-season living. In this area, you can be outdoors for a good nine months of the year: spring, summer if you have bug protection, and then into fall, when it's really beautiful. Create spaces that will let you enjoy that three-season living; don't just contain the house within the walls, but let a portion of it reside outdoors as well."

4. Employ adaptable comfort strategies. "With a hot summer and cold winter, there is no single solution for heating and cooling in this climate zone; you have to employ a range of strategies. Cross-ventilation is great for most of the summer, but on those hot, sticky days it makes sense to have ceiling fans or air conditioning."

CHAPTER 13
Construction Planning for Natural Remodeling

Adopt the pace of nature. The secret is patience.
A bottle fills drop by drop.

—Max Steingart

To paraphrase permaculture visionary Bill Mollison, planning your construction process beforehand is a process of "protracted and thoughtful observation" that helps avoid "protracted and thoughtless action." Put differently, an often-repeated maxim in construction circles advises, "Fast, affordable, beautiful ... pick two out of three." If you want a project that is affordable and beautiful, be prepared to spend adequate time in the planning and preparation stage.

Some features, such as a green roof, should be installed by an experienced, knowledgeable contractor.

Planning Your Construction Project

Every hour you spend educating yourself and planning ahead will save you money and time during construction and bear fruit in the form of a well-orchestrated, satisfying project. Start by addressing these questions:

Who will manage the project?

If you have a builder on your design team, congratulations; you're already talking with him or her about your plans for a *green* project. If not, you may be planning to hire a general contractor, hire subcontractors directly yourself (acting as an owner-contractor), or even do all the work yourself. When you select a general contractor or subcontractors, make sure they have experience with or an interest in green building.

What materials will you use?

During the design process, you thought about which materials would best fit your heating/cooling strategy, your climate, and your lifestyle. Before construction begins, you'll finalize those decisions in light of your cost breakdown, material availability, and other late-stage factors. Researching and selecting suitable, durable, locally available, sustainable materials *will* take more time than purchasing their unsustainable counterparts off the

MAKE IT EASY ON YOURSELF

Chances are that you'll be hiring someone to help with some aspect of your project. Finding a construction professional (architect, designer, general contractor, or subcontractor) who shares your commitment to natural remodeling can make the difference between a fabulous project and a frustrating one. Employing professionals with "green" experience takes the pressure off you to know everything. They can offer alternatives to improve the project, guide you to local material sources, and connect you with a world of resources.

Michael O'Brien of the Portland, Oregon, G-Rated green building program, says, "If you, the client, are in the position of having to drag an architect or contractor through green building when they're unfamiliar, suspicious, or skeptical of it—or they don't really want to do it—that's just a guaranteed set of problems. A lot of green building comes down to small decisions, and you can never think of everything. You have to have a contractor whose job that is, so every little decision is made following the sustainability principles you've established. This isn't about spending more money. This is about getting things to happen because there's agreement and communication."

Like any relatively new product, installation of plastic composite decking differs from that of wood decking.

shelf, especially if you're working with reclaimed or recycled materials. Here's where a local architect or builder familiar with green remodeling can save you time and money by helping you identify and obtain materials.

Where will you get your materials?

Even after you choose the right materials, you need to know where to obtain them. Some materials, such as FSC-certified wood and natural linoleum, may not be available through your regular building material suppliers. Call the manufacturers of your chosen materials and ask for the distributor nearest you, or approach your local building supplier and see if they can order the material for you. As noted in the previous chapter, it may not make good ecological sense to use the "greenest" low-embodied-energy material if it has to be shipped across the country.

Who will install the materials?

If you've hired a general contractor, he or she will complete the work or hire subcontractors. If you are acting as an owner-contractor, find a skilled craftsperson who has experience installing the specific material you've chosen; you don't want someone experimenting on your dime, in your house. Manufacturers and

As the market grows, green material supply businesses, like this one in Portland, Oregon, are opening all over the country and online.

At environmentally conscious building supplies stores, you can browse among a wide array of eco-friendly building products.

230

Sustainably harvested woods, like the cedar slats used on this pavilion, can take time to find.

suppliers often have a list of trained installers. If you are doing your own construction, request full installation instructions and don't hesitate to call the technical support number if your conditions are different from those described.

How much will it cost?

Natural remodeling needn't cost more than standard construction if you plan ahead. In fact, natural heating and cooling systems and durable materials will save you big bucks in the long run. Before you start work, get cost estimates (based on a clear understanding of the scope of work and materials to be used) so that you can weigh alternatives and make decisions. For example, the price of high-quality windows or extensive insulation may be offset by the related savings on a smaller furnace or air conditioner. When you estimate costs, don't forget to include building permits and associated fees.

When will it happen and how long will it take?

It's important to create a detailed and realistic schedule for the construction phase of your project. Construction is a sequential process. For example, plumbing and electrical work must be done before insulation can be installed. Furthermore, many materials have long lead times (the amount of time between when you place an order and when materials are delivered); unusual green materials and custom items like windows and cabinets may have lead times of 6 to 12 weeks. Planning every stage of construction increases the likelihood that people and products will show up when they're needed. General contractors are particularly experienced at creating such schedules.

Matts Myhrman and Judy Knox employed German craftsman Axel Linde to oversee the earth-and-lime plastering of their house.

231

Portland, Oregon's green building program, "G-Rated," supports green building projects with information, design advice, and even incentives.

What are the local planning and building codes?

Building codes exist to protect public health and safety by addressing hazards related to fire, building collapse, and unsanitary conditions. However, codes can also slow the adoption of nonstandard materials and systems. If your remodeling project includes "alternative" approaches, be proactive; visit your building department well ahead of time to discuss your plans. Most building officials are receptive to new ideas if you can show that they're safe. And many building officials are concerned about the negative impacts of building, too. Several jurisdictions are developing green building programs, some with preferential permit processing or even rebates.

SHOULD YOU DO IT YOURSELF?
CONFESSIONS OF A DIY QUEEN

When I'm not meeting with clients, talking with building officials, or designing homes and remodeling projects, I'm a DIY weekend warrior queen. When I was growing up, my family was always in the midst of some home improvement project—from building a storage shed, to repainting the back bedroom and putting up wallpaper in the half-bath, to building a spec house on the lot next door. It seems like I've always known how to use a speed square, chalk line, drill, and circular saw. I'm happiest in a tool belt, surrounded by power tools. When I bought my first house—a major fixer-upper—I started small by tearing up carpet, installing a ceiling-fan light fixture in the living room, replacing the locksets, rewiring the stove burners, and retiling the shower—trowel in one hand, DIY book in the other. I didn't know anything about natural remodeling then, but I always focused on installing durable materials in a way that would stand the test of time, improve the comfort of my home, and save me money in the long run. I guess I was pretty "green" after all!

Hand-colored walls, decorative tile, and cabinetry at the Lerner residence.

Every job I did was more complicated and took hours (if not days) longer than I anticipated and I learned a ton. Nothing beats the satisfaction of kicking back with a cold one after a long day and admiring a successfully completed project—and nothing is worse than the frustration of a DIY project gone wrong. So here's my two cents' worth, to help you learn from my mistakes:

- *Doing it yourself means you have complete responsibility for the quality of the job. Educate yourself on best practices and materials for the task at hand. Buy how-to books, take classes, and read articles in trade magazines, such as Environmental Building News, Fine Homebuilding, Journal of Light Construction, or Remodeling Magazine. Get a building-code reference book—the Code Check series from Taunton Press is good—and visit your local building department to ask about green building resources. Call the technical support number on the back of a product box or visit the manufacturer's website, if need be.*

A larger DIY project at the Lerner residence.

- *Construction takes time; the less experienced you are, the more time it will take. Give yourself enough time to do the job right. With construction, everything takes twice as long as you expect. After 20 years of experience with my DIY projects, my family asks how long I think a job will take, then triples it! Be realistic; painting the dining room until 4:00 a.m. on Thanksgiving morning when the guests are due at noon takes some of the fun out of a project.*

- *You may not even know what you don't know. Invest in professional expertise on unfamiliar or complicated tasks. Many skilled professionals are willing to consult on an hourly basis. They enjoy sharing their expertise. A remodeling contractor with experience using green materials and techniques can provide the best information on methods, materials, and local sources. Experienced eyes can immediately pick out the particular issues that a remodeling task could trigger, such as needing to reroute a plumbing vent, upgrade a circuit, or change the size of a header. They can also suggest the best materials or sequences, point out potential code violations, and explain a few tricks of the trade. A small investment in expertise can go a long way toward speeding up the job and preventing unforeseen problems.*

Kelly in her natural environment—a construction site.

Finding Experienced Green Professionals

The community of architects and builders with green experience is growing, but be prepared to search for them. As you interview professionals, look for demonstrated experience in green building. Short of that, look for someone who is excited about learning sustainable methods and using green materials. Here are some tips to guide your search:

Contact Local Groups

Local or regional green building organizations often have professional resource directories. Check with the local chapter of National Association of the Remodeling Industry (www.NARI.org) for NARI Certified Green Building Professionals. Friends and acquaintances can often provide referrals as well.

Interview Several Architects/Designers and Contractors

Ask to see examples of their sustainable projects, and look for design features and materials that address challenges similar to your own. Does she belong to a green building organization? Are there green building books, magazines, and material samples in his office? What are her areas of specialization within green building (someone who knows passive heating and cooling inside-out may not know about green materials or indoor air quality)? Can he provide you with client references on previous green building projects?

Check References from Previous Clients

Are former clients happy with the process and the final project? What problems came up during design and construction, and how were they resolved?

Don't Abdicate Your Responsibilities

Make your priorities and preferences clear. *Unless you make a special effort to communicate your ecological goals and the methods for achieving them, your architect or contractor is likely to do whatever she or he does habitually.* Point out the unique aspects of your project at the beginning—unusual materials, waste-recycling sys-

Some professionals specialize in green design, like the designers of this addition.

tems, or advanced energy-efficiency techniques. Make a written agreement (contract) that describes the project in detail. Check the written specifications to confirm that they reflect your goals for your remodeling project.

Hydronic heating in the walls is common in Europe, but a relatively new practice in the United States.

Work with Someone Who Communicates Well

A remodeling project is a long, intense, somewhat intimate process. You'll be telling your architect all about your family's daily life and preferences. The construction crew will be in and out of your living space for the duration of the project. When you're doing something cutting-edge, a contractor's communication skills may be just as important as an ability to budget, plan, and execute the work. As you interview contractors, pay close attention to how well they listen.

Keep the Lines of Communication Open

Have frequent meetings. Ask questions; if the answers don't make sense, ask for more details. Offer your input clearly and respectfully. Make decisions in a timely manner when requested. Continue your educational efforts throughout the project, and extend them to each subcontractor and crew member. Explain to the floor refinisher why you are choosing water-based finishes. Brief the insulation crew and drywallers about how air-sealing can prevent moisture problems in walls. Let the painter know that you chose no-VOC paints to improve your indoor air quality.

Plan to Stay Sane

All your planning can't prepare you for the messy process and harsh realities of construction. Remodeling turns your cherished haven into a loud, dusty, chaotic work site.

Many families report that the most difficult aspect of a remodeling project is having workers in and out of their house; it feels like a violation of their space. If you are away from home most of the day, this may be less of a problem. But in any case, you may need to set up alternative cooking, washing, or bathing facilities—or move out. Establishing clear boundaries with workers (like a set work schedule and what constitutes your private space) can prevent misunderstandings from the beginning.

Plan ahead for remodeling disruption by leaving extra time in your schedule. Keep your ecological remodeling project fun and sustainable by taking care of yourself and your family during the process.

In a mild climate, it's possible to move your kitchen outside for the duration of your remodeling project.

Ready, Set, Build

Though remodeling is never as quick or easy as it looks on TV (one trip to the hardware store takes longer than a whole episode of *This Old House*), planning and preparation are more than half the fun. From hunting down great used materials, to meeting contractors, to the camaraderie of a team of like-minded people, putting together an eco-remodeling project can be an exciting process. Great things happen—often unexpectedly—when you have a strong vision of what your home can be. In the words of owner-builder Charles Kingsley, "We've been amazed by the power of holding an intention and being brave enough or dumb enough to talk to people about it and assume that we can do an elegant ecological restoration that can be affordable." Start early, do your homework, and hold fast to your vision. Your project just might come together even better than you imagine.

Do what you can, with what you have, where you are.

—Theodore Roosevelt

Construction is messy and disruptive, even in the best of circumstances.

YOUR NATURAL DESIGN is fully fleshed out and you're ready to build. You've analyzed your house, your lifestyle, and your climate; assembled your team; crafted your plans for human comfort and environmental regeneration; signed on the dotted line with a contractor who shares your sustainable vision (or blocked out your weekends for the next 6 months); and found the best local sources for recycled wood, no-VOC paints, healthy insulation, and reclaimed lighting fixtures. It seems like you've been planning for years (and maybe you have). The fun is about to begin—if you like loud noises, power tools, and mountains of dust, that is. Your job site is where the nitty-gritty, real-life stuff of rebalancing your home comes together.

Communicate, Communicate, Communicate

Communication is *key* during construction—between you and your family members, and between you and the professional team (designer, general contractor, subcontractors). An eco-remodeling project will make more demands on your time than a conventional one. Because you're asking for something out of the ordinary, you'll need to make your preferences known every step of the way and be available to answer questions and make decisions. Even if you make most material and design decisions beforehand (and you should), a hundred little decisions will come up during construction—especially in a remodeling project, where unforeseen conditions are routinely uncovered during deconstruction.

The decisions involved in remodeling a kitchen are a good example. The basic design and materials selection may be done, but you'll still need to do the following:

- **Find and acquire** recycled flooring, hardware, or fixtures

- **Meet with the cabinet subcontractor** to confirm construction materials, and the configuration of drawers, shelves, glass style, finish, and hardware

- **Meet with the countertop subcontractor** to look at colors and finishes

- **Select energy-efficient windows** that match your existing house

- **Visit tile shops** to choose floor and backsplash tile or other flooring

- **Meet with the electrician** to confirm outlet, switch, and light locations

- **Visit lighting shops** to select light fixtures

- **Choose** your sink, stove, refrigerator, dishwasher, and vent hood

- **Find the best local source** of no-VOC paint and pick paint colors

- **Meet with the contractor** at least weekly to review the work, the schedule, the budget, and any changes

- **AND attend to your regular job and family responsibilities**

An unexpected find, like this peeled tree trunk, can require design changes during the course of construction.

Be sure to leave time in your schedule for these details. Planning ahead and going at a sane pace can make remodeling fun instead of frustrating.

Before construction begins, talk about and establish a communication model. The following questions will help you address most issues.

- If you're working with a general contractor, what individual will be your primary contact person?

- How often will project meetings occur? (It's a good idea to meet at least once a week.)

- How often will you be needed on the job site to make decisions?

- What's the procedure when unforeseen conditions affect construction costs?

- What is the system for requesting and approving change orders (agreed-on changes to the specified materials, design, or scope of work)?

- How will verbal decisions/agreements be documented?

Some contractors prefer that written communication be in the form of a job book or diary, in which you can leave notes and questions and the contractor can reply in writing. Some contractors like phone calls for their ease and flexibility, but verbal communication should be documented with some sort of written notes. If your contractor is computer-savvy, e-mail can be efficient, and it leaves a written trail of discussions and decisions.

The "Three Rs" on a Natural Remodeling Job Site

All construction involves destruction. Nationwide, building renovations generate 44 percent of building waste. A typical 300-square-foot kitchen remodeling can easily produce 28 cubic yards of debris—imagine a room 10 feet by 10 feet by 7½ high, full of debris!

Let's say you decide to open your kitchen to the dining room and install a new window in the dining room. Before you know it, you have a huge, dusty pile of 2x4s, lath and plaster (or gypsum board), insulation, tile, old cabinets, vinyl flooring, used electric wire, light fixtures and switches, and a door and window. But wait, it doesn't all need to go to the dump. With a little planning, you can pass some of those materials along to another user and recycle the rest.

Recycling waste from construction and demolition ("C&D waste," as it is commonly called) has been a steadily growing practice over the last decade. In addition to environmental values, this trend is driven by increased fees for dumping, shrinking landfill space, and government initiatives

Using local artisans and materials can lead to wonderful designs, like this rock retaining wall and reclaimed wood bench.

It's getting easier to recycle materials that you remove during demolition. Salvage yards like this one in Portland, Oregon, will pass them on to others.

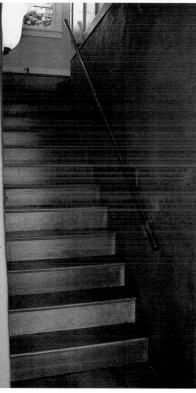

The risers of these Douglas fir stairs were once the treads of the previous (steeper) stairway.

There are two main types of "waste" generated during remodeling: the debris from demolition of the existing building, and the debris generated during construction. Here are the keys to managing your C&D waste:

- **Reducing** the amount of waste generated, through good planning and design (see page 178)

- **Reusing** materials on your own project, or passing them along to others

- **Recycling** materials that can't be reused intact but that need to be reprocessed before they can be used again

Short recycled studs are used as dividers in this entry floor.

DECONSTRUCTION: OPPORTUNITIES AND HAZARDS

During deconstruction, you have a rare opportunity to inspect the "guts" of your house and look for clues to ongoing or past problems. Mold or rot inside the wall indicates a moisture issue that should be addressed; sawdust or feces show an insect or rodent infestation; dirt on fiberglass insulation indicates an air leak. This is the time to address those problems.

When you open your walls, nasty stuff that's been trapped inside may escape into the air. If you have old insulation, textured ceilings, or acoustic tiles, have the materials tested for asbestos content. David Johnston, author of *Green Remodeling*, shares his experiences with deconstruction hazards:

> *"The construction process unearths all kinds of things. Take an attic, for example. No one's been in the attic in 30 years, and all of a sudden a contractor's up there moving stuff around, and it kicks up dust, rodent feces—who knows what has gotten into it? The freeze/thaw cycle may have dripped moisture into the insulation and mold has started to grow. People don't realize how sensitive they are to their own home. Then, behold, their immune system goes off! They develop allergies, maybe even asthma. Their body reacts in some dramatic way. And the only variable in their life is remodeling. They go to the doctor, who says, "well, you've got a cold" or "you've got an allergy. Take this medicine, take these drugs," and no one identifies the real causal elements. Of course, we know that sometimes the symptoms just don't go away; once the immune system is assaulted, some people just don't recover. Their life is different from that point forward. That's probably the biggest thing that happens unbeknownst to homeowners when they start the remodeling process."*

To minimize such problems, wear protective gear and the proper mask when opening, inspecting, or cleaning out cavities (attics, walls, crawlspaces). Take special care to isolate construction areas from living areas. Seal off all connections—doors, windows, ducts, electrical boxes, attic accesses—with tape and plastic; two layers is best. If air can move from one area to another, it *will* take dust, mold, and feces with it. If you are especially sensitive to dust, plan on relocating to an apartment temporarily or taking a trip during the worst parts of demolition and construction. For more information on existing hazards in homes, see Hazards, page 263.

Deconstruction for Salvage and Reuse

As in nature, "waste" products can simply be food for the next process. A typical kitchen remodeling, for example, can yield a treasure trove of salvageable materials: cabinets, knobs, countertops, light fixtures, windows, and appliances. Do your part to ease the pressure on landfills by finding new homes for these items.

Reusable building materials can be found at your local salvage yard.

Walk through the area you plan to remodel and make a list of the elements that could be reused. Some things, such as light fixtures, hardware, cabinets, and doors, can be used as is. But don't forget less obvious items, such as studs from a demolished wall that would be perfect for reframing a window opening, or siding that could be used as a patch where you've

moved a window. In order to salvage materials for reuse, you must take a more careful approach than usual; think in terms of *deconstruction* rather than *demolition*.

Deconstruction means taking a structure apart piece by piece, usually by hand, from the skin down to the bones. You need to pay close attention to protecting the elements you want to salvage. For example, a wood floor that you plan to save needs to be removed or protected to avoid damage before you start taking down walls.

If your deconstruction process will yield materials that you won't reuse yourself, make sure they go to a salvage yard; look in your phone book under "salvage," "recycling," "waste management," and "used materials." Depending on the type of material, some organizations will pick up items and give you a donation receipt—providing a tax deduction for you or your contractor. And don't overlook the possibility that your neighbors will be happy to have your castoffs; post a "FREE, You Haul" sign on working appliances or on a giveaway bin that contains clean, sorted materials.

The wide, hinged door that opens the end of this renovated garage was built by carefully deconstructing and rebuilding the previous flip-up garage door.

Many subfloors where once constructed with Douglas fir. While it is a soft wood, it ages gracefully and is perfectly serviceable as a finished floor.

The ReBuilding Center used an array of salvaged windows and siding when they constructed their new building in 2005.

Recycle What Can't Be Reused

Sorting makes the difference between a pile of trash and materials that are recyclable or sellable. The key to job-site recycling is having an organized system of material separation, and education for everyone working there. Sorting wood offcuts, pipes, wire, and gypsum board into bins by size and type makes it easy to see what is available for reuse on site and simplifies recycling. This requires both space (which can be at a premium during remodeling jobs) and commitment on the part of the contractor. Here are some tips to smooth the process:

- Call ahead to recycling centers; ask what materials they receive, whether they pick up materials, and how they would like materials sorted.

- Create conveniently located bins and storage areas (protected from weather if necessary) to facilitate sorting.

- Clearly label recycling bins or areas and educate workers about what goes where.

Most recycling centers want (and might even pay for) "clean" loads—deliveries that have been separated according to material type (concrete, wood, metals). Some yards are designed to receive, sort, and recycle mixed loads, which makes your job much easier.

Ask your contractor if he or she has experience with deconstruction, salvage, and job-site recycling. If your contractor is inexperienced in this, you can facilitate the process by finding local recycling centers and salvage yards and obtaining their guidelines.

Many salvage yards stock used lumber and siding for projects of all scales.

Ted Baumgart glued and wired together used plastic containers as molds and used them to craft a series of gargoyles around his home.

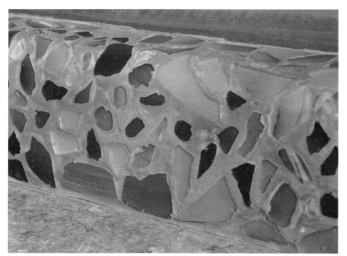

This mosaic backsplash is made of tumbled pieces of recycled glass.

THE REAL POOP ON REUSING OLD TOILETS

Toilets manufactured before 1994 can use 3.5 to 7 gallons of water or more per flush. Leaks in old toilets can account for another 10 per cent of residential water usage. New toilets use only 1.6 gallons per flush, and some have a dual-flush option that matches the water flow to the type of waste being removed. Replacing a pre-1994 toilet can save 9,000 to 26,500 gallons per household annually. While older 1.6-gallon/flush toilets sometimes didn't make the grade, manufacturers have recently optimized their 1.6-gallon designs (for toilet effectiveness testing, see www.cuwcc.org). Do yourself, your wallet, and your water district a favor. When it comes to toilets, don't reuse—replace!

KELLY'S EXPERIENCE *Replace, reuse, or recycle old single-pane windows? I'm a sucker for old windows. Their small panes and wavy, bubbled glass make me sigh with delight. But the single glazing and leaky seals of old windows can be an energy drain in old houses. If you decide to replace your windows with energy-efficient models, what can you do with the beautiful old ones? Here are a few ideas:*

- *Interior windows, which are used to share daylight and aid ventilation, don't need to be weather-tight.*

- *Single-pane windows can enclose a sunroom that's outside your thermal envelope.*

- *An old window sash can become a stylish mirror frame, or even a picture frame.*

- *Old windows can be used to make greenhouses or cold frames.*

At the ReBuilding Center, salvaged single-pane windows were used to bring daylight into the open-air warehouse.

243

MATERIALS TO BE RECYCLED

MATERIALS	Generated During	From What?	To Where?
CARPET and PAD	Deconstruction, new construction (scraps)	Carpeted rooms	Salvage yard if in good condition, C&D recycling center if in poor condition. Reuse under pond liner or green roof, or as permeable weed block under stone paths.
WOOD	Deconstruction, new construction (scraps)	Pallets, concrete forms, framing, interior finishes	Salvage yard for larger reusable pieces, C&D recycling center for small pieces. In some cases, must be clean of all metals and paint.
BROKEN CONCRETE	Deconstruction	Driveways, sidewalks, walkways	C&D recycling center, or reuse on site as pavers, low retaining walls for gardens, or "fill"
ROOFING SHINGLES	Deconstruction, new construction (scraps)	Roofs	C&D recycling center
DRYWALL/WALLBOARD/ PLASTER	Deconstruction, new construction (scraps)	Interior walls and ceilings	C&D recycling center, or pulverize gypsum and add to compost
CARDBOARD and PAPER	Throughout	Packaging, office supplies	Recycling center
NONFERROUS METALS	Deconstruction and new construction	Old hardware, wiring, plumbing pipes, conduit, connectors	Metals recycling center, salvage yard
PLASTICS	Throughout	Packaging, building parts in newer buildings	Recycling center (check ahead; not all plastics can be recycled)
FERROUS METALS	Throughout	Rebar, nails, screws, connectors	Metals recycling center, salvage yard
PLANT DEBRIS FROM CLEARING LAND	Deconstruction	Plants, trees, etc.	If small, dig up and donate. Chip and use on site or take to yard-waste composting program.
BRICK	Deconstruction and construction	Chimneys, walkways, veneer	Salvage yard or reuse on site (e.g., paths, patios, walls, benches)
BEVERAGE CANS and BOTTLES	Throughout	Thirsty workers	Recycling center

The End Is in Sight

Remodeling can take a long time. In fact, it often takes longer than anyone expects. All those finishing touches seem to take forever. To see your way through to the end, keep in mind how much you will enjoy living in your new home. Time spent on doing the construction job right will pay off for decades to come. As a client of Carol's put it, "Remodeling is like having a child: when you're in labor, you just want it to end. But once your child is born, you forget all the pain, and the joy takes over."

Debenham-Kingsley Residence
Portland, Oregon

Anna Debenham and Charles Kingsley have always enjoyed finding things that need some loving care. But when they moved to Portland, Oregon, and went looking for a home, they had no idea just how dramatic such a process could be—or how profoundly it would affect the course of their lives.

Anna and Charles's remodeling projects take the neighborhood into consideration as well as the house itself.

The couple went about househunting with a passion, first considering the whole city of Portland fair game and gradually refining their focus until they found the one neighborhood that felt most like home to them. That spirit of community and interconnectedness permeates everything Charles and Anna undertake.

Walking their favorite neighborhood looking for "ignored and neglected" houses, the couple spotted what appeared to be a fixer-upper's dream: a deserted house in a yard overgrown with ivy and surrounded by a chain-link fence. They learned that it was built in 1909, had been converted illegally from a single-family home to a duplex, had last been inhabited by drug dealers and a prostitute, and had sustained fire damage from a Molotov cocktail. It had been empty for two years. The owner was ready to deal.

This house on Woodward Street was the first of two back-to-back houses that Charles and Anna eco-rehabbed.

"The neighbors welcomed us with open arms," recalls Charles. "There's little you can do to feel more appreciated than to take over and restore an old drug house." They took possession of the house in April of 2001, and then things got even more interesting; the little house just over the back fence came on the market at a reasonable price. At first they thought they couldn't afford it, but when they considered the inconvenience of living in a house under renovation, they decided to buy and move into it while fixing the larger house.

The Woodward House

For the next eight months, Anna and Charles threw themselves into uplifting their two-story faded beauty on Woodward Street. Their goal was to restore its original elegance while updating it for contemporary living, all in a sustainable way that anyone could appreciate, no matter what their environmental values—and within a reasonable budget.

Charles and Anna found themselves sitting on the floor of the Woodward house looking around. "It looked like we were going to have to redo it from top to bottom," recalls Charles. "It felt like a privilege, and we wanted to start by honoring the roots of this house: 'What did it look like? What does it want to look like? How can we integrate a more open, country-style kitchen with the smaller kitchen that was built here in 1909?' It was actually easier than new construction, because it wasn't a blank slate. We sat there and looked at bad paneling, bad carpeting, and really cheap fixtures, but we also noticed that they hadn't redone many walls. The basic bones of the house seemed pretty good."

Anna and Charles discovered that they had a talent for redesigning spaces. Acting as their own contractors, they tore out the relatively recent alterations—partition walls, upstairs kitchen, crummy finishes—then made further changes to the house, aiming to remain sensitive to its spirit. They brought in more daylight via new windows; added a half-bath to the first floor; opened up walls into a little old porch in back and extended the kitchen into it; and created a second-story deck from a bad roof over the back of the house, with a great view over downtown Portland.

"One of the most ecologically sound things people can do is to not have more space than they need," observes Charles. "That saves on materials, and it means less space to heat and less house to maintain. There's often a lot of unused space in these older homes; by moving back a wall into

Though the house had been mistreated for years, Charles and Anna sought to honor its roots—in this case, with period tile and a clawfoot tub.

Extending the kitchen into an old enclosed back porch brought more light and useful space to a formerly small kitchen.

The new kitchen eating area opens to a new back deck, introducing a strong connection with the garden.

247

Lots of natural ventilation and shading are all the summer cooling you really need in Portland's mild climate.

unused attic space, opening up walls where appropriate, or reconfiguring awkward storage and circulation areas, we've been able to create more living space without adding square footage. We also love creating a more spacious feeling by bringing natural light and ventilation deeper into the house." In addition to adding windows, they used glass in several of the interior doors to allow light to penetrate farther into the house than usual.

Thermal Comfort

In Portland's moderate climate, the need for cooling is minimal; Charles and Anna found that by emphasizing natural ventilation and shading—primarily by having operable windows everywhere and planting trees on the south side for summer shade—they didn't feel a need to add air conditioning. However, winter heat is important in such a damp climate.

The house's furnace was ancient and had no ducting to the second floor. This left Charles and Anna free to install a hydronic radiant heating system—considered by many to be one of the most comfortable, healthy, energy-efficient options. The heart of the system is an efficient Polaris water heater, which feeds hot water to four zones via PEX tubing. On the main floor, the tubing runs under the wood flooring, and on the upper floor it runs in the ceiling. When installing the water heater, they plumbed it for a future connection with a rooftop solar water heater.

Insulation was another important feature of energy-efficient thermal comfort. The house had no insulation when Anna and Charles acquired it, so they insulated its top, bottom, and sides with blown-in cellulose.

The old windows were leaky single-pane models, so the couple replaced the glazing with double-pane, low-E windows in the existing wooden frames. They also added a few well-placed windows for more light and air, and they reused the original glass in a greenhouse.

Materials

Charles and Anna kept existing materials and used reclaimed materials wherever they could. Under the old carpet, they found beautiful Douglas fir floors with some damaged areas. They were able to find reclaimed fir flooring and piece it in to match the existing floors.

Working with several local architectural salvage companies, they found reclaimed sinks, tubs, lights, and doors, as well as beautiful pine for making countertops. Not wanting to reintroduce lead paint into the house, they had the salvaged doors stripped with the least-toxic products available. The new front door was custom made from salvaged pine, and the front porch sports beautiful recycled wood banisters. For the kitchen, they located and refurbished an old Wedgewood stove.

Removing the old carpet revealed beautiful Douglas fir floors worth saving and refinishing.

Using "waste" materials can lead to uncommon creativity and beauty, as seen in this fence made from cedar slabs cast aside at the mill.

The couple also purchased new products from local businesses wherever possible. The kitchen cabinets are made of wheatboard (from waste straw), and the fronts are made from wood certified by the Forest Stewardship Council (FSC). They painted the walls with low-VOC and no-VOC paints made by a local company. Anna and Charles feel that buying locally is a key element in ecological restoration, whether it involves locally harvested materials, crafts from nearby artisans, or just shopping at stores with local ownership. Buying locally minimizes transportation costs, builds community, and supports stronger connections with place.

The side yard fences are a work of art, made from "slab sides" of old cedar trees—the outer edges of trees normally considered waste in the milling process. "The slab sides have a sensual shape," notes Charles. "They're the outer edges of the trees, so the bark is still on them and they have an organic shape."

Rescuing the back garden from overgrown English ivy presented opportunities to sculpt peaceful outdoor rooms using native plants.

Landscaping

Anna and Charles began their landscaping by removing the invasive English ivy that had taken over the yard. At the back of the property (between the big house and the smaller house they were living in), they created a living fence. Wanting to honor the landscape that preceded human habitation in the area, they brought in native species such as vine maple, wax myrtle, white oak, and Oregon grape. At the same time, the living fence isn't a barrier. "We wanted to create some privacy, but we also wanted to open up and create stronger relationships between neighbors," says Charles. "We got the best of both worlds."

They also designed their back deck, which opens off the revised country kitchen, to playfully interact with the landscaping. "We made the deck floor in the shape of a leaf, with the decking boards running in the direction of the leaf's veins," says Charles. "It kind of flows off the back of the house."

Speaking of flowing, another strategy well suited to the Pacific Northwest is to use the abundant winter rainfall to water gardens during the dry summers. The pair installed a gutter system that routes rainwater to a 1,700-gallon cistern, located partially belowground under the kitchen deck (a hatch in the deck gives access to the cistern). "We end up using that rainwater to water the lawn for half the summer, and it only takes 2 inches of rain to fill up the cistern again."

The Northwest's abundant rainwater is collected from the roof and stored in a cistern under the back deck for summer garden watering.

249

Over the back fence, the house on Taggart Street was Charles and Anna's next project.

The Taggart House

As work proceeded in the Woodward house, Charles and Anna found themselves giving their little residence over the back fence a step-by-step eco-facelift. The two projects make for an interesting contrast. Whereas Woodward was a full-out gut-and-remodel project, the house on Taggart Street was done on the "incremental, doing-more-with-less" model. Whenever their carpenters had to stop work on the Woodward house for a few days (while insulation or heating was going in, for example), Anna and Charles had them work on the Taggart house. "There was kind of a nice ecology in that, too," notes Charles. "It made for really productive use of time, and there was no commute—just move between backyards. So that was sweet."

Though livable, the Taggart house had "bad vinyl, bad carpet, bad paint, and a drywall finish so rough that we almost grazed ourselves on it," recalls Anna. It was also dark, small, and awkwardly laid out. The first thing they did was add windows and a double French door to bring in some west light. Though there was a garden area on the west side of the house, virtually no windows looked onto it.

At the same time, they reconfigured the floor plan. About a third of the main floor had been taken up by a dark hallway and a laundry room, which blocked access to the west garden. They moved the washer/dryer into the basement and turned the liberated space into a sitting area overlooking the garden. "It allowed us to bring in more light and gain nearly 300 square feet of living area on the main floor," says Charles. "It was like creating an addition without increasing the house's footprint. We love stuff like that." Upstairs, removing the wall of a walk-in closet/office space created a more open space that aided cross-ventilation and natural lighting.

The gardens of the Woodward and Taggart Street houses are connected by a curving path.

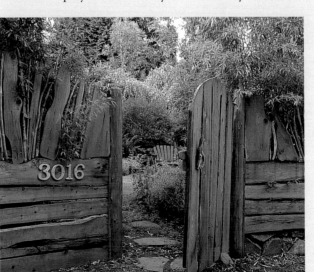

Crafted of salvaged cedar slabs and branches, the entry gate and fence at the Taggart Street house display creative use of reclaimed material.

When the Woodward renovation was complete, the couple moved into the larger house and turned their attention to further improvements in the Taggart house. They replaced the kitchen cabinets with wheatboard cabinets, doing the painting themselves to save money. They chose a fun color to add interest. Taking out the unappealing vinyl kitchen flooring and removing the sitting-room carpet revealed oak flooring underneath. They then found salvaged oak and pieced it in for a kitchen floor that blended right into the sitting room floor. They had a kitchen countertop crafted from salvaged whiskey barrels and made open shelves out of old bleacher seats.

Sometimes subtraction is a plus; here, removing some walls added openness, natural light, and ventilation.

A previous owner had replaced several of the Taggart house's windows with double-pane vinyl windows, presenting a challenge. "We knew we wanted to bring in more light and air," recalls Charles, "but we really preferred wood windows, both aesthetically and in terms of environmental impact. 'Should we throw away all these new vinyl windows, or finish the restoration with vinyl windows to match?' That was tricky. We ended up adding vinyl windows. It was a trade-off that honored the embodied energy of the windows that were already there." The couple mitigated the plastic look by adding wood-slat blinds to the windows. For Anna, there's still an unsettled feeling about that decision. "We had good reasons for the choices we made, but windows are the way you look outside. A view to the garden that's framed in plastic is different from a view framed in wood."

Colorful wheatboard cabinets, salvaged oak flooring, a countertop made from old whiskey barrels, and shelves that were once bleacher seats combine to make a lively, functional kitchen between the living and dining areas.

A glass-block window admits light to the dark hallway beyond.

The pièce de résistance is the porch that Anna and Charles created on the west side of the house, with a roof designed to provide both summer shade and winter sunlight for the house. The porch posts are two old cedar trees from a clear-cut, and the beams are salvaged. The next step was to install a "green roof"—a sod-covered roof (with a system of waterproofing below) that allows rooftop gardening so that a person upstairs looks out over plantings. "It was part of the experiment in 'How do you design something that responds to and supports the original design of the house and yet is different?'" explains Charles. "How can we design a transitional space that models more of nature that we're moving into, and yet doesn't feel out of place and still feels close to being an original part of the house?"

At the new front porch, salvaged, peeled tree trunks support milled timbers with a delightful balance of whimsy and solidity.

"It's also nice that it's so low to the ground that it doesn't need a railing," adds Anna. "There's just one step down into the yard, so the porch feels like an extension of both the garden and the house. And the garden has become a lovely, amazing place. In summer, expanding out into the garden creates many more rooms. We both love it."

That little enchanted garden on the west was once a driveway. Because the house had two parking areas and no yard, Charles and Anna reclaimed this driveway for living things. In the bargain, they were able to improve the water situation on both lots. Rainwater used to run straight down the driveway from the Woodward property and into the basement of the Taggart house. Charles and Anna tore out the paving, installed French drains, terraced the yards with low rock walls, brought in topsoil and compost, and planted a nitrogen-fixing clover ground cover to break up the compacted soil and add nutrients. This slowed the rainwater down so that it filters into the soil and groundwater, and the soil was nourished in preparation to receive native plantings. What was once impenetrable soil is now rich with earthworms and plant life—including a vegetable garden—and less water runs into the city's storm water system.

Formerly a secondary driveway, this garden now contributes positively to food and water cycles while providing a lovely environment.

Thermal Comfort

For a while, Charles and Anna put up with the funky old furnace and water heater that came with the house. Later, they found a used furnace and water heater that were relatively new and energy-efficient, and convinced an HVAC contractor to install them. They also added a soapstone wood stove to the living room. "On particularly cold mornings, we'd turn on the furnace first thing in the morning just to heat the space," says Anna. "Then if we planned to be there during the day, we'd turn down the furnace and build a fire. The soapstone stove puts out a wonderful, slow radiant heat. And because the house has only 1,100 square feet, it heats the whole house."

"There's also something about the feeling of a wood fire," says Charles. "I think it must go back to our ancient DNA—sitting around fires when we were first learning how to walk on our feet. It's an amazing feeling. And wood stove technology has gotten so good, in terms of emissions and efficiency, that it feels appropriate to us in this wooded area. We placed the wood stove in the corner of the living room, where it's visible from the kitchen and the dining area."

Building Community

As Anna and Charles revived these two forlorn houses, they were also feeding a social network. "Whenever we wondered how to do something or where to find something we needed, we asked lots of people," recalls Charles. "We met some great people that way, and found really unusual materials, like those cedar off-cuts that are now our fence. People steered us toward information, toward great salvaged stuff, toward Portland's Office of Sustainable Development and their G-Rated Homes program (in which Charles and Anna participate).

A rain chain from the gutter celebrates the frequent Oregon winter rains with motion and sound.

When they had finished most of the work on the Taggart house, they moved back into it. The 1,800 square feet of the Woodward house felt too large for their needs, so they rented it to friends. "One of our goals from the start was to support community and a sense of neighborliness. We came up with the idea of renting the Woodward house to like-minded people at a below-market rate, making up the difference with barter for yard work and small building projects. That way, we could create a form of affordable housing while having friends nearby and continuing to improve the houses." The plan has worked well. Their first tenants built the fence, the back deck, and a bench and helped with the landscaping.

The new soapstone wood stove puts out a wonderful radiant warmth that heats the whole little house.

253

Reflecting on the Process

Anna and Charles endorse keeping an eye on the connections among the parts of the home when remodeling. "Don't look at anything in isolation," says Charles. "Keep asking 'How does all this stuff relate to the rest of it? How does the design of the kitchen relate to how we're handling storm water, and how does that relate to the design of the deck?' We had to stretch ourselves and our subcontractors all the time." The approach has paid off. When the Woodward house was included in a green home tour, a group of designers said, "We've been around to all these other houses, and a number of them have a menu of green features, but yours is the only house that actually feels like a whole; it feels really sweet to be here."

To Anna and Charles, that's what all the hard work is about. "That kind of elegance of design and how things fit together is far more than just 'do we have salvaged wood and insulation and whatever else is on the checklist.' There's a whole deeper conversation about ecology and the feel of a space and the soulfulness and how it relates to the outdoors and to the neighbors."

Charles Kingsley and Anna Debenham's
Top Five Tips for a Rainy Marine Climate

1. Insulate.

2. Bring in natural light (getting light into the heart of the house is dramatic in this climate):
    • Energy-efficient windows
    • Indoors, half-walls and glass-block walls to bring light deeper into the house
    • Skylights; they make a tremendous difference.

3. Landscape sensitively.
    • Native plantings
    • Terracing, to slow water down and let it soak in, rather than just diverting it or burying it
    • Rainwater catchment—a cistern or a pond or whatever you dream up

4. Bring in as much color as you can.

5. Don't be afraid to use wood; it's a local resource here, and there's a lot of it; use salvaged wood; expose it and let it sing.

Charles and Anna plan their next remodeling project while relaxing in their cozy, handcrafted garden shelter.

Conclusion: Living There

There can be no greater happiness than to live a life that follows the natural order of things.

—Sengai

I F YOU'VE CHOSEN to remodel your house in one grand effort, you will eventually arrive at a point when your remodeling project is "done." If you alter your home in phases, or as a series of little projects, you may instead find yourself settling into a long-term relationship with a constantly changing home. In either case, the larger endeavor of inhabiting and maintaining your natural home—of living in harmony with nature—is a joyous process that lasts a lifetime.

Natural Living

What do you first see when you wake up in the morning? What do your feet feel when you walk around your home? What do you hear when sitting in your favorite spot? What do you smell when you step out your front door? Your senses are constantly tuning you into the world and bringing you messages. Every now and then, tune in to whether your senses are bringing you messages of beauty, vitality, and oneness with nature.

To Everything There Is a Season

One way to increase your vitality is to inhabit your home differently at different times of the day and year. Some areas might feel most comfortable in the morning and others in the evening—some in winter and others in summer. Rather than using fossil fuels to bring the light and temperature to the same level in all parts of your house at all times, consider migrating throughout your home to find comfort and pleasure.

Another way to participate in natural cycles is to honor the arrival of each season. Seasonal rituals have been celebrated since the dawn of humanity. When life revolves around hunting and gathering what's in season—or on planting in spring, tending the fruits of summer, harvesting in fall, and storing up for winter—people develop an intense relationship with these annual cycles.

Modern lifestyles and technology have largely divorced us from such survival-based seasonal behavior. For most urban dwellers, the main cycle is a daily one: go to work, come home. But many people find that marking the seasons brings them deep satisfaction. Whether it's hanging Indian corn on the front door and placing a pumpkin on the stoop to welcome autumn, laying out a special gift of seeds and nuts at the winter solstice for the birds and squirrels, giving your house a fresh start with spring cleaning, or moving a table onto the porch for evening meals in summer, look for ways to enjoy the natural cycles around you.

KELLY'S EXPERIENCE *In my house, remodeling isn't a one-time act; it's an ongoing process. Even after the large projects are finished, each act of maintenance—painting a bedroom, fixing a leaky faucet, replacing a gate—becomes an opportunity to bring my home into better harmony with nature. The more I remodel, the more opportunities reveal themselves. With each change, I become more connected to my house. It's regenerative—and addictive. When I began work on this book, my friend Athena Steen told me about her experience with this phenomenon in a different context. Athena is a pioneer in the natural building world and coauthor of* The Straw Bale House *and* Built by Hand. *She has both built and remodeled several houses using natural materials.*

As a teenager, Athena worked with her grandmother, the Santa Clara Pueblo potter Rose Naranjo, etching intricate geometric designs on burnished pots. Sometimes Athena's tool would hit a grain of sand and skid astray, marring the design. "There was already a lot of work in this pot," says Athena. "I couldn't just throw it away, but it was ruined—messed up. Unable to figure out how to fix it, I'd set the pot aside and go on to the next 'fresh' pot. A few days later, able to let go of my initial preconceived ideas, I'd return to the scratched pot and create a new pattern that incorporated the flaw. These pots always became my favorites. The flaw not only inspired a more beautiful, unique design, but also a deeper connection between the pot and myself."

While my own house often seems "messed up," working with an imperfect house sparks my creativity in ways that starting with a blank slate never does. The result is a rich, ever-evolving design and a deep connection and satisfaction with my home every time I walk through the door.

Caring for Your House

The things you use every day in your home are just as important as the materials and systems you used in your natural remodeling project. It makes little sense to carefully select salvaged building materials and recycle your job-site waste, then bring lots of short-lived, disposable products into your home. It's equally counterproductive to create a healthy home, then use toxic personal-care and cleaning products. Check the Resource Appendix in this book and learn more about the products you use at home—and where to get eco friendly, durable replacements for toxic or resource-ineffi cient items. Be as kind to yourself and the earth on a daily basis as you were in remodeling.

Remember to keep your home in good repair, too. Durability— a key element of sustainability—comes from a combination of choosing good materials, installing them well, and maintaining them over time. After you've gone to the trouble of finding and installing good materials, protect your investment—and your enjoyment—with regular maintenance. An occasional coat of paint, new caulking around the windows, replacement washers, and an annual furnace tune-up are all a part of keeping your home and your life in balance.

CAROL'S EXPERIENCE   *When I lived in a downtown apartment, many of the views from my windows were of other buildings. But I managed to place my bed near a window so that I looked onto a tree-top and the sky from my bed. It meant everything to me to lie there gazing at the tree as I gradually came to consciousness.*

I later moved to a suburban house where my bedroom had a view through glass doors into a verdant yard. I loved waking up to the sunlight, greenery, and birds. One night I drew some curtains over the glass doors when I went to bed. When I awoke the next morning, the feeling in my bedroom was so flat, so dull that I will probably never close the curtains again before going to sleep.

Community Is Wherever You Are

You may wonder how remodeling your home can help the rest of the world. One of the best ways is to bring your neighbors into the conversation. Many cities and suburbs could use some natural remodeling, too, and you can join with others to multiply your positive impact—perhaps even creating an eco-village right where you live.

One great example of this is Los Angeles Eco-Village, which has been growing since 1992. Lois Arkin, one of the founders, had lived in an inner-city Los Angeles neighborhood of apartment buildings for 14 years. Neighbors from 15 ethnic groups often feared each other; the children didn't even play together. Esfandiar Abbassi, one of the early Eco-Villagers, recalls, "It literally started with people talking to each other: 'Hi, I'm so and so, I've seen you on the streets, what's your name?' Some of us were interested in gardening, so we started planting things, and gradually the neighbors said, 'Can we help out too?' When the first garden was put in, we had Saturday potluck brunches there—and watched the biology of the neighborhood change as butterflies and bees and birds started coming in."

Before long, a sense of community began to grow. A core of Eco-Villagers gently made information available on sustainability issues: housing, water, gardening, trees; the economic, social, and physical systems; and a sense of how to integrate them. Over the years, Eco-Villagers have planted a dozen organic gardens and more than 100 fruit trees in their two-block neighborhood; developed a community revolving loan fund that made it possible to purchase and eco-rehab two apartment buildings (which will be converted to co-ops); composted 60 cubic yards of green neighborhood waste; diverted 20 tons of brick from the landfill (from the 1994 earthquake) for Eco-Village beautification projects; and held weekly potlucks to build a sense of community. And more projects are in the works.

In Davis, California, N Street Cohousing is a good example of ecological community growing on a street of single-family houses. This project began in 1986, when two neighboring families with a shared interest in permaculture took down the fences between their yards. As homes on the block came up for sale, they found like-minded buyers to move in. Their community now includes 16 homes, several retrofitted with solar collectors, and one huge backyard, enhanced by play areas, outdoor dining patios, organic gardens, laundry lines, compost bins, and a chicken pen. One house was transformed into a "common house" with a large kitchen, a group dining room, an office, and upstairs rooms for rent.

Another inspiring project is OnGoing Cohousing in Portland, Oregon. It includes seven existing homes whose inhabitants share meals, work parties, and celebrations. Together, they are rehabbing their houses (upgrading insulation, adding double-pane windows, recycling building materials, adding solar water heat and low-flow toilets), sharing amenities (tools, electric mulching lawnmower, pickup truck), growing gardens and orchards, capturing rainwater, and recycling greywater to irrigate the gardens. A food-buying club initiated by the group has now turned into an organic cooperative storefront.

If you're not feeling quite that ambitious, keep in mind that big changes begin with little steps. Maybe your ripple effect will start when a neighbor asks a question while you're gardening one morning in your front yard. Maybe people will start looking to you for advice as their heating and cooling bills go through their uninsulated roof. Maybe they'll just ask your secret for staying so healthy and happy. Whenever your neighbors show an interest, you'll be ready with information and inspiration.

Coming to Life

Our overarching point is that, while this book appears to be about your house, it is actually about how you live. Your house is not a thing; it is one aspect of your personal and community ecosystem.

Whatever makes your heart glad—the rising sun, the changing seasons, caring for your home, knowing your neighbors—know that life is happening in you and all around you all the time. Nature isn't somewhere far away; it's everything. Every choice you make, every moment you spend can nurture you and the world.

While we do need to acknowledge and respond to the threats to our biosphere, it's equally important to affirm love, kindness, life, fun, and joy with every opportunity. Every day, we can appreciate the turning of the earth, the dew on a leaf, the song of a bird. And it helps to know that there are many others who not only care but also are doing something to heal their separation from nature. Even if you never meet them, your deep commitment to life adds to theirs in an ever-growing and unstoppable groundswell. We love life, and we intend to help it thrive. Welcome home.

Appendix A
Pre-Design Questionnaire

I. Personal Environmental History

1. Describe the physical and emotional qualities of the house and landscape where you grew up. If you had many homes, pick the ones that evoke the strongest feelings.

2. Close your eyes and recall the most beautiful, comfortable room you've ever been in. "Walk around" in it for a while, then describe the room and your feelings about it.

3. Describe one of the most beautiful sights you've ever seen (not necessarily a building).

4. Describe the best environment you've lived in (if different from above) and why you found it so.

5. Describe your patterns of well-being, health, illness, energy, and tiredness in terms of where and when you tend to feel various ways. Are you aware of any environmental sensitivities (allergies, chemical sensitivities, etc.)?

6. What have been the predominant color schemes where you've lived? How have you felt about them?

7. Through your own cultural background or travels, do you have an affinity for any particular historical period or ethnic style, building materials, or symbolism?

II. Your Self

1. How close to nature do you feel? Which elements do you respond to most (water, air, fire, earth)?

2. Are you more an outdoor or an indoor person? What are your favorite activities, indoors and outdoors?

3. What hobbies, special interests, and sports are important to you (alone, with others)?

4. What are your favorite colors?

5. Where and when is heat/warmth most important to you? Coolness?

6. If you could not control your environment, would you prefer to be too warm or too cool? In a brightly lit room or a dimly lit one?

7. When at home, do you tend to be active or passive?

8. Are you more comfortable with a certain amount of clutter and disorganization, or with more neatness and organization? Explain/describe. What kinds of storage do you prefer?

9. How important is it to you that the materials and systems of this home reflect concerns for indoor health, ecology, and/or political issues? Explain.

10. Do you have any pets? What environment(s) do they need? Are there parts of your home that are off limits to pets?

11. Where are you and what are you doing when you feel your best?

III. Other People

1. Who will be living in this house (include part-time)? How will this change over time?

2. How does your family or living group spend its time during the day and evening (work, separate projects, computer games, reading, listening to music, watching TV together, etc.)?

3. How do you entertain guests? Would you like to change your entertainment patterns?

4. How often do you have overnight guests? How do you want to accommodate them?

5. What do you want your home to say about you to others?

IV. General Planning

1. What functions do you want your home to include?

cooking	eating	conversation
sleeping	bathing	grooming
reading	hobbies	business
laundry	relaxing	games
meditation	music making	gardening
TV watching	artistic creation	parties
meetings	children's play	car housing
storage	sports	_____
_____	_____	_____

Check all that apply, add important functions that are not included here, and circle the one (or a combination) that is the heart of the home. Draw lines connecting the functions that should be adjacent to each other.

2. What functions or areas of the house require the following.

  • privacy
  • quiet
  • views (what kind?)
  • outdoor access
  • a deck, porch, or other outdoor living area
  • a lot of space
  • little space
  • access to storage
  • being at ground level
  • warmth
  • coolness

3. Will you use existing furniture? If so list and give exact dimensions (length, width, height). (Only one person in the family needs to complete this.)

4. Do you have any special collections that need to be housed?

5. Do you have a piano? What room will house it? (Remember to include its dimensions in IV.3)

6. Where do you want.

  • television(s)
  • telephones
  • sound systems
  • fireplaces or woodstoves
  • computers

7. Would you like to have outdoor (or partially outdoor) areas for cooking, eating, sitting, sleeping, etc.?

8. Do you plan to remodel your home in phases? Explain.

V. Kitchen

1. Who cooks in your house? How often is there more than one cook at work simultaneously (how many maximum)?

2. What types of cooking do you tend to do (baking, vegetarian, barbecue, gourmet, etc.)?

3. Do you like to see your pots, pans, dishes, and foods, or to have them hidden, or some of both? What kinds of storage do you prefer (upper cabinets, lower cabinets, drawers, pantry)?

4. What are holidays like in your kitchen?

5. Do you want to encourage or discourage guests congregating in your kitchen at parties?

6. How much connection do you want between the kitchen and other functions (eating, garden, hearth, entry, sitting, television, views, etc.)?

7. What appliances do you want in your kitchen? (specify gas, electric, or other; give name brands or types if important)

   - range/oven combination
   - cooktop (type?)
   - eye-height oven
   - sink (type, number)
   - refrigerator/freezer
   - freezer
   - dishwasher
   - microwave oven
   - espresso machine
   - food processor

VI. Dining

1. Do you want one eating area, or more than one for different purposes? Explain.

2. What type and size of dining table(s) do you want? Would it be extendible? (Give sizes in both positions above.)

3. Describe the ways in which you want to use your dining area, both daily and on special occasions. Will it be used during nonmealtimes (if so, for what)?

4. Do you want to see into the kitchen from the eating area(s)? From other areas?

5. What kind of storage areas do you need near the dining area?

VII. Living Room

1. What activities will occur in the living room?

2. Describe the qualities you'd like to experience in the living room.

3. How many people will typically use the living room? What maximum number would you like to accommodate?

4. Do you prefer armchairs, couches, or both? How many of each?

5. Will the living room accommodate a TV, extensive sound system, and/or media center? If so, please provide dimensions and any special clearances, adjacencies, or other related needs.

VIII. Bathrooms

1. Do you prefer to think of a bathroom as an efficient space for performing necessary functions, or a sensuous place to luxuriate and care for your body? Elaborate.

2. What sort of tub and shower arrangement do you prefer—separate, combined, sizes?

3. Do you want a separate toilet compartment?

4. Do you want special views from particular places in the bathroom?

IX. Sleeping Area(s)

1. What is your typical sleep pattern (early riser, night owl, etc.)? Does it vary much?

2. Are you a morning or a night person? Do you like to be awakened by the rising sun?

3. Are you a heavy or a light sleeper?

4. Do you like to read in bed?

5. Do you like to have moonlight shining into the bedroom or not? Do you want to see the stars from your bed?

6. How spacious a bedroom do you want? What do you want in the bedroom besides your bed (desk, chairs, vanity, mirrors, sink...)?

7. How big a closet do you need in or near the sleeping areas?

X. Laundry

1. What other functions would you like your washer/dryer to be near (bedrooms, kitchen, etc.)?

2. Do you want an outdoor (or indoor) clothesline?

3. Do you want a separate laundry room? If so, what other functions/spaces/appliances would you like in that room?

4. What type of laundry equipment will you use? (stacked or side-by-side, front-loading or top-loading, size and brand if known)

5. Will you use an ironing board? If so, how frequently? Do you want it built in?

6. Should your laundry area include a utility sink or folding area?

XI. Transportation Area(s): Bicycles and Automobiles

1. Do you want a garage? Carport? Parking area? Turnaround?

2. How many cars and bicycles will be housed? Do you work on your own vehicles?

3. Do you want a garage workshop or similar area?

4. Do you need a solar charging station or other renewable-fuel accommodation?

5. Do you have other vehicles that need to be housed? What are their spatial needs?

XII. Home Office

1. Will you conduct business at home? If so, full time or part time?

2. What sort of space and office equipment will you need?

3. Will clients, employees, and/or coworkers be coming to your home office? Does your office need a separate entrance?

XIII. Gardens

1. Are you (or do you want to be) a gardener?

2. Describe the sort of yard and gardens that you would like to have.

3. Will you need garden-related areas (garden tool shed, potting bench, compost area)?

4. Do you want any "outdoor rooms" (for eating, entertaining, sleeping, bathing, etc.)?

XIV. Activity Patterns

Take note of your daily activity patterns for a week or more. Notice what you're doing, when, and where. Notice whether your pattern varies much from day to day. Think about whether it varies with the seasons or for special circumstances. You might even want to map these personal migrations on a floor plan of your house. Once you become more aware of the climatic shifts in and around your home, you may find ways to alter how you use your home, bringing your life into greater harmony with nature.

XV. Resources

1. What is your financial budget for this project?

2. What other personal resources do you bring to the project (design or construction skills, other skills that you can trade for same, organizational ability, etc.)? Be creative about what you can bring to the project in addition to money.

3. Who can you call on for help, and what are their skills? Again be creative; you may know someone who can lay bricks, a family with an empty garage where you can store salvage finds, or even a great cook who will happily feed friends who come for a "barn raising."

XVI. Other

Please add any other thoughts you have, special interests or needs you want accommodated, or anything else that's important to you that hasn't already been covered. Please describe additional rooms/spaces not yet mentioned (family room, den, utility room, mudroom).

Appendix B
Checking For Household Hazards
By Mary Cordaro

If you are planning to remodel your home—or if you want to buy a house to remodel—there are a number of potential hazards to assess. I call it "getting a baseline," or learning whether the house has lead, EMFs (electromagnetic fields), mold, toxic chemicals, pests, asbestos, or air-pressurization problems.

Also look for deal-breakers—anything that would make it unwise to proceed. If you're considering buying a house, a deal-breaker would mean that you don't want this house; if you're assessing your current home, a deal-breaker could mean that your money would be better spent on a different house.

You may not want to invest in a particular house if the cost of mitigating the health hazards will be too high. Get estimates up front and roll them into your overall budget. This may have an impact on your other remodeling decisions.

Lead

If the house was built before 1978, when lead was banned from building materials, it's likely that there's lead in the paint or ceramic tile. If you'll be tearing out walls or otherwise disturbing those surfaces, you should get a lead test. Here's why: when you disturb any lead-containing material, it could contaminate the whole house. It's important to remove them under containment during demolition.

Lead can also be a problem in your yard. If someone has scraped off exterior paint, including any layer that was applied before 1978, lead dust may have fallen into your soil. That can affect your vegetable garden, or any children and animals that play in your yard.

The Issue

Lead is a neurotoxin, meaning that it can harm nerve tissue. Lead can affect anyone, but its effects are most dramatic in children and small animals; ingesting or inhaling the tiniest amounts of lead can create serious neurological problems. What's worse, children are constantly touching and licking things and putting their hands in their mouths.

Detection

First, determine the age of the house; if it was built before 1978, it may have lead paint. The areas with the highest potential are painted woodwork and anything painted with shiny (or formerly shiny) paint, such as in bathrooms and kitchens—even if it's buried under layers of post-1978 paint. Another potential problem area would be double-hung windows, doors, and cupboards—any place where regular friction may rub off old lead paint.

Second, if you do have pre-1978 paint and it has been disturbed or is bubbling—or if it's likely to be disturbed during remodeling—you should call in a lead inspector (see page 266).

What to Do

A lead inspector will write a remediation plan and refer you to appropriate professionals. This may include a certified painter or a lead-abatement company that can remove the lead-containing materials under containment during demolition. After the work is completed, the lead inspector should perform clearance testing to ensure that the work was done properly.

Deal-Breakers

Lead can usually be dealt with, but the question is whether you want to spend the time and money involved. Lead could be a deal-breaker if you can't easily do remediation using affordable methods.

EMFs

EMF hazards fall into two categories: outdoor sources and indoor sources. It's a good idea to test for EMFs before planning a remodeling project, and avoid elevated EMFs if you can.

The Issue

The effect of EMFs on health is a very controversial topic. Here's how one expert I respect sees it: For every study that says that there are no health effects from EMFs, there are six that say there are. There is enough evidence to suggest a correlation between elevated EMFs and Alzheimer's disease, childhood leukemia, lymphoma, other forms of cancer, and many other health issues. Stress to the immune system is a less dramatic effect, which could show up in a variety of ways depending on a person's weak areas—joint problems, sleep disturbance, or chronic fatigue.

Detection

To some extent, it's possible to test for EMFs yourself; you can take a class or read a book, and buy your own meter—then perform a simple screening to indicate whether to invest in a professional EMF inspection for greater accuracy.

First, assess the outdoor environment around your home. Check for EMFs in areas where you or your children spend a lot of time. Also look for outside sources of EMFs that may affect you inside your home. For example, there might be high EMFs from an outside power line or a transformer, even if it's underground. There could even be current traveling on the water supply pipes coming in from the street.

Second, if you've ruled out exterior EMFs, test for fields inside your house. Carry your meter into every room, especially bedrooms, areas where you spend most of your time, and at floor level wherever children play. First check for outside sources of EMFs by turning the power off (stand to the side as a safety precaution). Then turn the power on and check for indoor sources of EMFs.

If you detect high levels of EMFs, or if you're in the line of sight of a cell phone tower or antenna, you may want to call in a trained EMF consultant* to find out if the problem can be solved. You might also want a consultant to check for EMFs from digital microwave frequencies.

What to Do

For minor problems, such as a bedside clock that emits a high field, you can take simple measures: move the clock away from the bed—or, better yet, replace it with a battery-operated clock. But for more systemic problems, you'll probably need to call in a qualified EMF-remediation professional.

Deal-Breakers

The first category of deal-breakers would include living in the line of sight of a cell site or a cell tower, or high EMFs from overhead or underground wires that can't be remediated. If you have really high ambient levels outside, chances are that you won't be able to do much about it.

The second category of deal-breakers involves indoor EMFs that are difficult to fix. It basically comes down to time and money.

Moisture And Mold

Mold has its place in nature. If we didn't have mold, we'd all be living in undisintegrated compost. However, when indoor mold levels are too high, too much of a good thing can become a bad thing.

The Issue

Mold can be a serious problem for people who have allergies and asthma. But even for someone who starts out with a pretty good immune system, long-term exposure to mold can eventually cause problems, from upper respiratory difficulties and sinus infections to—in rare cases—brain damage.

Stachybotris atra is the big, mean, bad mold that is mentioned most in the media, but in too high a dose, any mold can be bad for you. And dead mold can be just as toxic as live mold.

Detection

You can do your own initial screening whenever you can be out of the house for 24 hours: close up the house, turn off any fans or ventilation systems, and close all the windows. Then, after it's been sealed up for 24 hours, go in with a fresh nose—or take along somebody who has a sensitive nose. If you smell any mustiness, you have mold. After four to five minutes, your nose will become desensitized, so you should go outside again and give it a 10-minute break.

Sometimes you can see mold. The question would then be how serious it is. For example, if you have small areas of mold on a windowsill or in a shower, it may be a localized issue that doesn't indicate a larger, systemic problem.

If you have any concerns about mold, get your home and site inspected for water intrusion and mold by a reputable mold inspector — preferably one with a background in building science (see page 266).

As with EMFs, you need to look at both outside and inside sources of moisture and mold. Outside problems include having a high water table, being in a floodplain, or being in the path of hillside runoff (above or below ground). Inside sources could include past flooding, plumbing leaks, or poor air circulation in regions with high humidity.

What to Do

If you are certain that a mold growth is limited and only on the surface—such as from condensation on bathroom tile or a windowsill—you may be able to address the problem yourself. First, clean up the mold with hydrogen peroxide (wearing a mask). Then make sure you remove the source of moisture: get a vent fan, install double-pane windows, squeegee the shower walls, wipe up the condensation more often—whatever's appropriate.

Generally, it's better to err on the side of caution where mold is concerned. If you have any doubts, bring in a pro. If a problem is detected, find out if you can afford to have the moldy areas cleaned out. If so, you can roll the remediation work into the rest of the remodeling.

It's crucial that mold mitigation work be done well; a botched job can waste your money and may even make things worse over time. After any mitigation work is done, be sure to get clearance-testing by an independent mold inspector.

Deal-Breakers

Sometimes there are cases in which you'd practically have to knock the house down to get all the mold out. And if you're especially mold-sensitive, even the best cleanup might not be enough. Another deal-breaker would be outside sources of water that can't be controlled; it can be very expensive to stop water that's coming from a high water table. Canyon properties and lots at the bottom of a hill can be particularly problematic.

Toxic Chemicals

One of the worst toxics you may find around a house is pesticides. But there's a long list of other toxic substances that may be in your home. Your remodeling project might disturb urea-formaldehyde foam, or interior wood surfaces may have been treated with PCP (pentachlorophenol). Or maybe your property had an underground gas tank. If you're buying a home, and the seller just painted, carpeted, and installed new cabinets, the indoor air may be loaded with formaldehyde and other volatile organic compounds (VOCs). Each property should be evaluated to determine whether there's cause for concern.

The Issue

The potential health problems are as varied as the many kinds of poisons that are or ever have been used in and around homes. Indoor toxic chemicals may cause reactions ranging from flulike symptoms to cancer.

Many people are unaware that semivolatile organic compounds (SVOCs) can be problematic in both new and older homes. People tend to think, "Oh, it's an older house, so the toxic chemicals have offgassed by now." But SVOCs have a high boiling point, so they don't volatilize into the air; they adhere to house dust, which you can then inhale.

Detection

You may want to find out the history of the house and what has been done to it. The pesticide chlordane was banned in 1988; an older house might have been treated with DDT. These things just don't go away. You can probably deal with pesticide residues in a crawlspace, but it's good to know what's there so you can find out whether it's possible to keep them out of the house—and, if so, how.

One of the best ways to detect toxic chemicals is by sampling the house dust. To find a qualified expert, go to www.buildingbiology.net.

What to Do

If you have any concerns, get a qualified inspector to check out your house for toxic chemicals.* In addition, have someone check your house's air pressure balance. If your house is negatively pressurized—in other words, if your forced-air system pulls out air so that make-up air has to come in through cracks in your house—you should remedy that problem. When a house is negatively pressurized, microscopic airborne particles and toxic chemicals can be sucked in from the crawlspace, attic, and wall cavities. (See HVAC below.)

If you have pests, look into least-toxic control methods. For rodents, trapping is a better strategy than poisons. If you have termites or other insects, call a pest control company that uses least-toxic strategies—sand barriers, heat treatments, electrical treatments, nematodes, and so on. But be careful; many companies advertise nontoxic methods, then try to sell you a chemical treatment. Here's my advice: Get a pest inspection report, including suggested treatment methods. Then pay the nominal fee to join the Bio-Integral Resource Center, and call them; their resident chemist will tell you whether the suggested treatment is really low toxic—and if not, they will give you some other suggestions. Another option is to check the Pesticide Action Network (see Resources, page 269) website and do some research in its database.

Deal-Breakers

If previous owners have regularly sprayed pesticides indoors, it can be very difficult to remove them. If a house has a strong chemical smell—particularly in the absence of new materials—you may find the problem too expensive to solve.

Asbestos

Asbestos was once a widespread component of building materials, some of which may still be in your home. If you plan to remodel, you may disturb asbestos-containing materials, so it's a good idea to be aware of its presence. The good news is that asbestos has long been recognized as a potential health problem, so the infrastructure for testing and abatement is well established.

The Issue

The hazards of asbestos are fairly widely known: little pointed fibers can lodge in lung tissue, and depending on the motility of the person's mucus and the mucous membrane lining, some people can't get it out. In such cases, it can cause enough irritation to create cancer down the line.

Detection

Asbestos in household materials could be out in the open, such as in vinyl-asbestos floor tile, acoustic ceilings, or fireproofing. It could also be in less obvious places, such as inside a gravity floor furnace or as duct-wrapping in the attic or crawlspace.

If you get a home inspection, check the contract; many say that they don't look for asbestos, but homeowners often assume otherwise. If the home was built before 1978, when asbestos was banned from use in homes, it's a good idea to have an asbestos inspection.

What to Do

Not all asbestos needs to be removed. Generally, if it isn't broken up or won't be disturbed by your remodeling project, leave it there. It's only when the fibers get loose in the air that they cause problems.

Asbestos is much easier to remove than mold because it doesn't grow. The problems can almost always be solved, and it's relatively easy to find trained asbestos professionals. However, there is one thing to watch out for: asbestos wrapping your ducts. Many asbestos professionals will tell you not to worry about it if it's on the outside of the ducts. However, most ducts are not airtight. My opinion is: If you've got asbestos on your ducts, get rid of that ducting.

Don't do asbestos removal or encapsulation yourself; this is a job for a professional.

Deal-Breakers

Asbestos is rarely a deal-breaker; the industry is so well developed that it can handle almost anything. The question will come down to whether you want to pay the price of mitigation; get a bid and find out what the price-tag is.

Heating, Ventilating, and Air-Conditioning Systems (HVAC)

If you have a ducted system for forced-air heating, air-conditioning, or both—and your remodeling project doesn't involve removing it—you should get a good HVAC assessment. Ideally, you should revamp the system so that it meets building science criteria for positive pressure, fresh-air dilution, and airtight ducting (see chapter 7). That way, you'll also save a lot of energy.

The Issue

The last thing you want is to remodel your house so that it's clean and energy-efficient, then be sucking up pesticide residues from your crawlspace. That can happen if you have leaky ducts, negative pressure, or a return-air duct that brings in polluted air.

Detection

You should have someone with a building science background inspect your HVAC system.

What to Do

If negative pressurization, blocked return-air pathways, or leaky ducts are causing indoor air quality problems in your home, be sure to get a qualified professional to upgrade your HVAC system (see chapters 7 and 8).

Deal-Breakers

If an entire HVAC system needs to be replaced, get a price to determine whether this is a deal-breaker for you. Sometimes ducting or air-handling units are in areas that can't be reached without demolition (under slabs, in soffits, in walls).

Conclusion

Whatever the problem, my advice is: get an inspection, get a report, and get an estimate for remediation work. Budget it out so that you know whether you can afford to have the work done. Time might also be a factor. If you're buying a house, you may need to move in by a certain date. Find out whether you can get the mitigation work (and any other remodeling work that's crucial to living there) done before you move in.

In many cases, you can save money and time by having mitigation work done concurrently with other remodeling work. For example, if you have high EMFs that can be fixed, and your remodeling project will also require some electrical work, you can combine the projects. This may not only save you money but could also prevent your electrician from creating new EMF problems.

If you need both inspection and mitigation work—for mold, lead, asbestos, EMFs—hire two different companies to do those jobs. Otherwise, there's a conflict of interest that's not in your favor.

If you have a worst-case scenario—say you've got mold, lead paint, and a return-air duct sucking pesticides in from the crawlspace —then you should have all the mitigation work done under containment prior to the rest of the demolition. That way, you'll have all the toxic demolition completed and contained, and you can proceed with the rest of your remodeling.

Mary Cordaro is a consultant and an educator who helps people diagnose and solve environmental home problems and select healthy, green alternatives to conventional building and interior materials. Mary is the president and founder of H3Environmental (www.h3environmental.com).

*How to Find Home Inspectors:

Lead:
- Before hiring anyone, ask for proof of EPA certification.
- For information and links to qualified inspectors and abatement companies: www.epa.gov/lead/
- For lead inspectors, look in the Yellow Pages under "lead inspection
- For lead abatement companies, look in the Yellow Pages under "environmental inspection" or "environmental testing."
- For more information or updates, call The National Lead Information Center at (800) 424-5323.

EMFs:
- For all types of EMFs, see buildingbiology.net
- For AC magnetic fields only: www.theramp.net/nefta/

Mold:
- Inspectors should have building science background, if possible. They should show proof that they follow current mold-remediation practices established by the IICRC (Institute of Inspection, Cleaning and Restoration Certification: www.iicrc.org); at this point, the standard is called the SB500.
- Inspectors should be separate from mold abatement professionals so that there's no conflict of interest; the inspector should do the clearance testing after the abatement procedures.

Appendix C
Resources

Ecological Remodeling

Eco-Renovation: The Ecological Home Improvement Guide, by Edward Harland (Chelsea Green, 1999).

Green Remodeling: Changing the World One Room at a Time, by David Johnston and Kim Master (New Society Publishers, 2004).

Healthy Housing Renovation Planner: Renovate the Healthy Way, by CMHC/SCHL (Canada Mortgage and Housing, Natural Resources Canada and Canadian Wood Council, 1999).

Home Ecology: Simple and Practical Ways to Green Your Home, by Karen Christensen (Fulcrum, 1990).

A Manual for the Environmental & Climatic Responsive Restoration & Renovation of Older Houses in Louisiana, by Edward Jon Cazayoux, AIA, CSI (Louisiana Department of Natural Resources, 2003).

No-Regrets Remodeling: Creating a Comfortable, Healthy Home that Saves Energy, by The Editors of Home Energy Magazine (Energy Auditor & Retrofitter, Inc., 1997).

Redux: Designs that Recycle, Reuse, or Reveal, by Jennifer Roberts (Gibbs Smith, 2005).

The Resourceful Renovator, by Jennifer Corson (Chelsea Green, 2000).

Green Home Guide: www.greenhomeguide.com

The National Association of the Remodeling Industry (NARI): www.nari.org. NARI is developing a national Green Remodeler certification program. Information: Dan Taddei, (847) 298-9200 x 8145.

General Eco-Building

Alternative Construction, by Lynne Elizabeth and Cassandra Adams (John Wiley & Sons, 2005).

Design with Climate, by Victor Olgyay (Princeton University Press, 1963).

"Getting to Know a Place: Site Evaluation as a Starting Point for Green Design," Alex Wilson. *Environmental Building News*, Volume 7, Number 3, (March 1998).

Green by Design, by Angela M. Dean (Gibbs Smith, 2003).

The Natural House: A Complete Guide to Healthy, Energy-Efficient, Environmental Homes, by Daniel D. Chiras (Chelsea Green, 2000).

The Natural House Catalog, by David Pearson (Simon & Schuster, 1996).

The New Ecological Home, by Daniel D. Chiras (Chelsea Green, 2004).

The New Natural House Book, by David Pearson (Simon & Schuster, 1998).

A Primer on Sustainable Building, D.L. Barnett and W.D. Browning (Snowmass, CO: Rocky Mountain Institute, 1995).

Solviva: How to Grow $500,000 on One Acre & Peace on Earth, by Anna Edey (Trailblazer Press, 1998).

Designer/Builder: www.designerbuildermagazine.com
Environmental Building News: www.buildinggreen.com
GreenClips: www.greenclips.com
The Last Straw Journal: www.thelaststraw.org
Mother Earth News: www.motherearthnews.com
Natural Home & Garden Magazine: www.naturalhomeandgarden.com

Building Concerns Regional Resource Directories: www.buildingconcerns.com

Center for Maximum Potential Building Systems: www.cmpbs.org

Comfortable Low Energy Architecture: www.learn.londonmet.ac.uk/packages/clear/index.html

Development Center for Appropriate Technology: www.dcat.org

Ecological Building Network: www.ecobuildnetwork.org

Ecological Footprint: www.myfootprint.org

National Association of Home Builders (NAHB): www.nahb.org (case studies, indoor air quality, land development, and more).

Oikos: www.oikos.com (green building news, online information library, books, and product information)

Residential Green Building Discussion Group: www.buildinggreen.com/elists/gb_signup.cfm

Rocky Mountain Institute: www.rmi.org (advocacy, technology, and energy policy)

Sun Angle Calculator: www.sbse.org/resources/sac/index.htm

Sustainable Sources: www.greenbuilder.com (many green building resources, including *Sustainable Building Sourcebook*).

Wind rose data: www.epa.gov/ttn/naaqs/ozone/areas/wind.htm

Energy

"Bioclimatic Design," by Donald Watson and Murray Milne, in *Time-Saver Standards for Architectural Design Data*, seventh edition (McGraw-Hill, Inc., 1997).

Consumer Guide to Home Energy Savings, by Alex Wilson et al. (American Council for an Energy Efficient Economy, 2003).

Heating, Cooling, Lighting: Design Methods for Architects, by Norbert Lechner (John Wiley and Sons, 1991).

Insulate and Weatherize, by Bruce Harley (Taunton Press, 2002).

The Most Energy-Efficient Appliances (American Council for an Energy-Efficient Economy, annually).

Passive Solar Buildings, by J. Douglas Balcomb (The MIT Press, 1992).

Residential Energy: Cost Savings and Comfort for Existing Buildings, by John Krigger and Chris Dorsi (Saturn Resource Management www.srmi.biz, 2004).

The Solar House: Passive Heating and Cooling, by Daniel D. Chiras (Chelsea Green, 2002).

Solar Living Source Book, by John Schaeffer (Gaiam Real Goods, 2001).

Sun, Wind & Light: Architectural Design Strategies, by G. Z. Brown and Mark DeKay, second edition (John Wiley & Sons, Inc., 2001).

Thermal Delight in Architecture, by Lisa Heschong (The MIT Press, 1979).

Home Energy Magazine: www.homeenergy.org

Home Power Magazine: www.homepower.com

Alliance to Save Energy: www.ase.org

American Council for an Energy Efficient Economy (ACEEE): www.aceee.org (lists of the "best of the best" energy efficient appliances)

American Solar Energy Society: www.ases.org (Publishes *Solar Today Magazine*)

American Wind Energy Association: www.awea.org

Center for Renewable Energy and Sustainable Technology: www.crest.org

Climate Star: www.climatestar.org (calculate your carbon footprint and how to minimize it)

Database of State Incentives for Renewable Energy: www.dsireusa.org

Department of Energy Office of Energy Efficiency and Renewable Energy: www.eere.energy.gov

The Efficient Windows Collaborative: www.efficientwindows.org (window fact sheets that compare window performance for cities throughout the U.S.)

Energy Star appliance rating system: www.energystar.gov

Energy Guide: www.energyguide.com

Florida Solar Energy Center: www.fsec.ucf.edu

Green Power State-by-State Database: www.eere.energy.gov/greenpower/buying/buying_power.shtml

Light Site (energy-efficient lighting info): www.lightsite.net

National Renewable Energy Laboratories: www.nrel.gov

The Power Scorecard: www.powerscorecard.org (rating mechanism to assess the environmental impact of different types of electric generation)

Residential Energy Services Network: www.natresnet.org

Solar Energy International (SEI): www.solarenergy.org

Solar Living Institute: www.solarliving.org

Sustainable by Design: www.susdesign.com (design tools, including a sun angle calculator and overhang modeling for use in passive solar design)

Tax Incentives Assistance Project: www.energytaxincentives.org

Windows & Daylighting: windows.lbl.gov (estimate potential energy saving of window replacements using a simulation program

Building Science

EEBA Builder's Guide to Cold Climates, by Joe Lstiburek, (Energy and Environmental Building Association, 2004).

EEBA Builder's Guide to Mixed-Humid Climates, by Joe Lstiburek, (Energy and Environmental Building Association, 2005).

EEBA Builder's Guide to Hot-Dry/Mixed-Dry Climates, by Joe Lstiburek, (Energy and Environmental Building Association, 2004).

EEBA Builder's Guide to Hot-Humid Climates, by Joe Lstiburek, (Energy and Environmental Building Association, 2005).

EEBA Water Management Guide, Joe Lstiburek, editor. (Energy and Environmental Building Association, 2002).

Investigating, Diagnosing, and Treating Your Damp Basement, by CMHC/SCHL (Canada Mortgage and Housing, Natural Resources Canada and Canadian Wood Council, 1999).

Building Science Corporation: www.buildingscience.com (best construction practices for your climate)

The Energy Conservatory: www.energyconservatory.com

Kansas City Building Science Institute: www.kansasbuildingscience.com

Society of Building Science Educators: www.sbse.org

Green Building Programs

Build It Green: www.builditgreen.org (includes free Ask an Expert service)

Center for Resource Conservation: www.greenerbuilding.org (extensive list of product suppliers and green building programs)

National Association of Home Builders list of local residential green building programs: www.nahbrc.org/, click on green building

U.S. Green Building Council: www.usgbc.org (green building and the LEED Green Building Rating System)

Green Building Materials

Earth Plasters for Straw Bale Homes, by Keely Meagan (self-published, 2000).

EcoNest: Creating Sustainable Sanctuaries of Clay, Straw, and Timber, by Paula Baker-Laporte and Robert Laporte (Gibbs Smith, 2005).

Efficient Wood Use in Residential Construction, by Ann Edminster and Sami Yassa (Natural Resources Defense Council, 1998).

GreenSpec Directory, by the Editors of Environmental Building News (Building Green, Inc., 2005).

Lime in Building: A Practical Guide, by Jane Schofield (Black Dog Press, 2001).

Making Better Concrete: Guidelines to Using Fly Ash for Higher Quality, by Bruce King (Green Building Press, 2005)

The Natural Plaster Book, by Cedar Rose Guelberth and Dan Chiras (New Society Publishers, 2003).

Serious Straw Bale: A Home Construction Guide For All Climates, by Michel Bergeron and Paul Lacinski (Chelsea Green, 2000).

Environmental Building Supplies: www.ecohaus.com

Environmental Home Center: www.environmentalhomecenter.com

Environmental Depot: www.evironproducts.com

Forest Stewardship Council: www.fscus.org (includes *Designing & Building with FSC*, in the Green Building section).

Green Sage Sustainable Building Materials and Furnishings: www.greensage.com

Greenmaker Supply: www.greenmakersupply.com

Habitat for Humanity ReStore directory: www.habitat.org/env/restores.aspx (quality used and surplus building materials at low prices)

King County Washington, Green Building Website: www.metrokc.gov/dnrp/swd/greenbuilding/index.asp (useful green building information, no matter where you live)

Rainforest Alliance's SmartWood Program: www.smartwood.org

Healthy Homes

Better Basics for the Home: Simple Solutions for Less Toxic Living, by Annie Berthold-Bond (Three Rivers Press, 1999).

The Clean Air Guide: How to Identify and Correct Indoor Air Problems in Your Home, by CMHC/SCHL (Canada Mortgage and Housing, Natural Resources Canada and Canadian Wood Council, 1999).

Clean and Green: The Complete Guide to Non-Toxic and Environmentally Safe Housekeeping, by Annie Berthold Bond (Ceres Press, 1994).

Common-Sense Pest Control, by William Olkowski et al (Taunton, 1991)

Healing Environments, by Carol Venolia (Celestial Arts, 1988).

Healthy by Design: Building and Remodeling Solutions for Creating Healthy Homes, by David Rousseau and James Wasley (Hartley & Marks, 1998).

The Healthy House (and other books), by John Bower (The Healthy House Institute, 2001).

Home Safe Home, by Debra Lynn Dadd (Tarcher/Putnam, 1997).

Homes That Heal, by Athena Thompson (New Society Publishers/*Mother Earth News*, 2004).

Prescriptions for a Healthy House, by Paula Baker-Laporte, Erica Elliot, and John Banta (New Society Publishers, 2001).

The Sick House Survival Guide, by Angela Hobbs (New Society Publishers, 2003).

American Lung Association Health House: www.healthhouse.org

Clean It! Safer Cleaning Methods That Really Work: www.nasites.com/cmprojects/projects/bacwa/docs/10,024%20CleanItGuide%202003.pdf

Environmental Protection Agency (EPA): www.epa.gov/iaq

Covers general indoor air quality topics, including radon, asthma, and mold.

The Green Guide: www.thegreenguide.com

Green Home Environmental Store, www.greenhome.com

Healthy Building Network: www.healthybuilding.net

Healthy House Institute: www.hhinst.com

HealthyHome: www.healthyhome.com. Offers healthy home products and supplies, including EMF reduction supplies and cleaning products.

Indoor Air Quality (IAQ) Test Kits: www.aqs.com

Institute for Bau-Biologie and Ecology: www.bau-biologieusa.com ("how buildings impact life and the living environment")

Lead Safe Work Practices: www.nsc.org/issues/lead/leadsafework.htm

The Radon Information Center: www.radon.com

Sick of Dust: Chemicals in Common Products, a Needless Health Risk in Our Homes: www.safer-products.org

Water

Branched Drain Greywater Systems, by Art Ludwig (Oasis Design, 2004); www.oasisdesign.net

Create an Oasis with Greywater: Choosing, Building, and Using Greywater Systems, by Art Ludwig (Oasis Design, 2004); www.oasisdesign.net

Rainwater Catchment for the Mechanically Challenged, by Suzy Banks with Richard Heinichen, (Tank Town, 1997); www.rainwatercollection.com

Rainwater Catchment Systems for Domestic Supply, Erik Niseen Petersen and John Gould, editors (ITDG Publishing, 2000).

Rainwater Harvesting, by Arnold Pacey (ITDG Publishing, 1986).

Texas Guide to Rainwater Harvesting, Texas Water Development Board in Cooperation with the Center for Maximum Potential Building Systems (1997).

American Water Works Association's WaterWiser: www.awwa.org/waterwiser

American Rainwater Catchment Systems Association (ARCSA): www.arcsa-usa.org

City of Portland Rainwater Harvesting Code: http://www.bds.ci.portland.or.us/pubs/CodeGuides/Cabo/RES34%201.pdf

General Home Design

Building with the Breath of Life, by Tom Bender (Fire River Press, 2000).

Code Check series from Taunton Press (condensed building code information)

The Earth Path: Grounding Your Spirit in the Rhythms of Nature, by Starhawk (Harper San Francisco, 2004).

Home by Design, by Sarah Susanka (Taunton, 2004).

A Home for the Soul, by Anthony Lawlor (Clarkson/Potter, 1997).

Homing Instinct, by John Connell (McGraw Hill, 1998).

The Not So Big House: A Blueprint for the Way We Really Live (and others in the series), by Sarah Susanka (Taunton, 1998).

A Pattern Language, by Christopher Alexander et al. (Oxford University Press, 1977).

The Place of Houses: Three Architects Suggest Ways to Build and Inhabit Houses, by Charles Moore, Gerald Allen, and Donlyn Lyndon (Holt, Rinehart and Winston, 1974).

Places of the Soul, by Christopher Day (Aquarian Press or Thorsons, 1990).

Silence, Song, and Shadows: Our Need for the Sacred in Our Surroundings, by Tom Bender (Fire River Press, 2000).

The Temple in the House: Finding the Sacred in Everyday Architecture, by Anthony Lawlor, AIA (Jeremy P. Tarcher/Putnam, 1994).

The Wabi-Sabi House, by Robyn Griggs Lawrence (Clarkson Potter, 2004).

Gardens and Landscaping

Cultivating Sacred Space, by Elizabeth Murray (Pomegranate Communications, 1998).

Design for Human Ecosystems: Landscape, Land Use, and Natural Resources, by John Tillman Lyle (Island Press, 1999).

Energy-Efficient and Environmental Landscaping, by Anne Simon Moffat, Marc Schiler, and the staff of *Green Living* (Appropriate Solutions Press, 1994).

Garden and Climate, by Chip Sullivan (McGraw-Hill, 2002).

Green Nature, Human Nature: The Meaning of Plants in Our Lives, by Charles A. Lewis (University of Illinois Press, 1996).

Microclimatic Landscape Design: Creating Thermal Comfort and Energy Efficiency, by Robert D. Brown and Terry J. Gillespie (John Wiley & Sons, Inc., 1995).

Permaculture: A Designers' Manual, by Bill Mollison (Tagari, 1997).

Plants/People/and Environmental Quality, by Gary O. Robinette (U.S. Department of the Interior, 1972).

Sustainable Landscape Construction: A Guide to Green Building Outdoors, by J. William Thompson and Kim Sorvig (Island Press, 2000).

Water Gardens: Simple Projects, Contemporary Designs, by Hazel White (Chronicle Books, 1998).

Wild Ones, Ltd.: www.for-wild.org

LifeGarden: www.lifegarden.org

Bio-Integral Resource Center: www.birc.org (nonprofit educational institution dedicated to pesticide use reduction)

Pesticide Action Network: www.panna.org

National Wildlife Federation Backyard Wildlife Habitat Program: www.nwf.org/backyardwildlifehabitat

WindStar Wildlife Institute: www.windstar.org

Kitchens and Food

The Sacred Kitchen, by Robin and Jon Robertson (New World Library, 1999).

This Organic Life, by Joan Dye Gussow (Chelsea Green, 2001).

The Smart Kitchen, by David Goldbeck (Ceres Press, 1994).

The Sustainable Kitchen, by Stu Stein, et.al. (New Society Publishing, 2004).

The Slow Food Movement: www.slowfood.com
Solar Cookers International: www.solarcooking.org

Community

Block Parties & Poker Nights: Recipes and Ideas for Getting and Staying Connected with Your Neighbors, by Peg Allen (Clarkson Potter, 2002)

Creating a Life Together: Practical Tools for Starting Ecovillages and Intentional Communities, by Diana Leafe Christian (New Society Publishers, 2003).

Rebuilding Community in America, by Ken Norwood, AICP and Kathleen Smith (Shared Living Resource Center, 1995).

City Repair: www.cityrepair.org/about.html (have facilitated the creation of some wonderful residential public/private spaces and events)

Cohousing: www.cohousing.org

Neighbornets: riseup.net/neighbornets/ (affinity groups of people who live in the same general neighborhood)

Urban Ecovillage Network: urban.ecovillage.org

Appendix D
Eco-Remodeling a Mobile Home

By Carol Venolia

When you think of mobile homes, any number of thoughts come to mind, but "eco-home" isn't usually one of them. Yet plenty of folks who walk their green talk aren't in a position to bankroll a brand-new eco-home. If you want to own your house (maybe even mortgage free), eco-retrofitting a used mobile home just might be the ticket.

"You could go to a used mobile home lot and buy a 14-by-70-foot home for $1,000 to $2,000, then invest maybe $10,000 in it, and you'd have yourself a pretty dang nice house," says residential energy-efficiency expert John Krigger, author of *Your Mobile Home: Energy and Repair Guide for Manufactured Housing* (Saturn Resource Management, 1998). "I have a lot of respect for the way mobile homes use natural resources," he adds. "They're very lightweight, and they don't require much in the way of materials. The average site-built house probably uses three times as much material for a given floor area."

Another advantage is that, unless you're in a park with narrow lots, you can orient your mobile home so the long dimension runs east-west. That exposes the greatest wall area to warming winter sun and cuts down on the amount of wall area facing the cold westerly winds and hot summer-afternoon sun.

Canadian mobile-dwelling innovator Andy Thomson has observed that people living in mobile homes can use from 10 to 100 times less energy and resources (propane, water, materials, and electricity) than people who live in site-built houses. "Mobile home codes don't spell out minimum room sizes," he says, "so you can be really space-efficient, which automatically cuts down on material use, energy consumption, and impact on the land. They also use less water because fixtures are ultra-low flush, with low-volume delivery. Furthermore, mobile-home codes allow for more creativity in how you heat, cool, handle waste, and filter greywater."

The catch is you'll have to do some work. Even brand-new mobile homes aren't very energy efficient and are notorious for outgassing formaldehyde and other toxic substances, so your best bet all around is to buy a used mobile and upgrade it. Before undertaking any projects, however, be sure to consult a good book or a qualified professional—and be wary of existing mold and mildew.

Stay High and Dry

Dealing with moisture is the first step in improving almost any mobile home. Mobile homes can leak at roof vents, window perimeters, screw holes, and roof edges without overhangs. Water that collects under the home because of poor site drainage can also cause damage, and plumbing leaks and stray landscape watering can wreak their own havoc. To prevent this, site a mobile home well, making sure you:

• Provide good drainage
• Add gutters or overhangs to the roof
• Fix plumbing leaks
• Install a ground-moisture barrier under the home
• Seal leaks in the roof and walls

In many mobile homes, what appears to be water leaking in from outside is actually condensation from internal moisture buildup. Most mobile homes need some mechanical help:

- Use vent fans in bathrooms and in the kitchen, with backdraft dampers to avoid air leakage.
- Consider adding a whole-house fan.
- Install a heat-recovery ventilator to keep interior air fresh and pressure balanced without wasting heat.

Energy specialist Cal Steiner, who gives workshops in weatherizing mobile homes, points out that a furnace blower can drive moisture into wall, attic, or floor cavities, where it's likely to condense and cause structural damage. The solution is to create an air barrier around the indoor space by sealing cracks and penetrations in the home's interior membrane:

- Around heating ducts and registers
- At air conditioners
- In the underbelly or floor/chassis
- Around plumbing
- At building joints
- Around electrical penetrations
- Behind cabinets
- At loose siding, paneling, and trim

In addition, seal all penetrations in the furnace closet and provide adequate room under the furnace closet door to let air return to the furnace without building up pressure. These measures will also conserve heating and cooling energy.

And finally, a few simple lifestyle changes can reduce indoor air humidity.

- Cook with lids on pots.
- Open a window when cooking or taking showers.
- Don't keep too many of those water-loving houseplants.
- Leave wet clothing and boots in a mudroom.
- Vent the clothes dryer to the outdoors.
- Don't use a humidifier unless it has been medically prescribed.

Use Energy Well

Even when mobile homes have some insulation, it's often poorly installed with gaps that reduce its effectiveness. You can pull back a portion of the cladding to blow or foam in additional insulation. In some cases—especially if you're removing the interior or exterior surface—it may be practical to add fiberglass batts. The right way to approach an insulation project will depend on the mobile home, your climate, how handy you are, and whether you can find good contractors. Adding insulation may also facilitate the installation of a new air/vapor barrier.

Chances are, you'll want to increase the insulation level of your mobile home no matter when it was built. Even the most recent codes require only R-14 to R-22 insulation in the roof, depending on the thermal zone it's built for. So the most important thing to look at is the structural condition of the home; it's much easier to reinsulate than to repair kinks in the framing. And research performed at the National Renewable Energy Laboratory indicates that mobile-home dwellers can save up to 40 percent on their energy bills through good weatherization. To take it up a notch, add solar panels.

Park That Thing

Krigger sees rural areas as the best location for eco-mobiles; not only are mobile homes outlawed on many city lots, but paying site rent at a mobile-home park can negate the real joys of mortgage-free ownership. A big yard also allows you to correctly orient your home and landscape to enhance its appearance and energy efficiency. "In fact," says Krigger, "landscaping may be your best long-term investment for reducing heating and cooling costs."

Properly selected and placed, trees can reduce summer cooling bills by creating shade, and winter heating bills by acting as windbreaks. Deciduous trees provide shade in summer and admit warming sunlight in winter. A lattice or trellis with a climbing vine can block sun while allowing cooling breezes—and if you don't like the appearance of mobile homes, it can help a lot there, too! If summers are hot, provide shade plantings around patios and pavement to reduce reflection of solar heat from their surfaces.

What if you do want to live in town? As Thomson sees it, trailer parks have a lot of potential for eco-community: rent is cheap; hooking up to utilities is optional; lots are small (requiring less land and infrastructure); you're not digging foundations (therefore not disturbing the earth or reducing its capacity to take in water); and there are often shared facilities such as park space, swimming pools, and laundry facilities. The sense of community in a trailer park is often much greater than in suburbs—partly because of park rules that define appropriate behavior, including quiet hours.

Is There an Eco-Mobile in Your Future?

Ecology-minded people should think twice before dismissing mobile homes, suggests Thomson. "I realized the people who are most passionate about green building often have little money, and the people with the most money often have no passion for green living," he says. How do we reconcile that? Find ways to make housing cheaper. Eco-mobile homes are a good start."

Resources

Cal Steiner, Residential energy specialist, gives workshops in mobile-home weatherization,
(701) 227-7415;
csteiner@state.nd.us

Andy Thomson, Mobile eco-home ideas
www.Sustain.ca

Further Reading
Your Mobile Home: Energy and Repair Guide for Manufactured Housing, by John Krigger
(Saturn Resource Management, 1998)
(800) 735-0577
Residential-Energy.com

Glossary

Abatement. Eliminating or reducing the degree or intensity of something, often referring to pollution or hazards.

ACQ. Alkaline Copper Quaternary (or Quat)—a method of wood treatment that uses copper as the primary active ingredient; less toxic than the formerly standard CCA (chromated copper arsenate).

Active solar heating. A high-tech system in which heat from the sun is absorbed by collectors and transferred by pumps or fans to a storage unit for later use, or to the house interior directly.

Active solar water heater. A system in which heat from the sun is absorbed by collectors and transferred by pumps to a storage unit. The heated fluid in the storage unit conveys its heat to the domestic hot water of the house through a heat exchanger.

Advanced framing. A set of construction techniques designed to conserve materials by using alternative framing methods.

Agricultural fiber. Fibrous materials that are grown in agricultural operations. Agricultural fibers such as cotton have recently been used as insulation materials.

Air barrier. See "air boundary."

Air boundary. The elements in a building's thermal envelope that are designed and constructed to control airflow between indoor conditioned space and outdoor unconditioned space.

Air-sealing. Sealing the cracks and holes in a home's envelope to prevent uncontrolled air movement.

American Society of Heating, Refrigeration, and Air Conditioning Engineers (ASHRAE). A professional organization that writes many of the standards for installation of thermal comfort systems.

Annual Fuel Utilization Efficiency (AFUE). A measure of efficiency for heating appliances that accounts for chimney, jacket, and cycling losses. The higher the number, the greater the efficiency of the appliance.

Aquifer. A water-bearing stratum of permeable rock, sand, or gravel.

As-built drawings. Floor plans and elevations (side views), created after a house was built.

Asbestos. A mineral fiber that has been commonly used as insulation and fire retardant in many building materials. Invisible fibers of asbestos can be inhaled and have been connected to lung diseases and cancer.

Backdrafting. A negative-pressure situation that pulls combustion gases from a flue or chimney back into habitable space.

Batt insulation. Glass, mineral wool, or cotton, which may be faced with paper, aluminum, or other vapor retarder. Used in wall, ceiling, and floor cavities.

Berm. A mound or bank of earth, often used as a barrier or to provide insulation.

Bio-fuels. Fuels created from biological sources, such as corn or soybeans.

Bio-source. A biological source of raw materials; for example, soybeans used as a base for spray-foam insulation, adhesive, or bio-diesel fuel.

Blown-in insulation. Insulation that is placed with a machine that ejects the insulation with force. Examples include cellulose, fiberglass, and spray foams.

Building envelope. A building's enclosure formed by the roof, floor, and exterior wall.

Building pressurization. The air pressure within a building relative to the air pressure outside. Very slight positive pressurization is usually desirable to avoid backdrafting and infiltration of exterior air.

C&D. Abbreviation for construction and demolition.

Casein. A white, tasteless, odorless protein precipitated from cow's milk. In building, it is used to make natural paints and adhesives.

Catchment. See "rainwater catchment."

Cellulose. The fibrous part of plants, used in making paper and textiles.

Cellulose insulation. Thermal insulation made from recycled newspaper and typically treated with natural borates for vermin and fire protection.

Chemical sensitivity. See "multiple chemical sensitivity."

Chimney effect. See "stack effect."

Chlorofluorocarbons (CFCs). A class of compounds that has been used extensively (refrigeration, air-conditioning, packaging, insulation, solvents, and aerosol propellants). They are inert at low altitude, but they decompose in the upper atmosphere, destroying ozone, which protects us from harmful ultraviolet light.

Circadian rhythms. Cycles with a period of approximately 24 hours. As used here, the term refers to biological cycles.

Cistern. A tank for storing water.

Clerestory windows. A row of windows high in a wall, typically above head height and often above an adjoining roof.

Climate rose. A phrase coined by Carol Venolia to describe a circular symbol that summarizes important climate data for a given site—sunrises and sunsets at solstices and equinoxes, prevailing and storm winds, etc.

Color temperature. A numerical designation, in degrees Kelvin, of the visual "warmth" (yellow/orange/red) or "coolness" (green/blue/violet) of a given light source.

Combustion air. The air required to burn a fuel.

Combustion gases. The gases emitted when fuel is burned. Breathing combustion gas is harmful.

Compact fluorescent light (CFL). A small form of fluorescent light, available with a screw base; it uses 75 percent less electricity than an incandescent bulb and lasts 10 times as long.

Composite material. A building material made up of two or more substances (e.g., plastic laminates). These materials can be difficult to recycle and may be best applied in situations where they can be removed for reuse (not requiring remanufacture).

Composting. A process whereby organic wastes, including food wastes, paper, and yard wastes, decompose naturally, resulting in a product rich in minerals and ideal for gardening and farming as a soil conditioner, mulch, resurfacing material, or landfill cover.

Conditioned space. The indoor area of a building that is designed to be thermally modified for the comfort of occupants.

Conductivity. The rate of heat flow through a given material under specified conditions.

Contour lines. Lines on a map connecting points on the land surface that are the same elevation above sea level.

Cool roof. A roof assemblage made up of specialized materials designed to reflect the sun's heat away from the building, thereby reducing the cooling load and associated air-conditioning costs.

Cooling climate. A climate region in which cooling is the dominant comfort need.

Cooling/heating load. A building's demand for heating or cooling input in order to keep the conditioned spaces at a given temperature.

Cotton fiber insulation. Batt insulation made from post-industrial blue-jean scraps; it does not contain fiberglass, formaldehyde, or chemical irritants.

Cob. A building material made of earth, water, straw, clay, and sand, that is easy to sculpt into organic shapes.

Crawl space. The space below the floor framing and above the ground in a raised-floor building, where plumbing, wiring, and ductwork may be accessed; some people confuse crawl space with attic.

Cross-ventilation. The movement of air across a space, driven by the force of the wind.

Daylighting. A method of illuminating building interiors with sunlight so that the use of electric lighting is reduced in the daytime.

Deciduous. An adjective used to describe plants that shed their leaves in the autumn.

Deconstruction. The reverse of construction. The careful and systematic dismantling of a structure to maximize the recovery of valuable building resources.

Depressurization. See "negative pressure."

Desynchronization. A condition in which a person's circadian rhythms are out of synch with each other.

Diffusion. The movement of individual molecules through a material (e.g., moisture through drywall).

Dioxin. Any of several persistent toxic heterocyclic compounds, produced by a wide variety of processes including pesticide manufacturing, paper-making, and incineration.

DIY. Do-it-yourself.

Domestic hardwood. Deciduous trees that grow in the U.S.— the only type of wood that is typically grown faster in the U.S. than it is removed.

Double glazing. Two layers of glass set in a window sash to reduce heat flow.

Drip irrigation. An above-ground, low-pressure water system with flexible tubing that releases small, steady amounts of water through emitters placed near plant roots.

Drywall. Gypsum wallboard.

Dual-flush toilet. A toilet with two settings, usually 0.8 gallons for liquid removal and 1.6 gallons for full-flush solid removal.

Duct system. A continuous passageway for the transmission of conditioned air.

Electromagnetic field (EMF). A magnetic field produced by an electric current (e.g., in a power line). Investigators have correlated current intensity and damage to humans.

Embodied energy. All the energy required to grow, harvest, extract, manufacture, process, package, ship, install, and dispose of a particular product or building material. A useful measure of ecological cost.

Emission. The release of gas or particles.

Emissivity. The ability of a surface to emit radiation. Low-E windows have low emissivity.

Energy-recovery ventilator (ERV). A mechanical device that draws stale air from inside a building and, in winter, transfers the heat in that air to the air being pulled into the house; in summer, the heat transfer works in reverse. Use of an ERV can reduce energy costs and dilute indoor pollutants.

Energy Star. A voluntary labeling program designed to identify and promote energy-efficient products, introduced in 1992 by the U.S. Environmental Protection Agency (EPA) to reduce greenhouse-gas emissions.

Engineered lumber. Wood products created from the fiber of young, abundant, fast-growing trees, bound together via adhesives, heat, and pressure. Engineered lumber such as structural laminated beams or I-joists are built up of smaller pieces of wood, use 50 percent less wood, and save old-growth trees from being cut for large structural members. Engineered lumber is stronger and straighter than lumber from whole trees.

Envelope. The boundary that separates indoor conditioned spaces from unconditioned spaces. It includes both a thermal boundary that controls heat transfer and an air boundary that controls air transfer.

Environmental Protection Agency (EPA). The U.S. Government organization charged with setting and enforcing environmental regulations nationwide.

Environmentally preferable. A phrase that designates products or services with less negative impact on human health and the environment than competing products or services that serve the same purpose. This comparison may consider raw-materials acquisition, production, manufacturing, packaging, distribution, reuse, operation, maintenance, or disposal of the product or service.

Evaporative cooling. A passive cooling strategy that uses the evaporation of water to cool air; useful in climates with hot, dry summers.

Evapotranspiration. Movement of moisture from the soil to the air, through evaporation from the soil's surface and transpiration by plants.

Fan-coil unit. An HVAC system with a fan that blows air over coils that have been heated or cooled, typically by water.

Fly ash. The ash residue from high-temperature combustion processes, usually coal-burning power generation equipment. When mixed with lime and water, it forms a cementitious material that can substitute for a portion of the portland cement in a concrete mix.

Forest Stewardship Council (FSC). A non-profit organization that certifies various forests around the world that exhibit good sustainability and management practices.

Formaldehyde. Colorless, pungent-smelling, toxic substance.

Fossil fuel. Fuel, such as coal, oil, or natural gas, produced by the decomposition of ancient plants and animals.

Framing cavity. The spaces between building framing members, such as wall studs or floor joists.

French drain. A gravel-filled trench with a drain pipe, dug to a gradient that will allow surface water to drain away from a building.

FSC-certified wood. Wood obtained from lumber operations that have been certified by the Forest Stewardship Council.

Full-spectrum lights. Fluorescent tubes or incandescent bulbs that give off light with a spectrum approximating that of a standard noon sunlight.

Glare. Dazzling or uncomfortable brightness.

Glazing. Any translucent or transparent material in exterior openings of buildings, including windows, skylights, doors, and glass block.

Green building. An approach to building design and construction that aims to reduce negative impacts by decreasing resource consumption and pollution while increasing energy-efficiency.

Greenguard. A product certification program, overseen by the Greenguard Environmental Institute that presently provides the world's only guide to third-party certified low-emitting interior products and building materials.

Greenhouse gases. Gases in the atmosphere that contribute to global warming. Carbon dioxide is the most significant greenhouse gas.

Green power. Energy derived from natural sources that replenish themselves over short periods of time. These resources include the sun, wind, moving water, organic plant and waste material (biomass), and the earth's heat (geothermal). Also known as "renewable energy."

Green roof. A roof system that supports plant growth, utilizing a specialized undercarriage for a waterproof membrane and excess water removal. Various types of vegetation are set into a special growing medium to replace displaced vegetation in the building footprint and greatly reduce the heat radiated from the roof, especially in hot climates.

Greywater. Wastewater that does not contain sewage or fecal contamination and can be reused for irrigation.

Grid-connected. Attached to a centralized utility service.

Ground-source heat pump. A heat pump that extracts heat from subsurface water and soils to heat buildings in winter, and that discharges heat into the ground for summer cooling. Also called geothermal heating.

Gut, gutting. Removing all interior finishes of a building so that the framing is exposed on the inside.

Heat exchanger. A device that transfers heat from one medium to another without mixing, typically by conduction through a barrier.

Heating climate. A climate region in which winter heating is the dominant comfort need.

Heating Seasonal Performance Factor (HSPF). A rating of heat pumps that describes how many Btus they transfer per kilowatt-hour of electricity consumed.

Heat pump. A mechanical device that extracts heat from one place and distributes it elsewhere, using a refrigerant to absorb heat upon expansion and emit heat when compressed. When used to heat buildings, a heat pump may extract heat from air, water, or earth for distribution indoors. For cooling, heat is extracted from indoor air and discharged elsewhere.

Heat-recovery systems. Mechanical systems that capture waste heat from another system and use it to replace heat that would otherwise come from a primary energy source.

Heat-recovery ventilator (HRV). A mechanical device that exchanges heat between incoming and outgoing airstreams, recovering about 50-80 percent of the energy. Also known as an air-to-air heat exchanger or energy-recovery ventilator.

Housewrap. Any of the numerous spun fiber polyolefin rolled sheet goods, or perforated plastic films, designed to function as drainage planes and/or air barriers.

Human thermal comfort. A state in which a human being is satisfied with the temperature of his or her environment.

HVAC. The acronym for heating, ventilation, and air conditioning.

Hydrologic cycle. A sequence in which water vapor condenses from the atmosphere, precipitates onto the earth's surface, then evaporates back into the atmosphere.

Hydronic radiant heating. A system that warms people and interior spaces via heated water distributed through a system of tubes, typically beneath the floor but sometimes in walls or other building elements.

Impervious paving. A landscaping surface, such as concrete or asphalt paving, that promotes runoff by blocking the downward flow of water into the soil below.

Incandescent light bulb. A bulb that generates light by electrically heating a tungsten filament. Incandescent bulbs are less energy-efficient than fluorescent lights.

Indoor air quality (IAQ). The characteristics of the air inside a building, particularly as it affects occupant health and function. Indoor air may be polluted by cigarette smoke, dust, mites, mold spores, radon, and gases and chemicals from materials and appliances.

Infiltration. The uncontrolled leakage of exterior unconditioned air into a building through cracks and holes.

Instantaneous water heater. See "tankless water heater."

Insulated Concrete Form (ICF). Rigid foam, cast or injection-molded into various panel shapes, used as permanent forms for reinforced concrete walls. ICFs have R-values ranging from about 22 to about 40.

Insulated header. A box beam with a core of rigid insulation, designed to span door and window openings.

Insulating sheathing. Non-structural insulating board products with varying R-values and a wide variation in vapor permeability and drainage characteristics. Materials include expanded polystyrene (EPS), extruded polystyrene (XPS), polyisocyanurate (most often foil-faced), rigid fiberglass, and mineral wool.

Insulation. A material that resists the passage of heat, electricity, or sound. In this book, we primarily refer to insulation that resists heat transfer, typically by trapping small pockets of air.

Integrated pest management (IPM). A coordinated approach to pest control that is intended to prevent unacceptable levels of pests by the most cost-effective means with the least possible hazard to building occupants, workers, and the environment.

Joist cavity. The space between joists.

Joists. The parallel, horizontal framing members that support a floor or ceiling.

Kaolin. A fine white clay that has long been mined in many parts of the world for a variety of purposes, including ceramics. Here we refer to its use in plasters and paints.

Kilowatt-hour (kwh). A common unit of energy or work, equivalent to the use of 1,000 watts over a period of one hour. A light bulb using 100 watts for 10 hours consumes one kilowatt-hour of electrical energy.

Knee walls. The vertical side walls of an attic space, often less than full height.

Lead. A heavy metallic element that is a harmful environmental pollutant. It is often found in the home in paint or solder manufactured before 1978. Lead is toxic to many organs and can cause serious damage to the brain, kidneys, and nervous system.

Lead time. The time between when a product is ordered and when it is delivered.

Leadership in Energy and Environmental Design (LEED). A building rating system developed and administered by the U.S. Green Building Council. It evaluates the overall environmental performance of a building throughout its life cycle and provides a tangible methodology for evaluating how "green" a building is.

Leeward. On the side sheltered from the wind. See "windward."

Life cycle. The stages of a product, beginning with raw materials acquisition, continuing with manufacture, construction, and use, and concluding with a variety of recovery, recycling, or waste management options.

Life-cycle cost. The amortized annual cost of a product, including capital costs, as well as installation, operating, maintenance, and disposal costs discounted over the lifetime of a product.

Light pollution. Light that shines where it isn't wanted, such as streetlights illuminating a bedroom or city lights interfering with astronomical observations.

Locally sourced materials. Materials obtained from within a defined radius around a project site, in order to support the local economy and reduce transportation costs and energy expenditure.

Loose-fill insulation. Insulation that is loosely packed to allow pockets of dead air space; typically consists of vermiculite, perlite, fiberglass, mineral wool, or cellulose. Used mostly in ceiling cavities and attics.

Low-E, low-emissivity. Most often used in reference to a thin metallic-oxide coating that reflects radiant heat, and which can be placed on the airspace side of either pane of window double-glazing. The best location for the coating depends on whether the primary control of heat flow is from the inside out (heating climates) or the outside in (cooling climates).

Makeup air. The air required to replace air that is used for combustion in fuel-burning appliances.

Mastic. A thick, sticky cement, often used to seal duct systems and cracks in buildings. It dries to form a permanent, flexible seal.

Material Safety Data Sheet (MSDS). A form that provides information about chemical and physical hazards, health effects, proper handling, storage, and personal protection appropriate for use of a particular chemical in an occupational environment.

Mechanical ventilation. Controlled, purposeful introduction of outdoor air into a conditioned space via mechanical equipment.

Medium-density fiberboard (MDF). An engineered panel that can be used to make things such as cabinets and wall panels. MDF typically offgasses formaldehyde, unless specifically manufactured for low offgassing.

Microclimate. The climate of a small area, as contrasted with the climate of a region.

Mineral wool. A lightweight, fibrous material made from molten slag, volcanic rock, or glass, produced by drawing or blowing. Used for insulation and fireproofing. Also known as "rock wool."

Mitigate, mitigation. To reduce the force or intensity of a hazard, such as lead, asbestos, or EMFs.

Moisture barrier. A material, membrane, or coating used on a foundation, below ground level, to keep moisture from penetrating.

Multiple Chemical Sensitivity (MCS). Extreme sensitivity to low concentrations of chemicals, including those found in some building materials. Reactions may include tachycardia, sweating, fatigue, nausea, trembling, and difficulty concentrating.

Natural cooling. See "passive cooling."

Negative pressure. A condition in which the air inside a building is at a lower pressure than the air outside, typically caused by air being exhausted from a building or consumed more quickly than it can be replaced.

Net-metering. A program in which an electrical utility company buys power produced by customers (via on-site photovoltaic, micro-hydro, or wind generation) at the same price the company charges the customer for electricity.

Nonrenewable resources. Natural resources that are consumed faster than they can be produced; limited resources that could eventually be depleted.

Old growth. Wood from trees found in mature forests that have never been exposed to logging operations.

Oriented Strand Board (OSB). A manufactured structural panel, made of glue-saturated chips of wood that are oriented into a pattern for optimal strength and formed under heat and pressure to create sheets for roof, wall, and subfloor sheathing. Small, fast-growing trees are used, saving old-growth trees.

Outgas or offgas. To emit gaseous substances. Numerous building materials contain chemicals that outgas at room temperature.

Passive cooling. The use of building elements to permit increased ventilation, evaporative cooling, shading, and retention of coolness. The intention is to minimize or eliminate the need for mechanical cooling.

Passive heating. The use of building elements to allow natural thermal energy flows, such as radiation, conduction, and natural convection generated by the sun, to provide heat. The intention is to minimize or eliminate the need for mechanical heating.

Passive-solar water heater. A system that uses solar warmth to heat water for domestic use, without mechanical pumps or controls.

Payback period. The length of time it takes to recoup the cost of a feature or appliance via cost savings due to the energy efficiency of that item.

Percolate, percolation. The somewhat slowed passage of a fluid (e.g., water) through a permeable substance.

Permaculture. A system of perennial agriculture, emphasizing the use of renewable natural resources and the enrichment of local ecosystems.

Permeable paving. Pavement that allows water to pass through it and into the ground, recharging the aquifer and reducing the volume of water that must be treated by the municipal water-treatment system.

Permeance. The tendency of a given material to allow the passage of moisture, measured in perms.

Pervious paving. See "permeable paving."

pH. A measure of acidity or alkalinity; 0 represents strong acidity, 7 neutrality, and 14 strong alkalinity.

Phantom load. The flow of electricity to appliances that are turned off. More accurately called "standby loss."

Photons. The quanta (or packets) that make up electromagnetic radiation. Can be thought of as the smallest possible bit of light.

Photovoltaic (PV) panel. A panel that uses a layer of semiconductor to directly convert sunlight into electricity.

Pipe insulation. Insulation on hot-water pipes to minimize heat loss.

Plastic lumber. A lumber product made from recycled plastics, or a composite of wood fiber and plastic. Water-, chemical-, and pest-resistant, it is suggested for use as decking or in light construction; it is not suitable for structural framing. Also see "composite material."

Polyvinyl chloride (PVC). A thermoplastic polymer of vinyl chloride; a known human carcinogen that releases dioxins when burned. It is commonly found in electrical cable, plastic piping, flooring, upholstery, and siding, and identifiable by the number "3" inside a recycling triangle. Its use is banned in many parts of Europe.

Positive indoor pressure. A condition in which the air pressure indoors is greater than the air pressure outdoors, caused by delivering air into a space faster than it is exhausted.

Post consumer recycled (PCR) content. Material that has been recovered after its use as a consumer product. Examples of products with PCR content include fleece clothing made from pop bottles and reclaimed carpet tiles used for new tile backing. Products with a high percentage of PCR content are typically very resource-efficient.

Post industrial recycled content. Manufacturing waste that has been cycled back into the production process. Products with post industrial recycled content do not represent the significant resource savings that post-consumer recycled content does, but they are far preferable to those that use virgin materials.

Power grid. The system through which electrical power is distributed to users by utility companies.

Pressure-treated wood. Wood that has been chemically treated to prevent moisture decay or insect infestation.

Prevailing wind. The predominant wind direction in a given area.

Programmable setback thermostat. A thermostat that can automatically change the indoor temperature maintained by an HVAC system according to a preset schedule. The heating or cooling requirements can be reduced when a building is unoccupied or when occupants are asleep.

Radiant floor heating. See "hydronic radiant heating."

Radon. A radioactive, colorless, odorless gas that occurs naturally. When trapped in buildings, radon concentration can build up, causing health problems such as lung cancer.

Rain shadow. An area of reduced rainfall on the lee side of high mountains.

Rainwater catchment. The process of gathering the rainwater that falls on a roof or other surface, and channeling it by gutters or pipes to a storage tank or cistern for later use.

Reclaimed lumber. Wood that has been removed from defunct structures, or logs that sank long ago in rivers during transport and have been retrieved. This lumber can be used for nonstructural applications such as paneling and flooring; if regraded, it can be used in structural applications. Advantages: usually higher-quality surface characteristics (often from tight-grained, old-growth lumber), reduced logging of already depleted forests, sometimes lower cost than new lumber, and reduced landfill wastes. Disadvantages: often labor-intensive to "clean up," often difficult to nail after many years of drying.

Recyclable. Materials that can be recovered or diverted from the waste stream for recycling/reuse.

Recycled content. The percentage of recycled material in a product, generally determined by weight.

Recycled material. Material that would otherwise be destined for disposal but has been diverted from the waste stream, reintroduced as a feedstock, and processed into marketable products.

Recycling. The series of activities—collection, separation and processing—by which materials are recovered from the solid waste stream for use as raw materials in manufacturing new products. This does not include use as fuel for producing heat or power.

Relative humidity (RH). The ratio of the amount of water vapor in the air at a specific temperature to the maximum amount that the air could hold at that temperature, expressed as a percentage.

Remediate, remediation. To remedy, correct, or counteract a fault or hazard.

Renewable energy. Energy resources, such as the wind or the sun, that can produce indefinitely without being depleted.

Renewable resources. Resources that can be created or produced at least as quickly as they are consumed, so that their source is not depleted.

Rim joist. The structural framing member around the perimeter of a floor or ceiling. See also "joist."

Rock wool. See "mineral wool."

R value. A measure of the thermal resistance of a material. The higher the R-value, the more effective the material is as thermal insulation.

Sash. The framework in which panes of glass are set in a window or door. Also refers to the framework and glass together as the movable part of a window.

Sealed-combustion appliances. Fuel-burning appliances that take in combustion air from outside the building and vent exhaust to the outside via sealed ducts.

Seasonal Energy-Efficiency Ratio (SEER). The efficiency at which an air conditioner produces cooling; a ratio of the amount of cooling produced (in Btus) to the amount of electricity used (in watts). The higher the SEER, the greater the efficiency.

Setback thermostat. See "programmable setback thermostat."

Shell (as in "house's shell"). The weather-resistant outside face of the house. Often not the same as the thermal boundary.

Single/double/triple-pane. Refers to the number of glass layers that comprise a window unit.

Solar Heat-Gain Coefficient (SHGC). The percentage of the radiant heat that passes through a window assembly.

Stack effect, stack ventilation. Entry of cool air through a low opening in a space where warm air is escaping through a higher opening.

Sunspace. A glazed indoor area designed to collect heat from the sun to warm indoor air; may also be used as living space.

Sustainability. "Meeting the needs of the present without compromising the ability of future generations to meet their own needs." (World Commission on Environment and Development). A sustainable approach encourages people to behave as part of the natural flows and cycles of our planet, rather than seeking to overpower them.

Tankless water heater. An appliance that heats water when it is needed, rather than keeping a tank full of water warm 24 hours a day (as does the common "storage-tank water heater"). Also called "instantaneous" water heaters, they take up less space than a storage-tank unit.

Thermal boundary. The layer of a building enclosure that controls the transfer of heat between the interior and the exterior. It is a component of the building envelope that may or may not align with the air boundary.

Thermal envelope. See "thermal boundary."

Thermal mass. Building materials used to absorb heat during the daytime for release when air temperatures drop. Examples include stone, masonry, earth, and water.

Toxic. Poisonous. A toxic material can produce illness and/or loss of life if inhaled, swallowed, or absorbed through the skin.

Transom. A small window above a door or another window, typically operable.

Transpiration. The process of giving off water vapor through the pores of the skin or the surface membrane of a plant.

Treated wood. See "pressure-treated wood."

U-factor. A quantitative measure of a material's conductivity; the reciprocal of R-value. While R-values are used to indicate a given building material's resistance to heat flow, U-factors are used to summarize the conductive qualities of window assemblies or building enclosures.

U.S. Green Building Council (USGBC). A national organization, founded in 1993, whose mission is to accelerate the adoption of green building practices, technologies, policies, and standards. USGBC established the LEED Certification guidelines.

Vapor barrier. A material that is impermeable to vapor.

Vapor-impermeable. Materials with a permeance of 0.1 perm or less (rubber membranes, polyethylene film, glass, aluminum foil).

Vapor-permeable. Materials with a permeance of greater than 10 perms (housewraps, building papers).

Vapor retarder. The element of a building assembly that is designed and installed to retard the movement of water by vapor diffusion.

Vernacular. Native to or commonly used in a particular country, region, or climate. Characteristic of a particular period, place, or group.

Vinyl. See "polyvinyl chloride."

Volatile organic compounds (VOCs). Organic compounds that vaporize readily at ordinary temperatures. Examples of building materials that may contain VOCs include solvents, paints, adhesives, carpeting, and particleboard. Signs or symptoms of VOC exposure may range from such mild reactions as eye and upper-respiratory-system irritation, nasal congestion, and headaches, to memory loss, dizziness, or cancer.

Wabi-sabi. The Japanese art of finding beauty in imperfection and profundity in nature.

Wainscot. A facing or paneling, often of wood, applied to an interior wall—often at the lower three or four feet of the wall.

Wall cavity. The spaces between studs in a wall.

Water-conserving fixtures. Fixtures fitted with flow-reducers that constrict the volume of water to 1.5 to 2.5 gallons per minute. New water-conserving toilets use 1.6 gallons or less per flush, compared to 5 gallons for older toilets.

Wattle-and-daub. A wall construction system consisting of interwoven branches, laths, or dowels covered with earthen plaster.

Weather stripping. A thin piece of material—metal, rubber, vinyl, or foam—fitted around a door or window to prevent infiltration of air or moisture.

Wind catcher. A tower that rises above the roof to capture prevailing breezes and scoop them into the rooms below. Often found in traditional Middle Eastern buildings.

Wind-power system. A mechanical system that converts the energy of the wind into electricity via turbines. Surplus electricity is often stored in batteries for later use, or the power is passed back into the power grid, essentially making the electric meter run in reverse.

Wind rose. A meteorological diagram depicting the distribution of the wind direction and speed at a given location over a period of time.

Wind scoop. See "wind catcher."

Wind turbine. A mechanical device consisting primarily of rotor blades mounted on a tower in order to "capture" prevailing winds to generate electrical power.

Windward. On the side exposed to the wind.

About the Authors

Carol Venolia is an architect and educator who has been involved with ecological building for more than 30 years. Named a Green Design Trailblazer by *Natural Home & Garden Magazine*, she has designed numerous context-responsive homes of straw, earth, and "good wood" and consulted on schools, healing centers, and eco-villages. Her first book, *Healing Environments: Your Guide to Indoor Well-Being*, advocates restoring the vital connections between humans and the rest of the living world. In addition to her architectural practice, Carol currently co-directs the EcoDwelling program at New College of California and writes the "Design for Life" column for *Natural Home & Garden Magazine*. Her design work has been featured in numerous publications, and she travels widely to lecture and teach. For more information, visit www.carolvenolia.com.

Kelly Lerner is an innovative, award-winning architect who has been fixing up houses since she could hold a tape measure and pound nails with a toy hammer. Her firm, One World Design Architecture, designs delightful, energy-efficient, naturally sustainable remodeling projects and new homes throughout the Pacific Northwest. In 2005, *Natural Home & Garden Magazine* named her one of the top 10 eco-architects in the United States. Kelly also travels worldwide teaching natural building, passive solar design, and sustainable development. She received the World Habitat Award at the United Nations World Habitat Day for spearheading a project that introduced straw-bale construction to China and built more than 600 sustainable, straw-bale homes. Her designs have been featured in *Landscape Architecture Magazine*, *Metropolis Magazine*, *Natural Home and Garden Magazine*, *Mother Earth News*, *The Straw Bale House*, *Serious Straw-bale*, and *Green by Design*. For more of Kelly's work see www.one-world-design.com.

Endnotes

Chapter 3
[1] Zane Kime, M.D., M.S, *Sunlight*, World Health Publications, 1980.

[2] Balcomb, J. Douglas, Robert Jones, Robert McFarland, and William Wray, *Passive Solar Heating Analysis*, American Society of Heating, Refrigeration, and Air Conditioning Engineers, 1984.

Chapter 6
[1] Krigger, John and Chris Dorsi, *Residential Energy: Cost Savings and Comfort for Existing Buildings*, Saturn Resource Management, 2004, page 200.

[2] Krigger, John, *Your Mobile Home: Energy and Repair Guide for Manufactured Housing*, Saturn Resource Management, 1998, page 47.

[3] *Residential Energy*, page 199.

[4] Michael Reilly, quoted in John Tillman Lyle, *Design for Human Ecosystems*, Island Press, 1999, page 207.

[5] *Residential Energy*, page 199.

[6] *Your Mobile Home*, page 50.

[7] *Your Mobile Home*, page 48.

[8] *Your Mobile Home*, page 48.

[9] Based on material found in Moffat, Anne Simon et al, *Energy-Efficient and Environmental Landscaping*, Appropriate Solutions Press, 1994, and Krigger, *Your Mobile Home*.

[10] Thompson, J. William and Kim Sorvig, *Sustainable Landscape Construction: A Guide to Green Building Outdoors*, Island Press, 2000, page 280.

[11] *Energy-Efficient and Environmental Landscaping*, page 141.

Chapter 7
[1] Wilson, Alex, *Windows: LookingThrough the Options*, Environmental Building News, March/April (Volume 5, Number 2), 1996.

Chapter 8
[1] *The Dirty Folly of "Clean Coal"*. Natural Resources Defense Council, 2001.

[2] *Final Project Report, Pacific Gas and Electric Company's Advanced Customer Technology Test for Maximum Energy Efficiency (ACT2)*. 1990.

[3] *Electric Power Annual*, Volume II, Tables 4 and 5. Energy Information Administration. 1999

[4] *Natural Gas Annual*, Volume II, Table 14. Energy Information Administration. 1999

Chapter 10
[1] *National Waste Database Report 1998*, Environmental Protection Agency, 1998.

[2] California Integrated Waste Management Board, www.ciwmb.ca.gov/ConDemo/Wallboard

Chapter 12
[1] Alevantis, Leon. *Building Materials Emissions Study*, California Integrated Waste Management Board, 2003.

[2] Alexander, Christopher. *The Nature of Order, Book Four, The Luminous Ground*. The Center for Environmental Structure, Berkeley, CA. 2004

[3] Blanchard, Steven and Peter Reppe. *Life Cycle Analysis of a Residential Home in Michigan*, University of Michigan, 1998.

Credits

Photographers

Kelly Lerner
contents page (upper right); 7; 12 (right); 19 (upper right); 29; 30 (upper); 31 (upper); 32; 34 (right); 36; 37 (left); 70; 72; 75; 89 (upper); 93 (left); 100 (right); 101 (right); 102 (left); 111 (right); 138 (lower); 150 (lower); 154 (upper); 163; 164; 165 (left); 166 (right); 168; 170 (lower right); 189 (right); 191 (upper left); 199 (upper); 202 (lower); 206 (lower); 206 (upper); 208 (right); 209 (right); 210 (lower); 213 (right); 214 (left); 230 (lower); 232; 233 (upper right); 238; 239; 241 (upper); 242; 243 (right); 247 (upper); 248 (upper); 249; 250 (lower); 251 (lower right and upper); 252; 253 (upper); 254; 255; 257 (upper right); 260

Carol Venolia
19 (lower right); 31 (lower); 56; 60; 81 (lower); 86 (upper); 87 (upper left); 88 (center, lower left and lower right); 91; 92; 99; 101 (left); 188; 192 (left); 193 (lower); 195 (upper right); 197 (upper); 240 (upper); 258 (center)

Barley & Pfeiffer Architects
50 (right); 55 (right); 71; 81 (upper); 171; 176

Ted Baumgart
68 (right); 78 (lower right); 160 (lower); 200; 207 (lower); 212 (right); 243 (upper left)

Barbara Bourne Photography
9; 54 (right); 86 (lower); 87 (lower and upper right); 89 (lower left and lower right); 90; 174 (upper right); 193 (upper); 233 (left); 241 (lower left); 256

Michael Buchanan
13; 43; 46 (left); 47; 62 (right); 63; 131; 160 (upper); 169 (upper); 174 (lower); 19 (lower left); 192 (right); 203; 230 (upper); 236 (lower)

Jen Carlson
121 (lower); 173 (lower)

Don Carson
155; 199 (lower); 257 (lower right)

Dave Deppen
52; 53; 62 (left); 127; 130 (upper)

Phillip Gould
65 (right); 69 (right); 142; 143; 144; 145; 146; 212 (left); 259

Stephanie Gross
222 (upper); 226; 227

Emily Hagopian
title page (lower left); 12 (left); 20; 30 (lower); 46 (right); 67; 73; 106; 128; 134 (lower); 153 (right); 172; 173 (upper); 190 (lower and upper left); 191 (upper right); 194; 198; 201 (left); 204 (upper); 206 (middle); 210 (upper); 211 (lower); 217 (left); 241 (lower); 243 (lower left); 246 (lower and upper); 247 (lower); 248 (lower); 250 (upper); 251 (lower left); 253 (lower)

Rebecca Holland
8 (center); 45; 49; 165 (right); 201 (right)

Drew Hubbell
55 (left)

Image45
64 (lower)

Inscape Studio
222 (lower)

276

Acknowledgments

We want to begin by expressing our deep appreciation to the Graham Foundation for Advanced Studies in the Fine Arts, for recognizing the importance of our subject and funding the writing of this book.

Our warm respect and gratitude also go to John S. Reynolds, Professor Emeritus of Architecture at the University of Oregon. John, you awakened our awareness of climate, site, thermal comfort, energy issues, and resource use. Your example as an advocate, educator, and mentor has guided our careers. And your input to this book has been invaluable.

Thank you to David Eisenberg and Seth Melchert, for supporting our Graham Foundation grant application, and for your many other forms of encouragement and inspiration.

We couldn't have created this book without the devoted, talented team at Lark Books: our thanks to Carol Taylor for loving our proposal; Jimmy Knight for patient and tenacious editorial guidance; Deborah Morgenthal and Paige Gilchrist for caring oversight; Kathy Holmes for the beautiful graphic layout; Ronnie Lundy for eagle-eye editing; Rebecca Gutherie for editorial assistance; Olivier Rollin and Orrin Lundgren for their expertise in creating the illustrations for this book.

Robyn Griggs Lawrence, Editor-in-Chief of *Natural Home & Garden Magazine*, has been at the heart of this book from the start. She introduced us to Lark Books, contributed a wonderful sidebar, allowed us to try out our early material in the pages of NH&G, and encouraged us all the way.

Our appreciation goes to all our colleagues who contributed the sidebars you'll find throughout the book. We're also grateful to the owners of the homes we featured, who shared their experiences and opened their homes to us. This book comes alive because of you!

Several colleagues provided valuable input to the text. Warm thanks to Ann Edminster and Don Fulger for reviewing some of the technical chapters; any errors that remain are our own. David Johnston was a source of information, inspiration, and networking, through his NARI Certified Green Remodeler course. Mary Cordaro deserves kudos for the hard work and professional experience that went into creating the Checking for Household Hazards appendix. Lynn Elizabeth provided several items for the Community section of the Resources appendix, and Gina Ryerson made valuable contributions to the Healthy Homes section. Debra Lynn Dadd and Shay Salomon supplied many of the quotations that open our chapters. And Sarah Susanka kindly allowed us to use a play on her "not so big house" in our title.

Numerous photographers provided the images that make this book sing. In particular, Barbara Bourne contributed her luscious photographs to the proposal that launched this project, as well as many images that appear in this book. Emily Hagopian went beyond the call of duty, including us in her green building photography thesis. And Catherine Wanek shared striking images of natural remodeling in Europe and brought the Knox/Myhrman case study to life.

Athena and Bill Steen gave us special encouragement while we were incubating this book. Marcia Stewart and Richard Stim shared their wealth of experience as we navigated the maze of publishing contracts. Bonnie Aspen, who was moved to tears by our book proposal, gave rise to one standard for our writing: "What would make Bonnie cry?"

Linda Drew, Janie Lowe, and Ginnie Young provided warm hospitality, delicious food, friendship, and encouragement during key stretches of research, writing, and photography. And the folks at Brewery Gulch Inn on the Mendocino Coast provided an inspiring environment for creating our book's first outline.

Carol's Personal Thanks

While many authors thank their parents for their love and support, I want to thank my parents, Jan and Wayne Venolia, for all that and more. Mom, your professional editorial eye saved us from embarrassment countless times. Dad, your technical input is incomparable and invaluable. My deep love and gratitude to you both.

My appreciation also goes to my broad web of support. My colleagues and EcoDwelling students at New College of California have been unflagging in their enthusiasm and understanding as I've worked on this book. My clients have been wonderful; several became part of this book, and all were patient about the many hats I wear.

Thanks also to my friends and colleagues, who have given me everything from encouragement to Reiki treatments as I burned the midnight oil to complete this book. I especially want to acknowledge Mark Jackson, who cooked meals, made me get out for walks, and was incredibly tolerant of my book-induced distraction.

Finally, I want to thank my friend, colleague, and coauthor Kelly Lerner. I knew when I saw her remodeled home that we'd make a great team. It's been an incredible adventure, and I'm proud and pleased to have worked shoulder-to-shoulder with her. Kelly, I couldn't have done it without you.

Kelly's Personal Thanks

They say the acorn doesn't fall far from the tree, and I'm especially grateful for a childhood full of power tools, ingenuity, and duct tape. Though Dad, now 80, no longer crawls on his belly under the house to fix the plumbing leaks, and Mom, 81, hasn't repapered the bathroom recently, our family lore is built of side-splitting tales of remodeling mishaps, struggles, and ultimate triumph. Thanks, Mom and Dad, for the hands-on education and knowledge that I can do whatever I put my mind to.

Jennifer Helmuth and Deborah McCandless have supported this project and countless others—remodeling and otherwise—with boundless enthusiasm, humor, patience, and grace. I couldn't imagine having better accomplices on any adventure.

This book received invaluable boosts from my colleagues in the Northwest Eco-Building Guild (especially the infamous Ladies' Auxiliary), who generously and enthusiastically shared both their professional remodeling experiences and their friendship throughout this process. I'm also grateful to my many architectural clients who contributed their stories to this effort and patiently waited for drawings while I was writing.

I would never have taken off my tool belt or walked away from my drafting table to sit down at the keyboard and write about remodeling without the encouragement and support of my coauthor, Carol Venolia. Her great passion for concise, vivid communication and the healing power of nature inspired me at every turn. Thanks, Carol, for knowing we could do it.

Index

Index